1995

Adult
Personality
Development

To Bea

Adult
Personality
Development

Theories and Concepts

Lawrence S.
Wrightsman

volume 1

SAGE Publications
International Educational and Professional Publisher
Thousand Oaks   London   New Delhi

For information address:

SAGE Publications, Inc.
2455 Teller Road
Thousand Oaks, California 91320

SAGE Publications Ltd.
6 Bonhill Street
London EC2A 4PU
United Kingdom

SAGE Publications India Pvt. Ltd.
M-32 Market
Greater Kailash I
New Delhi 110 048 India

Printed in the United States of America

Library of Congress Cataloging-in-Publication Data

Wrightsman, Lawrence S.
　　Adult personality development / author: Lawrence S. Wrightsman.
　　　　p. cm.
　　Contents: v. 1. Theories and concepts — v. 2. Applications.
　　Includes bibliographical references and indexes.
　　ISBN 0-8039-4399-7 (v. 1). — ISBN 0-8039-4401-2 (v. 2). — ISBN
　　0-8039-4400-4 (pbk. : v. 1). — ISBN 0-8039-4402-0 (pbk. : v. 2)
　　　　1. Personality.　2. Adulthood—Psychological aspects.　3. Aging—
　　Psychological aspects.　I. Title.
　　BF724.85.P47W74　1994　　　　　　　　　　　　　　　　93-43076
　　155.6—dc20　　　　　　　　　　　　　　　　　　　　　　　CIP

94　95　96　97　98　10　9　8　7　6　5　4　3　2　1

Sage Production Editor: Yvonne Könneker

Contents

Preface

In teaching a course on adulthood, as I have done for the past 10 years, I emphasize to students the need to understand and adopt theories of development. We all have raw experience (for some of us, the experience is rawer than for others), but we all can benefit from the organizing and structuring of raw experience that theories can provide. The incorporation of this theoretical focus permits us to more easily compare our experiences with those of others, and theories may also serve, for some of us, as guidelines to possible changes and crises in the future.

This book contrasts three broad theoretical approaches to explaining psychological changes during the period from adolescence to the onset of late adulthood. Each of these approaches has some legitimacy for its claim that it accurately portrays the nature of psychological growth. But no theory can be completely comprehensive, and the overriding orientation of the book is an eclectic one, choosing whichever theoretical constructs that best explain the phenomenon at hand. A companion volume, *Adult Personality Development: Applications,* examines the relevance of these theories to several aspects of adulthood, including occupational and career shifts, marriage and relationships, and values.

The book's coverage does not seek to be exhaustive. Given the desired length of the book, that would have been impossible. Rather, specific topics have been included that reflect various aspects of major issues in adulthood. However, in this book, coverage has been greatly expanded and the number of new references equals that from my book *Personality Development in Adulthood* (1988, Sage).

Several uses for the book seem appropriate. This book may provide a feasible organizing structure for many of the rapidly increasing courses on The Psychology of Adulthood. Within the developmental sequence, courses on adulthood seem to be the last frontier; first we had courses on child psychology, then adolescence, then courses titled the Psychology of Aging and Life Span development courses, but only in the past 15 years has the void begun to be filled with courses that deal in depth with the remaining two thirds of our years of life.

Second, scholars who wish to have a review of current theoretical and research developments in the psychology of adulthood may find the book a useful source. The book is deliberately written in a nontechnical style, with terms defined whenever they are introduced. It is intended that the book will be accessible to scholars and interested readers from a variety of disciplines who wish an introduction to contemporary frameworks.

As one of the major theories (the dialectical approach) relentlessly emphasizes, human development is never completed. Likewise, no book can be a complete treatment of something as pervasive, complex, and important as the development of adult personality. But the aspiration motivating the writing of this book is, in a small way at least, to facilitate the task of psychological growth we all face.

–Lawrence S. Wrightsman

Acknowledgments

Charles T. Hendrix, Editorial Director of Sage Publications, encouraged me to write this book, and I am pleased that he did. I wish to acknowledge his patience in light of a project whose development took longer than either he or I anticipated or wished. The publication of this book marks the most recent manifestation of an editing and writing relationship between Terry Hendrix and myself that spans more than 25 years, a developmental period of its own!

Administrators and faculty at the University of Kansas also facilitated the development of this book. Michael Storms and Sharon S. Brehm, then Chair and Associate Chair of the Department of Psychology, supported my desire to teach an innovative course for adults in our evening program. I was awarded a travel grant from the University that permitted me to attend a summer institute on Psychology and Autobiography at the Andrus Gerontology Center of the University of Southern California. Conversations with faculty colleagues Franklin Shontz, David Holmes, Susan Kemper, James O'Neil (now at the University of Connecticut), Bill Tuttle (Department of History), Ann Schofield (Women's Studies), and Ray Hiner (Departments of History and Higher Education) have broadened my perspective and helped me clarify viewpoints. Scholars at other universities, particularly my friend Irwin Altman and the late Klaus Riegel, introduced me to the dialectical approach.

This is a book that emphasizes ideas, and it has been my delight to "meet" many distinguished scholars in the field of personality and development through reading their ideas in print and hearing them speak at conventions. Kevin Oldham, a talented composer and pianist who died of AIDS at the age of 32, said in an interview shortly before his death, "It seems to me that whether you stay alive or not seems to be the trivial part; it's your work that must have a life of its own." It is an honor for me to have had the opportunity to disseminate the work of these distinguished scholars to a wider audience. Any errors of interpretation in this book are, of course, my responsibility.

Katia Silva deserves my unconditional appreciation for her ability to interpret my almost unintelligible scribblings and her prompt production of each chapter of this revision.

The staff at Sage Publications has been solicitous and has nurtured the development of this project to a degree equaling the exceptional level of proficiency they showed on those books of mine previously published by Sage.

To each of these people I offer my appreciation. Writing is inevitably a solitary activity, but the production of a book permits a reassuring reentry into the real world of human relationships.

–Lawrence S. Wrightsman

1

Conceptions of
Personality Development in Adulthood

The life which is unexamined is not worth living.

Plato

Today, terms like *midlife crisis, generation gap,* and *thirtysome-thing* frequently appear in the popular press. But for many decades the field of psychology treated the topic of personality development in adulthood with benign neglect. Thirty years ago the assumption held by most psychologists, as well as by society in general, was that once people passed through the traumas of adolescence, completed their formal schooling, entered the world of work, got married, and "settled down," nothing much new happened to them until the inevitability of their death. But now all of us—psychologists and laypersons alike—recognize that things are not that straightforward, that adulthood is not a prolonged period of predictable sameness and constancy. As just one type of example, many middle-aged persons claim extensive personality and behavior changes that in some ways resemble a second adolescence. Adulthood—and especially the nature of personality development during this extended period—has become a topic worthy of scholarly study, as well as popular interest.

The phenomenon of the "midlife crisis" exploded into our consciousness in the middle of the 1970s, concurrently with social scientists reactivating a long dormant interest in adulthood. But even as the publication of *Passages* by Gail Sheehy in 1976 was leading many adults to contemplate their lives from a fresh perspective, social scientists began to disagree about just which theories and which sets of concepts to apply. How do psychologists properly conceptualize the processes by which we move through the several decades of adulthood? Do we simply unfold a scenario formed at an earlier age? Do changes reflect a smooth and seamless transition? Or are wrenching disjunctions and disruptive shifts inevitable? May apparent "changes" really reflect a manifestation of consistencies in the underlying structure of one's personality?

Three broad theoretical perspectives provide highly contrasting answers to questions like those above. These are, first, an early formation approach that assumes personality structure is established— and then remains essentially unchanged—in the first years of childhood; second, a stage theory of development, as represented in the concepts of Erik Erikson, Daniel Levinson, and Roger Gould; and third, a dialectical analysis that poses ongoing irreconcilable tensions between basic needs, meaning that development never ends.

Chapters in Volume 1 elaborate on each of these three approaches. Each theory has its merits. My goal is not so much to conclude which perspective is best, but to describe the approach, while examining the methods used to evaluate each theory and the quality of evidence for each. A second volume, titled *Adult Personality Development: Applications,* employs concepts and findings from each of the three perspectives to understand a multitude of aspects of adulthood, including occupational and career shifts, sex-role development, marriage and other intimate relationships, sexual behavior, changes in values, and attitudes toward death and dying. The second volume concludes with chapters on the use of personal documents to understand personality development in adulthood. Until recently, the science of psychology has been unduly restricted in the types of methods it has employed to evaluate differing theories of personality development. Throughout these volumes, I seek to demonstrate that the use of personal documents as sources of data can improve the knowledge base for each theory, and, not incidentally, provide each of us with greater understanding of ourselves. By "personal documents" I refer to materials such as autobiographies, memoirs, diaries, and collections of letters. Just as the topic of personality development in adults was neglected for many years, so too was the methodology for analyzing personal documents. It is not much of an exaggeration to claim that the "state of the art" regarding the use of personal documents in psychology has not, until recently, advanced beyond that level summarized in Gordon Allport's (1942) monograph review written about 50 years ago.

The major portion of this initial chapter presents an overview of the three divergent theoretical perspectives, including the basic assumptions underlying each. In selecting those theoretical conceptions that provide the structure of our analysis, my focus is on the global nature of personality, as defined in a classic Allportian sense (Allport, 1937). This personality paradigm, as described by Craik (1976), uses the person as the basic unit of analysis, seeks to understand the organization of the individual's behavior, and investigates the relationship of the individual's personality characteristics to his or her behavior and outcomes.

Early Formation Theories

It has been a staple of folklore for a long time that "as the twig is bent the tree is formed," that experiences during childhood structure one's orientation to life as an adult. An extreme reflection of this view proposes that you now *are* what you *were,* only bigger and more; whatever occurs later is just an elaboration or refinement of an early orientation. Psychological theories have contributed— sometimes intentionally, sometimes not—to this notion. In this section several approaches relevant to an assumption of "early formation" are introduced.

Personal Construct Theory

Early formation theories are usually associated with a psychoanalytic explanation of personality development, and that approach will be described in the next section. But Sigmund Freud and his followers are not the only ones whose contributions provide support for a view that adult personality is structured at an early age. Cognitive analyses of personality development also may emphasize early developmental processes.

Our behavior is influenced by our perceptions. We react to what we think we see or hear, not just what is actually there. Given the same stimulus—the same painting, the same song—each of us is likely to perceive it as somewhat different. In *personal construct theory,* interpretation thus results from cognitive determinants (in contrast to psychoanalytic theory, which emphasizes motivations).

Interpretation is inevitable, so this theory says, because the world is too complex to be perceived straightforwardly. There is too much going on to process everything; we can notice this but not that. We also have to make decisions rapidly on occasion, forcing us not only to perceive but to interpret. When a stranger knocks on our door, requesting to use our telephone, our response is influenced by his appearance, his demeanor, and our judgment of his credibility. As we drive along the freeway we notice drivers and cars that are behaving abnormally, and we anticipate the need to react to them if they lose control.

George Kelly (1955) developed personal construct theory as an effort to systematize these assumptions. As we attempt to superimpose some order on the complex world, we develop constructs, or organizing labels, that help us distinguish between and classify events (Jankowicz, 1987).

How does a construct develop? First, we notice general features or similarities in stimuli—whether in people, in events, in sounds, in tastes, in any broad type of stimulus. We note those that are alike; those that are different. A young child may grow up in a family that has both a dog and a cat. At first, the child views these as being alike, that is, in the same construct, and they are distinguished from other objects that the child is struggling to fit into other constructs. But later the child learns that separate constructs, "dogs" and "cats," are appropriate for distinguishing between and labeling these two objects. As children grow older they develop more specific constructs to deal with the different breeds of dogs, all the while maintaining and using their earlier, broad constructs, when appropriate.

This approach reflects, in a broad way, current thinking about cognitive development in young children (i.e., Keil, 1989; Markman, 1989; Stern, 1990). For example, even 3-year-old children use a kind of causal-explanatory framework—Wellman (1990) calls it a "belief-desire" theory of mind—in order to explain and predict the world. Flavell (1991) concludes that current research indicates that 3-year-olds can predict people's future actions and explain their past actions on the basis of relevant information about their beliefs and desires.

Kelly proposed that our assessment of individual people is based on the distinctive collection of constructs each of us has in our repertoire. Although we all apply order to the mass of individual differences—the variations in looks, age, gender, personality, interests, and so on—by applying constructs, each of us has developed a unique set of constructs. Each of us, in viewing the same behavior by another individual, may use radically different constructs to describe it; consider three people watching a brief film of a man in a parking lot who goes back twice to check that his car doors are locked. One viewer may call the person "suspicious," another may call him "overly careful," whereas a third may call him "absent-minded."

Central to Kelly's conception of human nature is the proposal that each of us is like a scientist, constantly developing, testing, and revising our constructs as we seek to predict and understand (and sometimes control) the behavior of important people in our lives. Kelly developed an instrument to identify the constructs each of us uses; the Role Construct Repertory Test (or "REP Test") is different from traditional personality inventories because the subjects, rather than the test constructor, generate the test's basic dimensions. As exemplified in Box 1.1, one person may use a great many constructs in describing the essential qualities of those around him; another may "explain" human behavior by using only a few constructs. Kelly (1963, p. 57) noted that a person might classify all people as either "good" or "bad," for example, but this broad construct might subsume a number of qualities (such as "intelligent-vs.-stupid") that other people might use as separate constructs. An example of the constructs used by one person is reproduced in Box 1.2.

(Text continued on page 8)

BOX 1.1

Rep Test Part A: Role of Title List

Instructions

Write the name of the persons indicated in the blanks provided below. Do not repeat names. If any role title appears to call for a duplicate name, substitute the name of another person whom the second role title suggests to you.

1. Your mother or the person who has played the part of mother in your life.   1. _____
2. Your father or the person who has played the part of father in your life.   2. _____
3. Your brother nearest your age. If you have no brother, the person who is most like one.   3. _____
4. Your sister nearest your age. If you have no sister, the person who is most like one.   4. _____
5. A teacher you liked or the teacher of a subject you liked.   5. _____
6. A teacher you disliked or the teacher of a subject you disliked.   6. _____
7. Your closest girl (boy) friend immediately before you started going with your wife (husband) or present closest girl (boy) friend (Ex-Flame).   7. _____
8. Your wife (husband) or closest present girl (boy) friend.   8. _____
9. An employer, supervisor, or officer under whom you served during a period of great stress (Boss).   9. _____
10. A person with whom you have been closely associated who, for some unexplainable reason, appears to dislike you (Rejecting Person).   10. _____
11. The person you have met within the past 6 months whom you would like to know better (Sought Person).   11. _____
12. The person whom you would most like to be of help to, or the one whom you feel most sorry for (Pitied Person).   12. _____
13. The most intelligent person whom you know personally.   13. _____
14. The most successful person whom you know personally.   14. _____
15. The most interesting person whom you know personally.   15. _____

BOX 1.1 (Continued)

Rep Test Part B: Construct Sorts

Instructions

The sets of three numbers in the following sorts refer to the numbers 1 to 15, inclusive, in Part A.

In each of the following sorts three numbers are listed. Look at your Part A sheet and consider the three people whom you have listed for these three numbers.

In what important way are two of these three people alike and at the same time, essentially different from the third?

After you have decided what that important way is, write it in the blank opposite the sort marked: Construct.

Next encircle the numbers corresponding to the two people who are alike.

Write down what you believe to be the opposite of the construct in the blank marked: Contrast.

Numbers

Sort	Part A	Construct (Emergent)	Contrast (Implicit)
1	9, 11, 14	_____	_____
2	10, 12, 13	_____	_____
3	2, 5, 12	_____	_____
4	1, 4, 8	_____	_____
5	7, 8, 12	_____	_____
6	3, 13, 6	_____	_____
7	1, 2, 9	_____	_____
8	3, 4, 10	_____	_____
9	6, 8, 10	_____	_____
10	5, 11, 14	_____	_____
11	1, 7, 8	_____	_____
12	2, 7, 8	_____	_____
13	3, 6, 9	_____	_____
14	4, 5, 10	_____	_____
15	11, 13, 14	_____	_____

SOURCE: G. Kelly, 1955. Reprinted with permission of the publisher.

BOX 1.2

Mildred Beal's Constructs

After a subject has completed the task described in Box 1.1, the psychologist may choose to analyze the responses in a rather subjective or impressionistic way, or, more desirably, apply a systematic analysis of the responses. When the latter is done, a pattern like the following might emerge. "Mildred Beal" is a subject whose responses are reported by G. Kelly (1955, p. 242).

Sort Number	Similar Figures	Similarity Construct	Dissimilar Figures	Contrasting Construct
2	rejecting person (10) pitied person (13)	very unhappy person	intelligent person (13)	contented
3	father (2) liked teacher (5)	very quiet and easy going	pitied person (12)	nervous, hypertensive
4	mother (1) sister (4)	look alike both hyper-critical of people in general	boyfriend (8)	friendliness
11	mother (1) ex-flame (7)	socially maladjusted	boyfriend (8)	easygoing, self-confident
13	disliked teacher (6) boss (9)	emotionally unpredictable	brother (3)	even temperament

SOURCE: G. Kelly, 1955, p. 242. Reprinted with permission of the publisher.

I stated earlier that early formation theories usually relied on a psychoanalytic conception of development and that Kelly's personal construct theory does not. In fact, he adamantly rejected revered psychoanalytic concepts, such as *unconscious, drives,* and *emotion.* So, does Kelly fit as an early-formation theorist? Yes and no. Yes, in the sense that one of his messages is that some simplification is a necessity; he wrote that without the creation of constructs, the world would appear to be an "undifferentiated homogeneity" (1963, p. 9). And once we form constructs, they have a tendency to become so internalized and self-perpetuating that we are not even aware that we are using them to generate decisions about behaving toward others. But Kelly would have dismissed my labeling him as an early formation theorist, because he believed that people can create alternative explanations of their world. In line with this view, his therapeutic procedure, called fixed-role therapy, encouraged people to develop new roles and try out new behaviors for themselves. We will see later that the therapeutic manifestations of other early formation approaches, especially the life script conception, also assume that their own brand of intervention can bring about a dismantling of prematurely formed approaches toward relationships with others.

Psychoanalytic Theory

The specifics of psychoanalytic theory are described in Chapter 2. At this point it is appropriate to discuss why I categorize psychoanalytic theory as an early formation theory. The reason is simple: Classic psychoanalytic theory, despite all its modifications, assumes that personality is largely formed during the first 5 years of life. The structure that is established then influences behavior for the rest of life. If *fixations* (see Chapter 2) occur at these tender ages, they have ramifications on our behavior as adults.

The Life Script Approach

Probably the most extreme variant of a psychoanalytic approach, with respect to the assumption of a premature resolution of personality dynamics, is the *life script approach,* formulated by Eric Berne, Claude Steiner, and other transactional analysts. A life script presupposes that the young child embraces a consistent orientation to others and to the social environment that is relentlessly "played out" throughout the rest of childhood, adolescence, and adulthood. As such, life script theory rests on the basic tenet of psychoanalytic theory that the sense of identity is established in childhood and that it produces a consistency in all behavior thereafter (Brim, 1977).

Eric Berne (1961, 1964, 1972), the author of *Games People Play,* defined a life script as a complex set of transactions by nature recurrent but not necessarily recurring, because a complete performance of a script may require a whole lifetime. Yet the life script is assumed to be formed within the first 5 years of life. For Berne, and other life script theorists, a script results from a repetition compulsion, or the tendency to repeat unhappy childhood events. Inherent to Berne's conception is that the person's life script is ultimately self-defeating.

Absolutely fundamental to life script theory is this assumption that people develop a characteristic interpersonal strategy in childhood, and that this strategy inexorably influences and makes understandable their interactions with others for the rest of their lives. Life scripts reflect Aristotle's principles of drama in the sense that, like the plot of a profound tragedy, they contain a prologue, a climax, and a catastrophe. Berne hypothesized that each of us battles between the nature of our script and the wish to avoid a personal disaster. Just like the tragic pattern inherent in Greek dramas, there is an inevitable outcome. Like the Greek hero, the individual intends to accomplish a particular result with his or her actions, but instead achieves the exact opposite. *Oedipus Rex* is a typical example of Greek drama; only long after accomplishing something apparently positive does Oedipus come to the shocking realization of what damage he has done to himself. Today the audience observes the reenactment of a Greek tragedy in horror, because members of the audience have the foresight to anticipate the tragic nature of the ending. But like Greek heroes, each of us encumbered by a life script does not possess the detachment to see its inherently counterproductive nature.

As noted previously, life scripts are developed early. Steiner (1974) proposes that the content of a life script is based on a decision by the child, who, with all the information at his or her disposal at the time, decides that a certain life course is a reasonable solution to an existential predicament; a dilemma results from the behavior of parents and family. Thus it is a seemingly healthy reaction that actually has unhealthy outcomes.

As an example, psychoanalyst Alice Miller (1990) offers the case history of Buster Keaton, the silent-screen comedian. When he was only 3 years old, Keaton started appearing on the theatrical stage with his parents, who were vaudeville actors. This act required the young child to be knocked about, to absorb physical abuse on stage, without batting an eyelash; the audience would roar its delight. But in his autobiography, Keaton (1960) describes his parents as his "first bit of great luck" (p. 14) and never realized that his parents had shamelessly exploited him. Furthermore, according to Miller (1990), this led him to make a lifelong career of entertaining other people even when he did not feel like laughing himself.

Recalling his childhood, Keaton later said:

> In this knock about act, my father and I used to hit each other with brooms, occasioning for me strange flops and falls. If I should chance to smile, the next hit would be a great deal harder. All the parental correction I ever received was with an audience looking on. I could not even whimper. When I grew older, I readily figured out for myself that I was not one of those comedians who could jest with an audience and laugh with it. My audience must laugh at me. (quoted in Kroszarski, 1976, p. 151)

He further stated, "One of the first things I noticed was that whenever I smiled or let the audience suspect how much I was enjoying myself they didn't seem to laugh as much as usual" (Keaton, 1960, p. 13).

What makes this a life script, in Miller's analysis, is that Keaton completely missed the significance of these scenes for his whole later life and for his art. Like Oedipus, he did not realize the implications of his behavior.

The support for the existence of life scripts comes from the case histories and clinical data that are rather informally reported in the books of Eric Berne and Claude Steiner. For example, Steiner (1974, pp. 69-70) provides an example of the creation of a life script involving a 4-year-old girl whose father had a strong influence on her. The father was quite annoyed, because his daughter wanted certain possessions, and he also believed that the best way to build character in the little girl—and hence to avoid spoiling her—was to deny her absolutely everything she wanted and to give her something else in its place. Thus, if he knew that the little girl wanted a teddy bear for Christmas, he would give her an equally lovely toy that she did not want, believing that this substitution would be good for her character development. Soon the little girl learned that none of her wishes were to come true; circumstances beyond her control made everything she desired automatically unobtainable. Furthermore, she also learned that if she restrained herself from expressing a true wish, the chances were enhanced that such a wish would be granted. Paradoxical as this may sound, it was the life script she developed. She also observed that even as she kept her wishes secret, she still feared that she would unwittingly reveal what she wanted by crying when she was disappointed. As a result, in order to keep her father from concluding what her true wishes were, she concluded that crying was undesirable. This little girl grew into adulthood, carrying within her these injunctions from her father against asking for anything and showing any feelings when disappointed. Steiner concludes that the life script served as a remorseless influence that guided every one of her significant decisions for years and years.

The actress Jessica Tandy, who received an Academy Award for her role in *Driving Miss Daisy,* reports a similar development. When she was a child in London and wanted something she could not afford, her mother would tell her, "Those who ask don't get." But her mother also used to say, "Those who don't ask don't want." Tandy's conclusion: "You lose either way," but she grew up learning to guard against false hopes (Darnton, 1990, p. 56).

Do many of us organize our responses to others in an unconscious effort to perpetuate a life script? Although few of us would overtly use such a term to describe ourselves, autobiographies and other personal documents do provide some examples. Some, as in Box 1.3, reflect an explicit link between the person's own characteristic style as an adult and a significant experience that person had as child, usually involving an interaction with a parent.

Like Buster Keaton's, other autobiographies reflect that the person, as an adult, maintains an orientation developed very early in life. Candice Bergen (1984), the movie and television actress and photographer, whose father was ventriloquist Edgar Bergen, chooses to describe as the first event in her autobiography an event when she was 6 years old. Her main concern then was "pleasing her father." The theme recurs throughout her book. "I am nervous about performing well for my father" (1984, p. 12). When, in her twen-

---

BOX 1.3

A Dramatic Life Script

The actor Sidney Poitier (1980), in his autobiography, writes:

> I was drawn to dangerous things. Ever since I can remember I have enjoyed being scared a little bit—an attitude I believe began in the tenth month of my life, when my mother threw me into the ocean like a sack of garbage and stood by expressionless in a dinghy boat watching me go under, sputtering, slashing, and screaming. My pitiful struggle for life seemed not to affect her; she looked calmly on while I clawed at the water, stricken with panic. Even as I gasped desperately on the way down for the last time, she made no move to help. Suddenly, mercifully, my father's hands scooped me up, held me above the water for a moment, then passed me to my mother—who promptly threw me back into the ocean again. (pp. 7-8)

On many occasions throughout his autobiography, Poitier demonstrates his willingness to take risks. It cannot be proved that the drowning incident at 10 months of age caused his characteristic risk-taking behavior, but it is clear that Poitier possessed a need to tie things together, to provide explanations for his characteristic behavior stemming from childhood experiences.

---

ties, she begins to live with a man who differs radically from her father's conservative political values, she is unable to reveal this to her father. "Not only did I not tell my father; I implied otherwise, inviting my parents to dinners at [my old house], where I rarely went now, to indicate that in spite of my relationship I had not strayed but had stayed close to home" (1984, p. 257). Even at her father's funeral, when she was 32, she notes that she is nervous, "wanting more than anything to please" her father (p. 13).

To summarize the life script conception, development is seen as playing only a limited role, because the content and structure of orientations toward others are formed early in life. Although the dominant script can be changed (through the therapeutic benefits of transactional analysis, of course!), Berne believed that some kind of intervention like this was required for the change to happen. Ironically, there is some anecdotal evidence that Berne felt that he too was playing out a tragic life script—one that called for him to die at an early age of a broken heart. Berne's death occurred when he was 60; he died of coronary disease (Steiner, 1974).

As implied earlier, the proposal that life scripts are "relentless"—a favorite description by their advocates—is extreme. As will be illustrated through the dialectical approach later in this chapter, many individuals struggle to free themselves of their life scripts even without therapeutic intervention. Also, there are even script theories, specifically Sylvan Tomkins's (1979, 1987), that explicitly reject Berne's assumption of the inevitability of a life script dominating one's life until death. (Tomkins's script theory is described in Box 1.4.)

Stage Theories of Adult Development

The second major conceptualization of adult personality development is the stage theory formulation. Erik Erikson (1959, 1963) gave impetus to a stage-oriented explanation that extended development throughout the life span by building on Freud's theory of psychosexual development and by generating a theory of eight stages of development. Erikson's theory serves in major ways as a prototype of a stage theory, in that each successive stage or period is not only qualitatively different, but is discontinuous with the previous stage. A crisis, or critical choice in each, leads eventually to a relatively abrupt termination of each period, even though transition to the next stage or period may take several months or even years. The stages build on each other, and the way in which each crisis is resolved affects the person's ability to attack successfully the conflicts of the next stages. Each new stage is seen as a wholly new level of structural integration. According to Erikson, then, personality development proceeds by "critical steps—critical being a characteristic of turning points, of moments of decision between progress and regression, integration and retardation" (Erikson, 1963, pp. 270-271).

BOX 1.4

Tomkins's Script Theory

Tomkins's conception of a script does not rely as much on heavy-handed processes as Berne's does; in Tomkins's conception the person is like a playwright constructing a dramatic narrative in order to make sense of his or her life (Carlson, 1981, 1988; McAdams, 1988). But like Berne's script theory, for Tomkins it is initiated in the earliest weeks of life.

The most basic unit of analysis in Tomkins's theory is the *scene:* "an idealized, affect-laden 'happening' that is constructed (rather than passively experienced and objectively recorded)" (Carlson, 1988, p. 107). A scene tells us "what is happening"; some scenes are more extensive than others; at the minimum a scene includes an emotion and the object of that emotion. Scripts are formed as people develop their individualized rules for "interpreting, creating, enhancing, or defending against a family of related scenes" (Carlson, 1988, p. 107). At first, a scene will determine what the script should be, but over time, the formation of scripts has so consolidated experience that scripts tell the person "what to do" about a number of scenes. The self-defeating nature of a script, present in Berne's conception, is not necessary, according to Tomkins.

As an example of a stage theory conception, Erikson's approach reflects at least three major differences from the early formation viewpoint reflected by life script theory. First, the mold is formed less concretely in childhood, although certainly all future development is affected by the way that the initial trust-versus-mistrust conflict (described in Chapter 4) is resolved. Second, stage theories propose tasks that we feel pressured to do at various ages. Third, Erikson acknowledges that the determinants of personality development extend beyond biological and family ones; the nature of society and its institutions are intrinsically intertwined with the stages of development; for example, parents and peers pressure us to form an identity in adolescence and to institute intimacy in young adulthood.

But what is common to these two conceptualizations is important. Erikson's writings can be interpreted as saying that the conflict or dilemma at each stage must be settled in one way or another before consideration of the task at the next stage—and, ideally, growth—can occur. This emphasis on resolution or closure seems to share the life script approach's assumption that the person develops a blueprint by which conflict is thwarted. In fairness, however, I should note that it is unclear whether Erikson unequivocally opts for a view that each stage's conflict must be resolved immediately; nowhere is he very explicit. The way that he expresses himself in *Childhood and Society,* first published in 1950, leads me to believe that at that time he assumed the resolution of conflicts was necessary. He discusses the absence of trust and "the firm establishment of enduring patterns for the *solution* of the nuclear conflict of basic trust versus basic mistrust" (1950/1963, p. 249, italics added). His leaning toward the necessity of closure is also reflected in his statement that "basic conflicts can lead in the end to either hostile or benign expectations and attitudes" (1950/1963, p. 251). But elsewhere he notes that earlier conflicts can resurface again much later in life.

Erikson's is not, of course, the only stage theory. It was chosen as an example for this overview, because it has been the most influential one, and Erikson, in his quest to test his theory, has been one of the founders of an approach to biographical analysis of personality called psychohistory. Erikson's stage theory is reviewed in Chapter 4 and the approach of psychohistory (better called, in this case, psychobiography) is critiqued in Chapter 5.

A number of other stage theories bear both resemblances to and differences with Erikson's approach. One type, developed by Marjorie Fiske Lowenthal and her colleagues (Lowenthal, Thurnher, Chiriboga, & Associates, 1975), focuses on those transitions during adolescence and adulthood recognized by society as "major," such as graduation from school, marriage, parenthood, grandparenthood, and retirement. Because resultant changes in behavior or personality are expected in light of the social norms operating in our society, the explanatory concepts used by Lowenthal and her associates are more congenial with a sociological perspective than the psychological one emphasized in this volume. (This point is elaborated in Box 1.5.)

Other examples of stage theories are evaluated in Chapters 6 and 7. Of particular usefulness here is the approach developed by Daniel

---

BOX 1.5

**Behavior: Does It Come
From Within the Person or From Outside?**

If given the task of explaining why individuals behave as they do, each of the theories described here assumes that internal determinants are central as people attempt to account for their experiences. They slight a contrasting approach, a social interactionist perspective that emphasizes the importance of close relationships with friends and family, along with those social roles that dominate people's lives (Whitbourne, 1991). The social interactionist approach receives emphasis in the text by Douglas Kimmel (1990); the social roles he considers as essential are those related to age. People have expectations for what is appropriate behavior at particular ages, and these influence our major decisions and life patterns, as well as our emotional well-being and our relationships with others (Whitbourne, 1991). They evaluate their accomplishments against a sort of "social clock," the increments of which are designated by social values, rather than an "inner clock" as emphasized by the theories introduced in this chapter. The social interactionist perspective would question, for example, whether stages are anything more than expectations for what should be our concerns at a given age.

Similarly, Ann T. Weick (1989) has proposed an alternative framework to the one that assumes growth occurs in sequential, age-related changes. According to Weick's growth task model, adults constantly redefine and rework tasks, for example, nurturance and productivity. Adults at midlife are not expected to be perfect just because they are "grownups." Rather than that, they feel challenged to change, and—through awareness of their own power in the change process—they can influence others to do the same (Weick, 1989).

J. Levinson and his colleagues (Levinson, 1978, 1980; Levinson, Darrow, Klein, Levinson, & McKee, 1977), because Levinson's theory reflects the influence of an Eriksonian-type stage model mixed with an emphasis on polarities in adult personality development. This dialectical approach represents the third major way to conceptualize personality development in adulthood, and it is to this approach that we devote the next section of this overview.

Dialectical Approach
to Personality Development

A dialectical conception of human behavior has had a long history, but a short life within psychology. Among the subfields within psychology, its greatest impact has been on developmental psychology; there, interest in a dialectical approach has advanced along with the recent focus on life-span development. Although dialectical ideas are implicit in some of the most historic theories of sociology, social psychology, and personality—for example, in the work of Georg Simmel (1950) and Freud's tension between the superego and the id—only recently have these influential ideas been systematically interpreted within a dialectical framework. Applications of a dialectical analysis to personality have been rather infrequent, but Irwin Altman and his colleagues (Altman, Vinsel, & Brown, 1981) have developed a dialectical analysis of interpersonal relationships. By building on their work and relying heavily on their operational definitions of a dialectic, I want to specify what a dialectical conception of adult personality conveys.

The following assumptions are basic to this approach:

1. Personality can be described as a collection of pairs of characteristics struggling for control within the individual.
2. Personality development reflects a striving toward the satisfaction or achievement of each of these forces, independently (perhaps even at the same time).
3. These characteristics that are in opposition do not simply reflect a presence versus an absence, but rather each is an entity that has a quality of its own; the tug is between two different poles representing, for example, affiliation and privacy, rather than a presence/absence state of being hungry or not hungry.
4. These contending characteristics are always in a state of tension; their relationship is cyclical and changing rather than stable. No matter how strong the pull from one motive or need at a given moment, some amount of the other oppositional force still exists and exerts an influence; thus—and perhaps this is the most important credo of the dialectical approach—the characteristic nature of the system is a never-ending struggle (Kimmel, 1980).
5. In a dialectical analysis, a concept of balance or homeostasis is of no permanent value, because it is the nature of behavior always to be

changing. In contrast to the two previous approaches that assume the resolution of a conflict, a dialectical analysis would propose (to paraphrase Gail Sheehy, 1976) that the whole idea behind the nature of psychosocial development in adulthood is that things can never be settled once and for all. The dialectical view also contrasts with a biological conception that values homeostasis, or the return to a state of equilibrium after any crisis, as a fundamental survival mechanism.

6. Change, in a dialectical analysis, can be assumed to be a cumulative process; that is, the long-term effects of conflicting forces may lead to a synthesis of opposites in the form of a new structural integration (Altman et al., 1981). Adler (1952) proposes that this new synthesis can lead to changes that incorporate the original opposites but also yield something distinctively new. I will examine this claim in detail as part of the consideration of Levinson's theory in Chapter 7. Yet it should be noted that there is an alternative view, held by some dialecticians, that dialectical processes do not necessarily culminate in this desirable higher order synthesis; Immanuel Kant stated, for example, that certain dialectical opposites may not be resolvable, but may continue to exist as "irreducible contradictions" (Adler, 1927).

What are some examples of the oppositional bipolarities so central to a dialectical analysis? Altman and his colleagues (1981) were primarily interested in interpersonal relationships; with respect to the ongoing relationships between two people, they proposed the dialectical concepts of openness-closedness and stability-change as most central. They also note that within social psychology, opposites include harmony and conflict, altruism and aggression, and competition and cooperation. But these authors note that social psychological research has mostly chosen to study one pole at a time, rather than the two in relationship with each other.

With regard to adult personality development, there are some bipolarities that are similar to Altman's interpersonal ones. Stability-change would seem to be reflected, for example, in Levinson's theory; as we will see in Chapter 7, it places emphasis on periods of entrenchment into a role, followed by questioning of one's outcomes, leading possibly to massive upheavals in one's personal and professional lives.

A conflict between individualism and being dominated by one's roles in life may reflect another dialectical issue. Again, the back-and-forth tasks of Levinson's theory are relevant. In certain periods, finding one's niche in the world of work or becoming an acceptable parent tug hardest at us; the role controls our behavior. But at other times not only must we escape the role or label, but our needs to be a unique individual take control (Snyder & Fromkin, 1980). Independence versus dependence and isolation versus community reflect other oppositional dimensions, to be elaborated in Chapter 8.

Such pushes and pulls are certainly not foreign to life script and stage theories, either. What makes the dialectical conception different is its assumption that no stability is ever achieved. In the life script approach equilibrium is the goal; in Erikson's stage approach disequilibrium seemingly serves only to move the person toward resolution of the conflict. By contrast, Klaus Riegel (1976), a radical dialectician, proposed that developmental tasks are never concluded; "at the very moment when completion seems to be achieved, new doubts arise in the individual and in society" (p. 697).

As I mentioned earlier, among contemporary theorists, Daniel Levinson best reflects a synthesis of stage-theory and dialectical ideas, because Levinson specifies four polarities whose resolution is the principal task of men in mid-life. These are attachment/separateness, destruction/creation, masculine/feminine, and young/old; Levinson (1979) writes:

> Each of these pairs forms a polarity in the sense that the two terms represent opposing tendencies or conditions. . . . Both sides of each polarity coexist within every self. At mid-life a man feels young in many respects, but he also has a sense of being old. . . . He feels alternately young, old, and in-between. His developmental task is to make sense of this condition of in-between to become Young/Old in a new way, different from that of early adulthood. (p. 197)

Levinson (1979) goes on to say, in a section most representative of his integration of these frameworks, "all these polarities exist during the life cycle. They can never be fully resolved or transcended, though some utopian thinkers have held out this promise" (p. 198). His statement may, to some readers, seem discouraging. But the dialectician shrugs and concludes that is the nature of human existence.

SUMMARY

The task of explaining why we, as adults, have the personality characteristics we do is a challenging one. Although both society in general and academic psychology in particular have recently increased their interest in adult personality, no one explanation of its causes is accepted by all.

Three alternative conceptions were introduced in this chapter. Early formation theories assume that our character as adults is determined largely by what happens in the first 5 years of childhood. The predominant example of an early formation theory is psychoanalysis; perhaps its most extreme extension, relevant to personality in adulthood, is the life script approach, which proposes that a child develops a characteristic way of responding to others. This life script is generated to protect the child from hurt, but in the long run the playing out of the life script is detrimental to mature adjustment.

A second type of approach is the stage theory, which proposes that development is reflected in reactions to a series of conflicts between choices of life goals. The choice at each stage, or resolution of the conflict, affects how the subsequent conflicts are approached and resolved. A prototype of this approach is Erik Erikson's conception of eight stages from infancy through late adulthood.

The third approach, the dialectical one, proposes that development can be conceptualized by an ongoing tension between pairs of goals. Central to this approach is the idea that no goal is ever fully achieved, because a tension always exists, pulling the person toward the oppositional goal.

Each of these approaches is examined in subsequent chapters of this volume.

2

Psychoanalysis as an
Early Formation Theory

Freud is the father of psychoanalysis. It has no mother.

Germaine Greer

This chapter examines psychoanalytic theory as a prototype of an early formation theory. How does personality develop? Are characteristics manifested in adulthood determined by experiences in childhood? Is psychoanalytic theory validated by empirical evidence? If the theory is correct, how much personality change in adulthood is possible? These questions will be considered in this chapter.

Basic Concepts
in Psychoanalytic Theory

One of the tasks for Freud, as for any personality theorist, was explaining the structure of personality. What are the basic building blocks in describing personality? How is it put together?

Personality Structure

Freud proposed that three systems within the person reflect different drives or motivations and these compete with each other for control of the person's behavior. It is important to recognize that these systems are concepts, not things or little people inside our heads; they are abstractions extracted from commonalities in behavior and inner experience.

Furthermore, they operate largely without our awareness; that is, the innate drives were seen as unconscious. Freud assumed that if the person is doing something that he or she cannot report or explain, then the mental processes necessary to "fill in the gaps"— the drives or motives—must be unconscious (Westen, 1990).

Toward the end of his life, Freud came to see the struggle between a life instinct and a death instinct as central; Westen (1990) effectively characterizes this view as follows:

> Perhaps what is most compelling about Freud's instinct theory is the notion that certain motives are simply rooted in the organism, and that there is nothing a person can do but to try to adapt to them, enjoy them or inhibit them when appropriate, and extrude them from one's experience of self when they are too threatening to acknowledge as one's own. (p. 24)

Freud could not escape the conviction that within every person exists an aspect of untamed, animal-like motivation. He conceived it to be there at birth—an instinctual set of demanding, selfish urges. This innate system he termed the id; he saw it as the reservoir of psychic energy and believed that it furnished all the power for the operation of the other two systems that developed later.

In young children, the id seems to rule, according to Freud's view. Young children, without restraint or regret, seek their pleasures and vent their unintentionally destructive impulses on the world. The id cannot tolerate tension; it seeks to discharge this tension immediately. This quest for immediate gratification is called the "pleasure principle." It is relevant to note that in the original German, Freud referred to this process as the "it," reflecting how his patients had expressed an impulse like an impersonal, uncontrolled force, as in "It just came over me" (Bettelheim, 1983).

But, in time, controls develop and restrain the operation of this primary process. At first, immoral and asocial behavior is inhibited only when disapproving and punishing adults are present. Later on, the individual internalizes these external controls. That is, they become his or her own and exert influence even when adults are not around to disapprove or punish. This system of controls Freud called the "superego," a construct that he defined as the *moral principle,* the conscience.

Right versus wrong is the only concern of the superego. Although its drives are almost always in conflict with those of the id, the superego and id share a nonrational quality; they tend to lack any concern with what is realistic or beneficial in the long run.

In Freudian theory two subsystems exist as part of the superego. In addition to the moralistic component, or conscience, the superego maintains an ego-ideal, a set of characteristics that the person seeks to attain for himself or herself.

The third basic system that seemed necessary to Freud to account for the behavior he saw is the ego. He found in his patients, as we have just noted, an array of primitive and unreasoning urges on the one hand, and rigid and sometimes equally unreasoning controls on the other. But he also saw the capacity to deal intelligently and rationally with reality. This reality principle is reflected in the actions of the ego. Freud saw the ego as something like an intelligent administrator, concerned with keeping the person going in the face of the conflicting demands of the id and the superego and in the face of the demands of reality. But the ego may not be up to this; it may lose control. After all, according to Freud, the ego came into existence in order to advance the aims of the id, and all its psychic energy was derived from the id. (Not all of Freud's later followers agree with this last proposition, instead proposing that the ego has its own instinctual source of psychic energy.)

Three principal elements, then, participate in the lifelong drama that Freud saw enacted within every person. The three components of personality are: the selfish, now-centered id that constantly threatens to spew forth its instinctual energies (Haan, 1989); the rigid, uncompromising voice of morality, the superego; and the sometimes weak but sometimes clever compromiser and arranger, the ego. The central goal of the game is control, and the central theme of the play is conflict; in fact, originally, Freud explained pathology and mental illness as caused by these structural conflicts. In general, he portrayed an everlasting and irreconcilable conflict between good and evil, between superego and id. (Contrary to his public image, Freud was essentially a moralistic person. His view of human nature was negative, and he felt that it is the function of society to restrain people from their basic selfish impulses.)

The opportunity for the ego to grow strong is rooted both in hereditary factors and in the experiences of the child. As noted in Chapter 1, in Freud's view, personality is largely formed by the end of the 5th year, and late growth consists mainly of elaborating the structure (Hall & Lindzey, 1970, p. 50). Thus the opportunities for the ego to develop control are tested by challenges to the young child as a result of biological changes during the early years.

An old saying claims that "biology is destiny." Because he proposed that inevitable biological changes during childhood can affect personality, Freud would have agreed with this constitutional imperative. Sigmund Freud was, of course, highly trained in physiology while he was in medical school, and furthermore, his concept for the basic psychological energy, the libido, reflected principles from biology and physics. Assuming, plausibly, that mental processes must be powered by energy, he then proposed that "this energy must follow the same laws as other forms of energy in nature" (Westen, 1990, p. 23).

In fact, the recent discovery of a speculative manuscript written by Freud in 1915 indicates that he saw anxiety, paranoia, and other types of emotional disorders as reflecting responses that were adaptive for the human species back in their evolutionary period around the Ice Age (Goleman, 1987a). Despite the fact that Freud came to conclude that some of the propositions in this manuscript were theoretical dead ends, it reflects the influence of the biological imperative on his thinking.

Stages of Psychological Development

The previous section reflected Freud's assumption that certain inborn motives propel humans and determine the direction that behavior will take (Freud, 1917/1963, 1933). Attempts to satisfy these motives formed the groundwork for the emergence of personality characteristics that, according to Freud, would continue into adulthood. The energy expended in satisfying motives is a psychological or psychic energy called "libido." This can be thought of as much like physical energy in that we have only a certain amount of it at any given time. Emphasis is on the conservation of this psychic energy. Hence the more energy that is devoted to one activity, the less there is available for another. Freud saw normal development as a process of redirecting the libido toward different goals as the person matures. Difficulties arise when psychic energy needed to work out problems in the present must be spent instead to achieve goals that should have been achieved in an earlier stage of development.

According to Freud, as children grow older they go through predictable and clear-cut stages of personality development. (Yes, Freud was a stage theorist; his theory did not, however, qualify for the second approach propounded in this book, because his stages did not extend into adulthood.) These stages reflect a timetable that is biologically determined.

Each of Freud's stages is centered on that part of the body that occupies the child's thoughts most at a particular developmental period. The first stage, which occurs during the child's first year, is the oral stage. The mouth during this stage is the center of the infant's universe, for it is used to ingest food and to express displeasure. Thus the infant's libido is directed toward the satisfaction of its oral needs (sucking, then swallowing, then biting). If these needs are satisfied, the child can shift his or her psychic energy toward a concern appropriate for the next stage. (That is, weaning is successful not only functionally, but also psychologically.) If oral needs are not fully satisfied, fixation occurs. This can result from improper weaning, an unsatisfactory feeding schedule, oral overindulgence, fears and anxieties, or other reasons. In fixation a certain amount of psychic energy remains devoted to the satisfying of an earlier need even though the child has moved on to confront the tasks of a later stage of development.

If fixation has occurred, the adult's personality and behavior reflect the continued lack of satisfaction of this need. For example, if a man became fixated at the oral stage, he might be very talkative, chew gum constantly, or smoke. He might seek out an occupation that permits him to talk excessively—such as salesperson or professor—or he might be sarcastic or biting in his conversation. That is, fixation could occur as a failure to satisfy either sucking needs (early part of oral stage) or biting needs (later part of the stage) or both. The concept of fixation is a prime example of Freud's relating personality factors to biological needs. But he also recognized that the child's environment would influence the degree of satisfaction or fixation.

The second stage in Freud's theory of personality development is the anal stage; here the 2-year-old or 3-year-old child, going through the self-discipline of toilet training, is learning self-control. The conflict emerges between the child's developmental awareness that the anus can be a source of pleasurable excitation and the efforts by parents or other caregivers to force compliance over toilet training.

Society places great emphasis on achieving "proper" toilet training. Again, we have a choice point, in that the child-rearing practices of the parents can lead either to fixation or to a shifting of the child's libidinal energy to other concerns. Hall and Lindzey (1970) indicate some of the outcomes of toilet-training methods that Freudian theory would predict:

> If the mother is very strict and repressive in her methods, the child may hold back his feces and become constipated. If this mode of reaction generalizes to other ways of behaving, the child will develop a retentive character. He will become obstinate and stingy. Or under the duress of repressive measures the child may vent his rage by expelling his feces at the most inappropriate times. This is the prototype for all kinds of expulsive traits—cruelty, wanton destructiveness, temper tantrums, and messy disorderliness, to mention only a few. On the other hand, if the mother is the type of person who pleads with her child to have a bowel movement and who praises him extravagantly when he does, the child will acquire the notion that the whole activity of producing feces is extremely important. This idea may be the basis for later creativity and productivity. (Hall & Lindzey, 1970, p. 51)

Thus are the traits of adulthood supposedly laid down during the anal stage.

The next stage of development, the phallic stage, usually occurs when the child is 3, 4, or 5 years of age. At this time, interests in one's genital organs come into prominence. (It is a manifestation of Freud's male bias that even while he tried to explain the development of each sex, he chose as the title for this stage a reference to the male sex organ, the phallus.) At these ages, masturbation and other kinds of self-stimulation may occur. The child may develop feelings of jealously toward the parent of the same sex and feelings of affection for the parent of the other sex. During this period a boy, according to Freud, "rather naively wishes to use his new-found source of pleasure, his penis, to please his oldest source of pleasure, the mother" (Schaeffer, 1971, p. 12). He envies his father, who is occupying the position he craves and is doing the thing he wishes to do. Freud called this the Oedipus complex, after Oedipus, the mythical king of Thebes who killed his father and married his mother.

According to psychoanalytic theory, attitudes toward the other gender and toward people in authority are largely influenced by the Oedipus complex and the person's way of resolving it. A boy's fear of his father—a part of which is castration anxiety—may lead to a repression of the sexual desire for his mother. Through repression, the unacceptable desire is removed from conscious awareness to an unconscious level of the mind. At the same time, the boy comes to identify or align himself with his father. This identification gives the boy some vicarious satisfaction of the sexual drives that he cannot satisfy directly. If fixation occurs, in later life the male may seek as companions and sexual partners those women who resemble his mother. Or he may carry over into adult life feelings of anxiety and self-doubt rooted in guilt about his sexual fantasies in childhood.

As he sought to explain the development of sexual orientation in females, Freud could not apply the same explanation, because both boys and girls start out attracted to the mother, the caregiver and source of benefits. He struggled over an explanation, and the resultant one was neither satisfactory to him nor acceptable to feminists (Chodorow, 1989). According to Freud, after the girl's original identification with her mother, she comes to blame her mother for the fact that she lacks the genitals of boys. She wishes she had a penis; she feels ashamed that she does not, and she feels inferior. Her feeling of deficiency extends to her whole self-concept. She concludes that she has already lost her penis, and she blames her mother for depriving her of this organ. In the process she comes to devalue her mother.

This state, called *penis envy,* generates a shift in attraction to her father, called the Electra complex. Electra was the mythical woman who incited her brother to kill her mother and her mother's lover. The transfer of love to her father occurs because he has the valued organ that she aspires to share with him. She gives up clitoral masturbation and represses a good deal of her sexual impulses in general. She becomes more passive, more "feminine." (Freud proposed that this lack of a penis is compensated for when the girl grows up and has a baby, especially if it is a boy baby.) Later in childhood, the girl again develops a feminine identification with her mother in a manner that Freud does not specify very clearly. Freudian theory has difficulty in explaining female development in biological terms. Perhaps that is one of the reasons why the examples Freud used were usually male-oriented, even though the vast majority of his patients were females.

The next of Freud's stages is the latency period. Between the ages of about 5 and the onset of puberty, the child's libido is tame, partly because the child represses unacceptable desires for the parent of the other sex. Sexual interests are replaced by interests in school, sports, and friends. In effect, the young person learns acceptable ways to sublimate sexual and aggressive drives. Freud felt that it was biologically determined that not much was to happen developmentally during these years, so he had little to say about them.

After the uneventful latency period, a person moves into the genital stage. The adolescent develops overt sexual interests. Concern is directed toward the biological goal of reproduction, and that part of the libido that is not still being devoted to earlier selfish needs may be channeled into love and into a genuine concern for others. Only those people who have most of the libidinal energy available for this stage can become realistic, well-socialized adults.

But many adults, said Freud, have so much of their limited psychic energy still being allocated to the satisfaction of the earlier needs that they have little left for the development of altruistic motives. They remain narcissistic or self-loving. Their "love of others" may be based on the ways others remind them of themselves.

Validation of Freud's Theory

One of the major contributions of Freud's writings to understanding of personality development was the comprehensive structure and richness of concepts. A contemporary observation (Gelman, 1991) views it as still providing the sturdiest framework for understanding personality development. Some of his critics would begrudgingly acknowledge that this was Freud's only positive contribution; other critics would not even grant him that!

Whether one concludes that our understanding has or has not been advanced by psychoanalytic theory, it can be agreed that Freud took a narrow view of attempts by others to substantiate his theory, and the theory's empirical foundations are one source of its criticisms (Edelson, 1988). When Saul Rosenzweig wrote Freud in 1934 about his attempts to validate Freud's hypotheses about repression through experimental procedures, Freud responded (on a postcard), "I cannot put much value on these [attempts at] confirmations, because the wealth of reliable observations on which these assertions rest makes them independent of experimental verification." He added gratuitously, "Still, it can do no harm" (quoted by MacKinnon & Dukes, 1963, p. 703).

The "reliable observations" on which Freud based his theory were, of course, the statements and nonverbal behavior of patients undergoing psychological treatment (Hall & Lindzey, 1970). As Westen (1990) notes, some psychoanalysts still view these as the only valid type of data for a theory of personality (see, e.g., Arlow & Brenner, 1988; Brenner, 1982; Edelson, 1988). But this is just as narrow as an experimentalist insisting on experimental data as the only valid pathway to truth. Marie Jahoda (1977) has, instead, suggested that the proper way to deal with limitations in one's method is to supplement it with other methods that possess other kinds of limitations or impurities. And many leading psychoanalysts welcome testing based on experimental research (see Holt, 1985; Holzman, 1985).

But that was not Freud's position. He carried out no experiments or controlled observations; he gave no personality tests and used no quantitative measures. But Freud did check for internal consistency; he did bring a critical attitude to his data; and he made an intensive study of single cases. Again and again he revised his theories in light of new observations. He did not revise enough, however, in the view of some of his critics; in 1984 it was claimed by Jeffrey Masson that Freud covered up some of his most sensational findings; Box 2.1 describes these claims in detail.

Empirical studies have examined virtually every aspect of psychoanalytic theory (Fisher & Greenberg, 1977). One focus here is on the assumption of early formation and the centrality of fixation in determining our personality as adults. Note that the hypothesis that adult personality patterns and characteristics derive directly from infant and childhood experiences is ingrained in modern thought; Freud tried to translate this platitude into a scientific finding (Stannard, 1980). Freud proposed specific childhood experiences that were related to specific adult character patterns.

Most psychologists would agree that maternal actions contribute to the child's development. For example, if a mother is protective and responsive, the infant will be more likely to explore novel environments (Buss, 1987). But psychoanalysts propose that these effects extend into adulthood, that, for example, physical abuse as a child raises the risk of aggressive behavior as an adult (Miller, 1990).

It is the case that the initial research that focused on specific linkages failed to show the presence of these predicted relationships. Using objective measures of adult personality and correlating them with accounts of activities during early childhood produced no consistent indication of a relationship (Eysenck & Wilson, 1974; Orlansky, 1949; Sears, 1943), although among this early work, a few isolated studies emerged that found relationships between particular measures, such as age at weaning and optimism/pessimism in adulthood (Goldman-Eisler, 1951). In reality, many of these initial empirical studies contained disabling methodological limitations (Cairns, 1983) and their results had little impact on the psychoanalytic perspective (Leichtman, 1987).

More recent work is more supportive. Runyan (1988) concludes there is evidence "about clusters of traits consistent with Freud's conception of oral character and substantial evidence about orderliness, obstinacy, and parsimony clustering together as Freud suggested in the anal or obsessive character" (p. 225).

In a more general sense, empirical verification exists for a psychoanalytic assumption that the kind of attachment that people

BOX 2.1

Freud and the Seduction Theory

In 1984 Jeffrey Masson, a psychoanalyst who briefly was project director at the Freud archives, claimed that Freud was a coward who tried to cover up his most explosive findings. Back in the late 1800s, Freud had speculated that all hysteria could be traced back to actual childhood sexual traumas, such as incest and rape. But Freud later claimed he rejected this explanation because of his increased realization that some of the "seductions" his adult patients reported were, in fact, fantasies. He came to place more emphasis on the theory that all children have sexual fantasies and sexual urges long before puberty. This was, of course, one of Freud's groundbreaking conclusions (Miller, 1984).

But Masson proposed that Freud rejected his earlier idea because he feared professional rejection and isolation if he were to continue publicizing it. It was "a personal failure of courage," Masson said.

Critics of Masson say that Freud did not suppress his own earlier hypothesis; he simply treated it as an open empirical question. Some neuroses of adulthood stem from the person having been raped or seduced when a child; some do not. (In a letter Freud wrote, "Such widespread perversions against children are not probable" [Masson, 1984, p. 264].)

In his introductory lectures, first published in 1916, Freud (1916/1966) acknowledges:

> Phantasies of being seduced are of particular interest because so often they are not phantasies but real memories. Fortunately, however, they are nevertheless not real as often as seemed at first to be shown by the findings of analysis. . . . You must not suppose, however, that sexual abuse of a child by its nearest male relatives belongs entirely to the realm of phantasy. Most analysts will have treated cases in which such events were real and could be unimpeachably established. . . . Up to the present time we have not succeeded in pointing to any difference in the consequences, whether phantasy or reality has had a greater share in these events of childhood. (p. 370)

Furthermore, it would seem that Freud's later view, that of infantile sexuality, was much more objectionable to people in the Victorian era than would have been a revelation of rape. The innocence of childhood has always been one of our cherished illusions.

form with their parents during childhood colors the nature of romantic relationships they have as adults (Hazan & Shaver, 1987). And the proposition that there exists a process known as the unconscious—a completely revolutionary idea when Freud proposed it—and that it can influence conscious thought and behavior is well accepted by psychologists of varying perspectives (Brody, 1987; Kihlstrom, 1990; Schultz, 1992).

But a contemporary viewpoint moves away from a search for a *direct* relationship between childhood limitations and adult personality. Thus the shift—and it is a pervasive one—is toward a lifespan interactionist position that emphasizes how early experience plays only one part in a cycle of unfolding events, with influences continuing throughout the person's life. William McKinley Runyan (1988) summarizes this new perspective:

> In contrast to earlier beliefs about the crucial aspect of childhood experience on adult behavior (Bloom, 1964; Bowlby, 1952; E. Kelly, 1955), there is a growing belief that the effects of early deprivation can be substantially modified by later experience and that behavior and personality are shaped and changed throughout the life course (Brim & Kagan, 1980; Clarke & Clarke, 1976; Mischel, 1968; Rutter, 1979). The argument is not that early childhood experiences have no effects, but that the effects of such experiences are mediated by intervening experiences and contingencies, and that personality and behavior are continually shaped throughout the life cycle.
>
> Early experience, of whatever form, rarely has a direct impact on adult personality, but early experience shapes early personality, which influences the kinds of environments one is likely to encounter, which in turn, influence later experience, which affects personality and so on in an interactive cycle (Wachtel, 1977). (Runyan, 1988, p. 226)

The problem with predicting behavior is not the only challenge to the validity of psychoanalytic theory. Critics complain that Freudian theory is so general that it cannot be pinned down enough to be empirically tested. For example, the philosopher of science Karl Popper (1957, 1963) labeled psychoanalysis as a pseudoscience, seeing it as unfalsifiable because any finding, even seemingly negative ones, could be explained away (Westen, 1990). But Nevitt Sanford (1980), a wise observer, has a different perspective on the difficulties in operationalizing psychoanalytic concepts. He writes:

The question is often put as to why Freud's theoretical scheme has persisted [more or less unmodified] for so long. Sixty years is a long time for a theory in science. . . . I think it ought to be conceded that the general theory has lasted because it was well conceived in the first place, and because it has been increasingly validated by objective studies and by clinical utility as the years have gone by. (pp. 250-251)

He goes on to observe:

No one will deny that the things Freud was talking about are things of perpetual, often consuming, interest. In conceptualizing them he seems to have made them just hypothetical enough, and just remote enough from anything directly observable, in order to insure the perpetuation of his theory; we cannot ignore his formulations, nor can we disprove them. The concepts can be defined operationally, in the modern sophisticated sense; and so they cannot be dismissed as vagaries of the imagination; yet it is extraordinarily difficult to devise any critical tests of them. (p. 251)

Although Sanford's perspective generally is justified, many would respond that Freudian theory has not remained rigid, despite criticisms that it has. Recent followers have provided new emphases, as Box 2.2 and Box 2.3 reflect.

Karen Horney's
Modification of Psychoanalytic Theory

As we know, Freud had many followers, some of whom developed their own theories of personality, albeit relying on his basic framework. In this and the next section are described two of these that I consider particularly relevant to the theoretical perspectives of this book.

Karen Horney (1950) proposed that neurosis resulted from a person's losing the thread of his or her guiding direction. Becoming too concerned with pleasing others, neurotic persons forget their own deepest satisfactions and needs. Horney's perspective is reminiscent of the life script approach described in Chapter 1; these two conceptions are similar in their assumption that the child forms a long-lasting style of responding to others, as a result of anxiety.

BOX 2.2

Object Relations Theory

The conceptions used in this chapter reflect Freud's own thinking about the ways that individuals' childhood experiences color their present behavior and relationships. In that sense these ideas are part of the classic Freudian model. Given that Freud began his writing in the last two decades of the 19th century, some of these ideas are more than 100 years old. More recently, some adherents to the basic guidelines of psychoanalytic theory have chosen to alter this mainstream viewpoint in several ways (Frosh, 1987). Among these revisionists, those who emphasize *object relations* theory are most important for the focus of this book.

As St. Clair (1986), the author of a text on psychoanalytic theory, notes:

> Object relations means interpersonal relations. The term *object*, a technical word originally coined by Freud, refers simply to that which will satisfy a need. More broadly, object refers to the significant person or theory that is the object or target of another's feelings or drives. Freud first used object in discussions of instinctual drives and in a context of early mother-child relations. In combinations with *relations*, object refers to interpersonal relations and suggests the inner residues of past relationships that shape an individual's current interactions with people. (p. 1, italics in original)

So it can be seen that object relations continues the focus on the effects of past experiences (here, the emphasis is on past relationships) on shaping of personalities. Yet there are differences, not the least of which is the proposal that the main motive a person has is for a relationship, not the satisfaction of a biological instinct. St. Clair (1986) provides us with a clever distinction between the two approaches by interpreting the "case study" of Cinderella through the constructs of each. Let us suppose, he proposes, that Cinderella seeks the assistance of a psychoanalyst because she is experiencing conflict in her marriage with the prince. He observes that "a traditional Freudian might investigate Cinderella's repression of her sexual instincts and unresolved Oedipal feelings that she had for her parents. This therapist or analyst would analyze Cinderella's problems in terms of defenses and conflicts between the structures of the ego and the id" (1986, p. 3).

(Continued)

BOX 2.2 (Continued)

In contrast, notes St. Clair, a psychoanalyst committed to the object relations perspective:

> would note that Cinderella suffered early psychological deprivation from the loss of her mother. Possibly this loss caused Cinderella to make use of the psychological defense mechanism of splitting, by which she idealized some women (such as her fairy godmother) and saw other women as "all bad" (her stepsisters and stepmother). She idealized the Prince despite knowing him for only a short time. A marriage based on such distorted images of herself and others is bound to run into problems as she sooner or later must deal with the Prince as a real person with human flaws. In object relations theory, the issue would center on the discrepancy between Cinderella's inner world and the persons and situations of the actual world. (St. Clair, 1986, p. 3)

Aspects of an object-relations approach—especially the theory developed by Otto Kernberg (1976)—reflect the development of more sophisticated cognitive representations reminiscent of George Kelly's personal construct theory described in Chapter 1. Kernberg proposed that development moves from a lack of distinction in infancy between concepts of self and other, to a distinction based on affective valence (whether a person or act is "good" or "bad") to eventually a mature cognitive representation reflecting an integration of mixed reactions.

Basic anxiety, for Horney (1937), is the feeling the child has of being isolated and helpless in a potentially hostile world. Anything that disturbs the security of children in relation to their parents produces basic anxiety. A person can become neurotic, and hence anxious, if he or she is raised in a home that lacks security, trust, love, respect, tolerance, and warmth. Conflict, then, is not inevitable, not built into human nature (as Freud believed); rather, conflict arises out of social conditions.

Horney theorized that people develop strategies by which to cope with the feeling of isolation and helplessness; this is done to mini-

---

BOX 2.3

**Psychoanalysis and
Developmental Psychology**

In the past decade, followers of psychoanalytic explanations have intensified their examination of concepts and theories from developmental psychology (Leichtman, 1987). Influential in this effort is psychiatrist Daniel Stern's (1985) book, *The Interpersonal World of the Infant,* a "work which draws on contemporary psychological research to construct a picture of the subjective experience of young children that contrasts sharply with the most influential theories of early development" (Leichtman, 1987, p. 1). For example, Stern reports findings leading to a conclusion that infants are born with a strong biological predisposition toward social relationships and thus rejects the self-centered id as "normal." He also extends the object-relations focus described in Box 2.2 backward, to the first 2 years of life, concluding that the infant and caretaker share efforts to achieve "affective attunement." He also questions the prominence of oral needs in shaping later experiences.

---

mize the anxiety of coping with others. One possible style or orientation toward others she called "moving toward people." This is the self-effacing solution to basic anxiety, in which the person shows dependency on others and seeks love from them. The person may become undemanding and be content with very little. Out of the desire to minimize the anxiety of coping with others, such persons may let others tread on them; afraid of being deserted and left alone, they avoid conflict.

"Moving away from people," a second type of strategy, is quite different. Here, the person becomes coldly aloof and withdrawn from any genuine interaction with significant others. A "lone wolf," such a person may reflect either resignation or rebelliousness. Whichever, there is a lack of commitment to others; the credo seems to be, "If I withdraw, nothing can hurt me."

The last type of strategy, "moving against people," reflects an orientation toward mastery and power. Hostility is a stronger component here, and this hostility may lead to a need to exploit others. The person seems to believe, "If I have power, no one can hurt me" (Horney, 1937, p. 98).

Horney believed that normal people integrate these three styles, but that neurotic persons, because of their greater degrees of anxiety, must use artificial or irrational solutions. Thus they consciously recognize only one of the tendencies and deny or repress the other two; that is, like the follower of a life script, the neurotic person is locked into a rigidly unshakable coping technique.

Are these styles universal? Probably not completely, but David L. Gutmann (1964, 1977), a clinical psychologist with training in anthropology, has identified three apparently universal styles that people in different cultures use to respond to demands placed on them (Chiriboga, 1989). These three styles, somewhat broader than Horney's, are:

1. Active mastery—or trying to change conditions in the environment.
2. Passive mastery—or accommodating to the environment.
3. Magical mastery—or a denial or redefining of the situation, rather than taking action to change it.

Carl Jung's Analytical Psychology

Carl Jung was one of the most innovative of Freud's followers. Even though he had been handpicked by Freud to become his "successor," Jung's ideas came to deviate from Freud's to such a degree that their relationship disintegrated. Jung came to conclude that Freud viewed the brain "as an appendage to the genital glands" (Westen, 1990, p. 25).

The following is only a selection of Jung's rich and extensive ideas, included particularly because Jung serves as a transition figure. Trained in an early formation framework, Jung was among the first to extend conceptions of childhood into adulthood. Many of the concepts described in Chapters 4, 6, and 7 reflect his ideas as a source. Another of Jung's relevant contributions was the distinction between the anima and the animus; as we will see, these provide a dialectical flavor, and are manifested in contemporary views of personality development, especially Daniel Levinson's (Chapter 7).

Jung proposed that in the late thirties or early forties a radical transvaluation occurs. Youthful interests and pursuits lose their value and are replaced by new interests that are more cultural and less biological. The middle-aged person becomes more introverted and less impulsive; wisdom takes the place of physical and mental vigor. Jung believed that this shift was the most decisive in the person's life, that this was a time of "immense growth and development, particularly for personal introspection, reevaluation, and spiritual discovery" (Hudson, 1991, p. xvii).

In introducing the concepts of the animus and the anima, Jung emphasized that there is both a masculine and a feminine side to personality, regardless of which sex you are. In most men, the anima is suppressed, and in women, the animus is less expressed. But recognition of the presence of both, and release of these values, gives the person completeness. Yet there is a tension between these two sets of values. One is more unconscious but is striving for expression; the psychoanalytic analysis of the life and character of Lewis Carroll, author of *Alice in Wonderland,* reported by Greenacre (1955) provides an illustration (see Box 2.4). The opposition of conscious and unconscious forces, as viewed by Jung, formed a kind of dialectic. Jung's conception of anima and animus in competition for expression was a significant recognition of polarities in personality development and expression.

S U M M A R Y

Psychoanalytic theory can serve as a prototype of an early formation theory because it assumes a structure that leads to personality formation early in life. Freud hypothesized that three systems—which have come to be called the id, the ego, and the superego—within the person reflect different motivations that compete with each other to determine behavior. These formed the groundwork for the emergence of personality characteristics that, in Freud's theory, continued into adulthood.

Freud used libido, or psychic energy, as a central concept in that shifts in its focus explained developmental task solution. The child was assumed to move through several stages—oral, anal, phallic, and genital—but if the satisfaction of the requisite motives was not

(Text continued on page 43)

BOX 2.4

A Freudian Analysis of
Lewis Carroll's Personality

Charles Dodgson was born in England in 1832 (he took the pseudonym "Lewis Carroll" for his nonsense writings). His father was an austere but witty minister in the Church of England; his mother, preoccupied with raising a family, was described as "quiet and devoted." They had 11 children in 17 years; Charles was the third, and the first boy. Two more sisters came next, one being born only a year after Charles's birth. Hence, the Freudians would note, he had a largely female world during his first 5 years. (Interestingly, only 3 of the 11 offspring ever married, and none did so until after the death of their parents.)

Charles was perhaps left-handed; at any rate, he was quite preoccupied with left and right, and became an accomplished mirror writer, puppeteer, and magician. A good child and well behaved, he went to a boarding school beginning at age 12. Seven years later, he received a "studentship" (a teaching fellowship) at Christ Church College, Oxford University, where he remained the rest of his life. To receive the fellowship, he was to promise that he should remain unmarried and take up the orders of the Church (that is, to become a minister). He never did the latter, although he occasionally preached at chapel.

Charles Dodgson never married; apparently he never had any kind of adult relationship with a woman. There is a hint that he once advanced the idea of matrimony but was refused. At the age of 25, he wrote in his diary, "If at any future period I contemplate marriage (of which I see no present likelihood) . . ." (Cohen, 1979).

Dodgson, after his formal training, became a professor of mathematics at Oxford. He wrote a number of mathematics books, but his contributions to the field were not profound or revolutionary; furthermore, Greenacre (1955) tells us, "He did not seem to make a real contact with his students, who respected him but regarded him as eccentric and withdrawn" (p. 140). In fact, Dodgson's sober personality was the very antithesis of what we think of as Lewis Carroll; he was meticulous and over-exact. A compulsive indexer, he made a record of all the letters—and he was quite a correspondent!—he wrote and received, cross-referenced according to content. At the time of his death, this registry contained 98,721 items (Pudney, 1976). For 40 years he kept a record of each dinner party he attended, including the menu and seating arrangements. He was also described as rather goody-goody; he would walk out of the commons room and return to his bachelor quarters at the mention of the least indelicacy or irreverence.

But he also enjoyed playing with children—the "Lewis Carroll" aspect of his personality. He enjoyed children ages 8 to 12 the most; he would tell them stories and act as a voluntary uncle. At first, he liked both sexes but later came to like only girls. In fact, he later came to describe boys as "not an attractive race of beings" and once said, "I am fond of children except boys." He would invite little girls to lunch with specific instructions to leave their brothers at home. Once the girl reached about 14 (i.e., the age of puberty) he lost interest in her.

Around 1856 he took up photography as a hobby and became quite skilled. He kept a wardrobe of costumes for his little girls to pose in, and also developed a penchant for photographing them in the nude (or as he once called it, "mother-naked")—until objections by parents to the latter terminated that. Nothing in his letters or diaries suggests that his interest was anything but an innocent one (Pritchett, 1980). At the age of 56 he recorded in his diary the new experience of sketching a nude model and concluded that "a spectator would really have to be in search of evil thoughts to have any other feeling about her than simply a sense of beauty as in looking at a statue" (quoted in Greenacre, 1955, p. 163).

In the presence of children, the stiff, stuffy academician became a witty, affectionate storyteller (Newman, 1991). *Alice in Wonderland,* published in 1865, his most famous nonsense writing, came from stories he told his child friends. There really was an Alice, the daughter of the Dean at Oxford; she and her friends were so delighted with the stories Lewis Carroll told them that they insisted he write them down. The success led to other nonsense writings, including *Through the Looking Glass,* published in 1871, when he was 39, which memorialized Tweedledum and Tweedledee, plus "The Walrus and the Carpenter." Much success, both popular and financial, came from the Alice books, so that at age 50 he quit teaching in order to write. But his later nonsense writing and fiction was not as successful.

One does not have to be a psychoanalyst to conclude that Charles Dodgson/Lewis Carroll had two separate personalities. Though not a multiple personality in the sense of "Sibyl" or "The Three Faces of Eve," in later years he tried to keep his two identities separate and became quite annoyed when he was addressed by one name while in the character of the other. In 1897 Dodgson more or less expelled Carroll from Oxford; he refused mail addressed to "Lewis Carroll" and marked it "not known."

(Continued)

BOX 2.4 (Continued)

The question is why did the separate identities develop? Universal questions of childhood, such as "Who am I?" or "How did I come to be?" became quite complicated for him. Psychoanalysts would note that he disciplined himself so thoroughly and cultivated self-control so successfully in his Charles Dodgson role that he might have been judged as a person of great steadiness with a restricted inner life. But in fact, this surface control disguised a precarious balance and much inner tension leading him to sublimate his unconscious drives in his nonsense writing and his photography (Hudson, 1954). For example, consider what the author must have been secretly feeling when he turned children into pigs or expressed the blind fury of the Queen of Hearts. The reason why he was not a success as a mathematician was that success requires "mathematical ability and imagination to work in harmony" and that for him, "the math interest was generally opposed to the imagination, probably carrying too much of the neurotic compulsive defense against the nearly mad imagination of Carroll" (Greenacre, 1955, pp. 140-141).

It thus required two identities to "integrate" these discordant elements. Interestingly, the stammer that Dodgson had all his life was not present when he interacted with little girls (Ellmann, 1979).

More speculative is the psychoanalytic proposal that an unresolved Oedipus conflict may have been present. Lewis Carroll was devoted to young girls, about 20 years younger than himself; his mother was 20 years older. Recall that young Charles Dodgson had a sibling born one year after his birth; he probably got little nurturance from his mother. Reversal of the Oedipus conflict is quite common, proposes Greenacre (p. 134) and other Freudians, some of whom even propose that the concern with Alice's changing size in *Alice in Wonderland* may be interpreted as a lament as to how his mother had betrayed him by having another child.

Such interpretations cannot be proved, of course; we will examine the problems of such a psychobiographical approach in Chapter 5. But it does seem that Charles Dodgson was maladjusted and neurotic; even his nonpsychologist admirers admit that. He must be considered an underachiever, even though he did leave us with so much. And, if he had been able to coordinate his imaginative fantasy world with his work activities, would he have given us *Alice in Wonderland?* We doubt it.

SOURCES: Gardner, 1960; Greenacre, 1955; Newman, 1991; Pritchett, 1980; Pudney, 1976.

achieved, fixation would occur. Empirical evidence for adult manifestations of fixations is mixed; recent thought tends to emphasize an interaction between early childhood events and other factors that occur later in the life course.

Karen Horney, as a follower of Freud, emphasized three possible responses to the basic anxiety the child feels; these are "moving toward people," "moving away from people," and "moving against people."

Carl Jung, one of the most innovative of Freud's followers, contributed to personality development through his concepts of anima and animus and midlife transitions.

3

Theorists' Lives

DO THEY

DETERMINE THEIR THEORIES?

The boy will come to nothing!

Sigmund Freud's father, commenting about his son

A college student, assigned the theme topic of "an unforgettable character," chooses to write about someone she knows well. A first-time novelist produces a literary work that is largely autobiographical. A philosopher's moral character contributes to his or her philosophy. Such decisions do not surprise us.

But what about the theorist who seeks to understand and conceptualize personality development? As Schultz (1992) notes, we might assume "that all personality theories, because they belong to a discipline that calls itself a science, are of the formal and objective variety," but "that conclusion would be incorrect" (p. 30). The sources of such concepts inevitably come from the theorist's experience; as Helson and Mitchell (1978) note, theorists rely on their

44

own lives as a primary source of empirical material. Some even view such theories as "disguised autobiography" (Page, 1983). Furthermore, the beliefs about human nature underlying these theorists' different theories of personality are determined "not only by certain empirical facts which can be agreed on by everyone, but also by a whole range of idiosyncratic factors and motivations affecting each theorist as an individual" (Atwood & Tomkins, 1976).

Theories as Human Constructions

Thus the theories and constructs represented in this book are human constructions. For example, as pointed out by St. Clair (1986), "The components of personality—the id, ego, and super-ego—are conceptualizations that exist only in writings about personality and are distant from people's experience of themselves" (p. 3). If we really believe our own theories—especially, that each of us comes to perceive the world through certain constructs—we must conclude that "universal" psychological theories often have a subjective origin. That is the theme of a provocative book titled *Faces in a Cloud,* by Stolorow and Atwood (1979). My view is that this subjectivity is inevitable and not necessarily undesirable; the degree to which theories receive acceptance by others is partly determined by whether the theoretician's subjectivity reflects the orientation of others. Stolorow and Atwood note that:

> every theory of personality constitutes a system of statements regarding the meaning of human life in the world. Each theory is founded on distinctive images of the human condition and the essential relationships between man and the world. These images are, at least in part, subjective and pretheoretical in origin; rather than being results of impartial reflection on empirical facts accessible to everyone, they are bound up with the theorist's personal reality and precede his intellectual engagement with the problem of human nature. . . . The personality theorist is a person and therefore views the world from the limited perspective of his own subjectivity. (1979, p. 17)

The term *personal reality* in the above quotation reflects George Kelly's assumption that each of us construes the world through idiosyncratic constructs. Furthermore, Stolorow and Atwood note that these views of the world develop prior to theorists' theories. Reading this quotation, George Kelly would have noted that theorists only do what all of us do, with two important exceptions: (1) They systematize their view of people in general, and (2) they seek to apply their construct system beyond just themselves, to people in general.

Where do theorists' constructs come from? Largely from their own experience. Although Freud certainly based his theories on the reports of his patients, his fundamental structure came before, and came from his quest to fathom his own nature. Stolorow and Atwood (1979) conclude that "personality theorists tend to rely upon their own lives as a primary source of empirical material. . . . No theorist offers definitive statements on the meaning of being human unless he feels those statements constitute a framework within which he can comprehend his own experience" (p. 18).

Freud saw humankind as conflicted, torn between yearnings for love and death, and besieged by unconscious impulses barely held in check by civilization. His conceptions were consistent with the ways that many others saw themselves; hence the theory survives.

I have argued that this development is natural and progressive. Theorists whose theories do not jibe with the ways that their audiences construe the world will not find acceptance for their theories. Stolorow and Atwood note the necessity of a common framework: "Other persons, in their reactions to theoretical ideas, are similarly subject to those influences" (1979, p. 18). Just like theory generation, theory acceptance is not entirely a rational act. A person's "eventual attitudes toward the material will be profoundly affected by its degree of compatibility with his own personal reality" (Stolorow & Atwood, 1979, p. 19).

Examples of the correlation between theorists' lives and their theories, although representing anecdotal evidence, are so prevalent that they lend strong credence to Stolorow and Atwood's propositions. In the following sections we examine Freud, Jung, and some non-Freudian theorists from this perspective. (Erik Erikson's life also impressively illustrates how theory derives from personal experience, but this example will be saved for Chapter 4, on Erikson's perspective.)

Freud's Life and His Theory

Sigmund Freud was born in 1856. His father, mother, and an older half-brother were the other family members. Another half-brother, Emanuel, was married and lived nearby. Emanuel's son, John, was to become Freud's first playmate.

As his mother's own first child, Sigmund Freud was her indisputable favorite. A prophecy had told her that she would bring a great man into the world, and the whole family was often reminded of this. Later, after Sigmund had several siblings, his younger sister was practicing her piano lessons, but the sound was so disturbing to young Sigmund that he insisted that the piano be removed, and his mother—despite her strong musical interests—agreed to do so (Fromm, 1959). As an adult, Freud (1952) once wrote, "A man who has been the indisputable favorite of his mother keeps for life the feeling of conqueror, that confidence of success which often induces real success" (p. 367). So be it.

But when Sigmund Freud was 11 months old, a younger brother, Julius, was born. No longer was Sigmund the sole recipient of his mother's adoring care. Freud reacted with jealousy (Fromm, 1959). In Freud's lecture on "femininity" in *New Introductory Lectures,* he wrote, "It is a remarkable fact that a child, even with the age difference of only 11 months, is not too young to take notice of what is happening, when two children are so close that lactation is prejudiced by the second pregnancy" (quoted by Stolorow & Atwood, 1979, p. 65). The choice of "11 months," while perhaps not a conscious choice, is also not a coincidence.

Eight months after birth, Julius died. Sigmund Freud, then age 19 months, blamed himself for his brother's death. He later described his self-reproach in detail. But he never expressed any feelings of betrayal or disappointment toward his mother—only very positive feelings; Freud was never able to acknowledge the ambivalent feelings that he possessed about his mother. Stolorow and Atwood believe that Freud developed hostility toward his mother but was unable to express it; "The central conflict in his emotional life had thus been established; namely, the conflict between an intense possessive need for his mother's love and an equally intense, magically potent hatred" (p. 52). But, in their view, he repressed the enraging disappointing qualities, and saved himself from the dreaded fear of losing her. This is reminiscent of Horney's "moving toward" interpersonal style. It is true that after Freud became an adult, he visited his mother every weekend for 50 years, and had her over every Sunday for dinner.

Regarding his other early ties, especially those with his father, Freud's feelings were openly ambivalent; he was able to express both love and hate toward his father. Erich Fromm (1959) recounts an example, a story Freud's father told him when Sigmund was 12:

> When he (the father) was a young man, a Gentile had knocked off his fur cap and then shouted at him: "Jew, get off the pavement!" When the little boy asked indignantly, "And what did you do?"; his father replied, "I went into the roadway and picked up my cap." Freud, in relating this story, continued: "This struck me as unheroic conduct on the part of the big strong man who was holding the little boy by the hand. I contrasted this situation with another which fitted my feelings better, the scene in which Hannibal's father, Hamilcar Barca, made his boy swear before the household altar to take vengeance on the Romans. Ever since that time, Hannibal had a place in my fantasies." (p. 57)

Every theory has to make decisions about the locus of causation in regard to psychological development. Stolorow and Atwood (1979) note that in Freud's theory of psychosexual development "the sources of evil were located not in the parents (in particular, the mother), but in the child himself, in his own sexual and aggressive impulses, which emerge according to an innate biologically predetermined sequence in relative independence of environmental influence" (p. 63). According to Fine (1973), this emphasis reflected Freud's wish to exonerate his parents, especially his mother. That is, by his choice to locate "badness" within the child, Freud "absolved his mother from blame for her betrayals of him and safeguarded her idealized image from invasions by his unconscious ambivalence" (Stolorow & Atwood, 1979, p. 63). Thus did he ward off his unconscious hatred of his mother.

Carl Jung's Life and Theory

Around the age of 50, Freud began a correspondence with Carl Jung; their interaction lasted for 8 years, during which time each wrote the other about 350 letters (Erikson, 1980b). Jung was different from Freud's other physician-followers. He lived in Switzerland rather than Vienna and was not Jewish; his father was a Protestant minister. Jung, born in 1875, was 19 years younger than Freud.

When Jung initiated the correspondence in 1906, Freud still felt markedly isolated from the tradition-bound medical school community; he probably saw in Jung the possessor of an academic connection (Jung had lectured at the University of Zurich) who could provide access to psychiatric centers abroad (Erikson, 1980b). Jung admired Freud as a genius free of academic encumbrances. Each benefited from the early correspondence.

Freud began to address Jung as his "spiritual heir" and "successor and crown prince" (McGuire, 1974, p. 218). In keeping with his own Moses complex (see Box 3.1), he also would call him his "Joshua" who would—in contrast to Freud—see the Promised Land of universal acceptance. Jung apparently considered Freud a father figure (Schultz, 1992) and their relationship, for several years, had many of the elements of an Oedipus complex (Alexander, 1982). But the mutually rewarding relationship soon soured.

Contrary to what Freud had hoped, Jung was not an uncritical disciple (Schultz, 1990); the older man's fears about the sure betrayals that threatened the immortality of his ideas were, in a sense, confirmed, and the relationship ended in 1914, just as the First World War began, because Jung began to develop an unorthodox theory of personality that was uniquely his own.

We find in Carl Jung's life other examples of the continuity between personal issues and later theoretical constructs. One overriding feature of Carl Jung's development as a child was his secret involvement in a world of religious fantasies (Stolorow & Atwood, 1979). In his autobiography, Jung (1961) refers to his secret world as "the essential factor of my boyhood" (p. 22).

At the age of 3, he was taught to say the following prayer before going to sleep each night:

> Spread out thy wings, Lord Jesus mild,
> And take to thee thy chick, thy child,
> If Satan would devour it,
> No harm shall overpower it,
> So let the angels sing.

BOX 3.1

Freud and Moses

Freud was a Jew, but the impact of his religious heritage on his personality and behavior is quite controversial (Rice, 1991). Yerushalmi (1991) argues that Freud deliberately suppressed his Yiddish identity for purposes of career advancement and acceptance by the scientific community of the period. He became what Yerushalmi calls a "Psychological Jew," wishing to both obfuscate and clarify his Jewishness.

Similarly, Jerry Diller (1991) portrays Freud as experiencing a tormented psychic struggle, because of the ambivalence he felt toward his religious and cultural traditions. As Segal (1992) summarizes the conflict:

> On the one hand, we are shown a man who rejected Jewish ritual and customs, attacked religious enterprises, and remained removed from the passions of Zionism. On the other hand, we are given a man who clearly sought out Jewish people as social and intellectual companions, struggled to protect his family from the ravages of anti-Semitism, and was addicted to collecting and telling Jewish jokes. (p. 886)

And it is clear that Freud was fascinated by the Bible, and especially by the figure of Moses (Robert, 1976). In his last important work, *Moses and Monotheism* (1939/1964), he argued that Moses was an Egyptian, that monotheism originated in Egypt, and that Moses was murdered by the Jews—once again causing observers to puzzle about the nature of Freud's identity.

The second phrase ("and take to thee thy chick") was confusing, and Jung thought that Jesus swallowed children. This view was supplemented by the child's observations of funerals and burials.

One day, playing outside, he saw a man in a strange black garment and broad hat coming down the hill toward him. The young Carl Jung rushed into the house and hid in the darkest corner of the attic. He was frightened for days, and it was years before he could set foot inside a Catholic church.

Those, and other religious dreams with frightening connotations, doubtless contributed to the emergence of his concept of the two-sided nature of God. In fact, this splitting process—dividing objects into positive and negative components—became a generalized feature of not just Jung's worldview, but also his conception of the nature of personality. Stolorow and Atwood (1979) state, "The world had been revealed in his mind as a polarized tension between above and below, omnipotent good and omnipotent evil. . . . We can therefore discern in these images an early source of Jung's later obsession with the reconciliation of opposites, the problem of wholeness, and integration" (p. 93).

During his childhood, Jung shared his secret with no one. His was a lonely existence; he had no siblings until he was 9; and at school he alienated himself from others. He came to distrust his mother and ridicule his father, whom he saw as weak. He spent many solitary hours in the attic of his home, confiding in a figure he had carved out of wood. As Schultz (1992) notes, his isolated nature as a child is manifested in his theory of personality, which emphasizes developments within the individual rather than relationships with other people. He came to see himself as possessing two separate personalities: "Personality No. 1," as he called one of these components, was the outer self which was known to his parents and other persons. " 'Personality No. 2,' on the other hand, was a hidden self which was unknown to others and which entertained secret fantasies about the ultimate mysteries of the cosmos" (Stolorow & Atwood, 1979, p. 98).

Jung's entire adulthood was obsessed with the competitions and contradictions between the two sides of his personality. His choice of psychiatry as a career was a compromise between these two self-images.

Given this perspective, it is quite understandable that one of Jung's major contributions to personality theory would be his emphasis on the bipolar nature of self-images. Staude (1981) observes:

> Jung was fascinated with polarities, probably in part because of his own split nature. He viewed development and the transformation of psychic energy as being a result of interaction among polarities in the psyche, such as male/female, light/dark, individual/collective, etc. He

found that developmental work with any one polarity usually opened out into other polarities. In his view dialectical-development conflicts within the psyche were transcended when both sides of the polarity were owned and acknowledged. In the course of the individuation process, in Jung's view, there is a gradual shift in the center of personality from the ego to the self, but neither side of this polarity is ever abolished; they remain in dialectical interplay. (pp. 100-101)

Following his conception of himself as two people, Jung did his dissertation on an interpretation of the personality development of Helene Preiswerk. She became the first example of what he came to call the law of enantiodromia, or polar reversal. Staude (1981) reports:

She went from one pole to another, her general weakness and silliness and her willingness to cheat, to the opposite pole where she was expressing the best in herself. . . . From this case he generalized another psychological law: in order to advance to a higher state of development we often have to commit some mistake so terrible that it may threaten to ruin our lives. (p. 29)

As noted earlier, Jung was one of the first theorists on adult personality to write about midlife crisis. Again, his own experience was related to his perspective. During World War I, Jung experienced an internal war and revolution of his own. He questioned everything he had done and believed in previously. "He went through a process of breakdown and transformation that we have since come to know, partly through his writings, as the mid-life transition" (Staude, 1981, p. 44). Prior to that time, he had appeared to be quite successful. In 1911 he had a stable marriage and family, and a flourishing private practice as a psychiatrist. He was the acknowledged heir-apparent to Freud.

But, approaching the age of 40, he broke with Freud, marital infidelities threatened his marriage, and he established a sexual relationship with a former patient—a young woman of 23 years of age—that was to last almost 40 years. He convinced his wife and his mistress that he needed both of them; his wife, Emma, provided the motherliness he missed in his own mother, whereas his mistress, Antonia Wolff, fulfilled the "female inspiration" for his creative work and awakened Jung's unconscious (Robinson, 1992). He even had his mistress as a regular guest for Sunday dinner with his family.

Jung's midlife crisis has been interpreted in various ways, "as everything from a heroic conquest of the unconscious to a psychotic breakdown. From his memoirs and sympathetic biographers it appears that Jung voluntarily made a conscious decision to confront the imagery of the collective unconscious at mid-life" (Staude, 1981, p. 47). That is, he saw the "quest for meaning" as the task of the second half of his life.

Jung also gave a great deal of thought to how the idiosyncratic personalities of Freud and of Alfred Adler led to their distinctive theoretical statements; in fact, he developed his concepts of introversion and extroversion on the basis of his comparison of Adler's and Freud's personalities (A. Elms, 1988).

We can best summarize the relationship of Jung's life and work by quoting Duane Schultz (1990), whose book *Intimate Friends, Dangerous Rivals* documents the turbulent Jung/Freud relationship:

> Jung's theory was established on an intuitive base, derived from his own experiences, memories, and dreams. It was then refined, along more rational and empirical lines, by data provided by his patients, nearly two-thirds of whom were middle aged and suffering from the same difficulties that Jung had faced. It is no surprise, then, that emotional changes at midlife became an important part of Jung's theory of personality. (p. 91)

Karen Horney's Life and Theory

Karen Horney made contributions to psychoanalysis beyond her theory of responses to basic anxiety, described in Chapter 2. She took issue with Freud's portrayal of women, especially that women suffer from penis envy (see also Box 3.2.). It was her observation that men are just as envious of women for their ability to give birth to children (Quinn, 1987). (She did not deny that women can envy men but more for their freedom of expression than their anatomy.)

The fact that Horney practiced both in her native Germany and later in the United States led her to note striking differences in the neuroses of her patients in the two countries. Personality, she

---

BOX 3.2

Freud's Views on Women

Chapter 2 noted that Freud had greater difficulty in explaining the psychosexual development of women than that of men. Perhaps that problem is related to his views toward women—views that they were a kind of castrated man, lacking a strong superego.

One example of his chauvinistic position is his reaction to the birth of his daughter, Anna Freud, in 1895. He wrote his long-term correspondent, Wilhelm Fliess, "If it had been a son, I would have sent you the news by telegram," but since it was only a daughter, a letter of announcement sufficed (Young-Bruehl, 1988). The letter condescendingly described her as "a nice complete little female" who "did not do her mother any harm." Ironically, of his seven children, only Anna, his youngest, followed him as a psychoanalyst. Anna Freud, in fact, came to make a unique contribution, by initiating (with Melanie Klein) the psychoanalysis of children. In fairness, it should be noted that her quick intelligence very early won her father's respect and encouraged him to admit her into his professional world (Young-Bruehl, 1988).

Anna Freud, when she was 22, even began to be psychoanalyzed by her father, a controversial relationship, to say the least, between a father and daughter. Her authorized biographer, Elisabeth Young-Bruehl (1988), concludes that such a procedure was not considered as outrageous as it would be today, but Peter Gay (1988), a biographer of Freud, labels the episode a "most irregular proceeding."

Anna Freud never married and, according to her authorized biographer, was chaste throughout her long life. She died at age 87 in 1982.

---

concluded, does not depend wholly on invariant forces, as Freud had argued (Schultz, 1992). From these perspectives she came to develop her position that the motivating aspect of personality is an effort to obtain security rather than sex or aggression.

Karen Horney's childhood was less unconventional than Freud's or Jung's but we still can discern idiosyncratic elements that contributed to her theoretical contributions. She was born near Hamburg, Germany, in 1885; as a child she was competitive and successful in school.

She rarely saw her father during her childhood; he was a busy shipping company executive. Susan Quinn (1987), author of a recent biography of Horney, notes that "her father's absence was a major factor in her development; she was a modern child in many ways—she lived at home with an absent father, and was not smothered, like the neurotics Freud treated, so much as left lonely, abandoned, like many of the patients analysts treat now" (quoted in Goleman, 1987b, p. 11). She decided at the age of 14 to become a doctor—a rare achievement for a woman at that time.

Even in her early diaries there are clues to her independence of mind. Her decision to go to medical school occurred against considerable family opposition. Prior to her marriage at age 24, there were many men in her life; the early years of her marriage were a time of personal distress, with feelings of oppression and overwhelming unhappiness. Her response was to have a number of affairs—which she called "vagabonding" (Schultz, 1992). The marriage ended when she was 40, and Horney moved from Berlin to Chicago.

Quinn's detailed biography offers a psychological (even psychoanalytic) explanation for this, arguing that Horney had a compulsive need for men but was not able to maintain a relationship because she was still searching for a replacement for her absent father. To use such an interpretation would have been seen by Horney as quite ironic (to put it mildly) as she disputed the traditional psychoanalytic view that adult character structure reflects direct repetition of childhood attitudes (Paris, 1989).

But even before the move to the United States, she was publicly disagreeing with traditional psychoanalysts over penis envy; she suggested that men repress their envy of mothering by overvaluing male sexuality. In doing so, she drew on her own experience as the mother of three daughters (Sayers, 1991).

Gordon Allport's Life and Theory

Our previous examples of the effect of life experiences on personality theorizing—Freud, Jung, and Horney—reflected psychoanalytic theory as the origination. But the basic theme of this chapter may be extended to those personality theorists who developed conceptions quite at variance with a Freudian approach.

As a more recent theorist, Gordon Allport (1937, 1961) emphasized the role of conscious awareness in the determination of behavior. One of Allport's basic credos was "If you want to know how
someone feels about something, ask them"; he saw human nature
as rational and the unconscious as effective only in neurotic persons.

A second critical difference was that Allport focused on *contemporary* influences of personality on behavior. He is quoted (by
Smith, 1993, p. 62) as saying, "I think the first three years of life
don't matter very much." There was no need to examine early
influences from childhood traumas. If a 29-year-old male is unmarried, shy, and self-deprecatory in his relationships with others, the
fact that an auto accident scarred and permanently disfigured his
face at age 6 is not relevant as an explanation. The young man's
present reluctance to date is, rather, a function of his present
feelings toward his appearance or his present awareness of humili-
ating comments about his face.

Without too much exaggeration, Allport's conception can be
characterized as clean and sanitized; it had none of the seamy or
"dirty" motivations inherent in psychoanalysis. So is there anything
in Allport's own life that is consistent with the basics of his theory?

When he was 22 years old, Allport was traveling through Europe
after teaching a year in Turkey. He wrote Freud and in an arrogant
and uncharacteristic way (for Allport was a gracious and modest
man) announced to Freud that "I was in Vienna and implied that no
doubt he would be glad to make my acquaintance" (Allport, 1968,
p. 383). Freud responded, inviting him to come to his office at a
certain time.

Let Allport (1968) then describe what happened, in what he later
came to call a "traumatic developmental episode":

> Soon after I had entered the famous red burlap room with pictures of
> dreams on the wall, he summoned me to his inner office. He did not
> speak to me but sat in expectant silence, for me to state my mission.
> I was not prepared for silence and had to think fast to find a suitable
> conversational gambit. I told him of an episode on the tram car on my
> way to his office. A small boy about four years of age had displayed a
> conspicuous dirt phobia. He kept saying to his mother, "I don't want
> to sit there . . . don't let that dirty man sit beside me." To him every-
> thing was *schmutzig*. His mother was a well-starched *Haus frau,* so

dominant and purposive looking that I thought the cause and effect apparent.

When I finished my story Freud fixed his kindly therapeutic eyes upon me and said, "And was that little boy you?" Flabbergasted and feeling a bit guilty, I contrived to change the subject. (pp. 383-384)

Allport characterized Freud's response as misunderstanding his motivation; "to ascribe my motivation in this case to the unconscious was definitely wrong" (Allport, quoted in filmed interview with Evans, 1970, pp. 4-5). But thanks to the thoughtful analysis of Alan Elms (1972, 1993), we may ask, did he really? Elms asks, what kind of little boy was young Gordon Allport? Allport's father was a physician whose office (and small hospital) was in the family home. Typical household activities included dealing with patients, cleaning surgical equipment, and maintaining an antiseptic environment. Gordon Allport lived as a child in an abnormally clean home/hospital. And this high-minded, clean child became a psychologist who avoided digging into the "dirt" of sexual activity or neurotic behavior (Elms, 1993).

Here is just one example of Allport's behavior as an adult, as reported by a former graduate student, Dan Ogilvie. In 1964, Allport had asked him to retrieve some copies of his first book from a dusty storage area (Elms, 1993). Then Allport handed the student a clean rag to remove the dirt from his hands while Allport autographed a book for him. Twenty years later Ogilvie recalled:

In the meantime I had removed the dust, but he insisted I use the rag anyway. I did that and seeing that the rag was in no worse shape than when it had been handed to me, I refolded it and placed it on the corner of his desk. With an expression of disgust, he gingerly deposited the rag in a waste basket. Suddenly I was glued to the floor with the realization that in a critical way the boy (of the Freud anecdote) . . . *did* represent an important aspect of Professor Allport after all. (Ogilvie, 1984, p. 13, cited in Elms, 1993, italics in original)

SUMMARY

This chapter has proposed that the theories described in this book stem from the personal experiences of the theorists. Every developer of an explanation for human behavior perceives the world through partially idiosyncratic constructs. Elements of the lives of Sigmund Freud, Carl Jung, Karen Horney, and Gordon Allport were described and related to their respective theories.

Readers may have varying reactions to the claim and purported demonstration that the ways that theorists view their own lives influence the theories they advance. For me, the claim is not disturbing. It reemphasizes three points:

1. There is no agreed-on reality, when we consider human experience. That is, there are many ways of explaining human development that possess some validity.

2. Subjectivity in generation of theoretical constructs is virtually inevitable; only humans can create explanations for human experience, and no one can, himself or herself, develop without having to interpret the world through certain limited constructs.

3. Theories survive or fail based on their acceptance by others. The very fact that the theories described here remain in the literature is an indication that, although their origin was partly subjective, they deal with experiences of enough commonality to be helpful in explaining personality development in others.

4

Erikson's Theory
of Psychosocial Development

*Anything that grows has a ground plan, and out of this
ground plan the parts arise, each part having its time of
special ascendancy, until all parts have risen to form a functioning whole.*

Erik H. Erikson

That type of approach that sees personality developing through a
series of stages dominates this and the next three chapters. After
evaluating Erik Erikson's conception in this chapter, we examine
in Chapter 5 the utility of psychobiography as an explanation of
personality, and in Chapters 6 and 7 other major explanations that
rely on psychosocial stages. Although different stage theorists high-
light different qualities, they possess a similarity in basic perspective. In general these conceptions view each stage or period as
qualitatively different, with relatively abrupt shifts from stage to
stage. Each of these stages is assumed to build on the earlier ones,
and a successful reaction to the crisis or major task of each stage,
in effect, gives the person the capabilities necessary to attack the

conflicts of the next stages. Thus each new stage provides a wholly new level of structural integration. But an unsuccessful or inadequate resolution of one "crisis" hinders the growth preferred at each subsequent stage unless some special intervention occurs (Dacey, 1982).

Erikson's Background
and Intellectual Development

Erik Erikson's life is so illustrative of Chapter 3's conclusion that theorists' concepts derive from their own experiences, it is worth detailed review.

Erikson's Life

The man who is now named Erik Homburger Erikson was born in 1902 in Frankfurt, Germany. He grew up in Karlsruhe, in southern Germany, as the son of a pediatrician, Dr. Theodor Homburger, and his wife, Karla, formerly named Abrahamsen. Erikson's mother was a native of Copenhagen, Denmark. The circumstances of Erikson's birth are not clear; Wright (1982) states that Erikson's Danish father abandoned his mother. Elkind (1982) notes that "not long after his birth his [real] father died" (p. 14). But this may be a rather sanitized version; Erikson has been reluctant to reveal the facts of his early life. Only when he was in his seventies did he state the following: "All through my earlier childhood, they kept secret the fact that my mother had been married previously, and that I was the son of a Dane who had abandoned her before my birth" (Erikson, 1975, p. 27).

Erikson has described his stepfather as coming from "an intensely Jewish small bourgeois family" and that his mother was a "Dane." We do not know whether his mother was Jewish. At any rate, he was brought up in a family that actively participated in Jewish traditions. He attended public schools, and religious services at the synagogue. The young Erik Homburger (for that was his name at that time) felt like an outsider in both settings. He says that he was "referred to as a 'goy' in his stepfather's temple while to his schoolmates he was a 'Jew.' "

Adolescence was not an easy stage for him; he says that "like other youths . . . I became intensely alienated from everything my bourgeois family stood for," but as Roazen (1976) notes, Erikson has not clarified for us what he was rebelling against. He was not a good student; he recalls that he was "selectively attentive."

Elkind (1982) tells us that Erikson's stepfather urged him to become a doctor, a pediatrician, like himself. But young Erikson deliberately chose to be different. After graduating from the "gymnasium," the German equivalent of high school, he enrolled in art school. Then he began to wander through Europe, earning a meager keep by painting portraits. He adopted what he later called a narcissistic lifestyle—sketching, making wood carvings, and avoiding the world's social and political problems (Wright, 1982).

The summer of 1927 was a critical period for Erikson. He had been working in Vienna, painting children's portraits. At the age of 25, he had not yet established any firm professional goals. An old school friend was at that time the director of a small progressive school in Vienna that had a tie-in with Anna Freud, who, like her father, was a practicing psychoanalyst. Many of the children in the school were in a therapeutic treatment program under Anna Freud's direction. Erikson had served as a substitute tutor at the school, and it was clear to all concerned that he—in contrast to most men at the time—was very good communicating with small children. So Anna Freud asked him whether he would consider becoming a child analyst—a profession that was only beginning and that he had not even heard of. He agreed to, and became a patient in analysis with Anna Freud. (All psychoanalysts, then and now, were required to be psychoanalyzed themselves.) Although Erikson also received a Montessori diploma, his psychoanalytic training remained his basic professional experience. Among influential theorists in adult development, he is unique in that he not only lacks a M.D. or Ph.D. degree, but he is also not even a college graduate. But even after his "adoption" by the Freudian circle, Erikson still considered himself fatherless (Roazen, 1976, p. 98).

Erikson remained in Vienna until 1933, when he and his wife moved to the United States. He hoped to establish himself among psychoanalytic circles and continue to practice, but he was discouraged by Freud's leading disciple in the United States, A. A. Brill of New York City. Hence he enrolled as a student in the graduate program in psychology at Harvard University, but he failed his first course. Roazen (1976) concludes that "his 'failure' can be attributed to his unwillingness to accede to what may have seemed to him some of the unnecessary demands of academic psychology, and in later years the Harvard psychologist Edwin Boring was embarrassed about how Erikson had fared in his department" (p. 8).

It was not until 1960, at the age of 58, that he changed his name from Erik Homburger to Erik H. Erikson. Why did he not revert to his natural father's name? Roazen (1976) observes that "his choice of a last name is obviously significant. One story has it that his children were troubled by the American tendency to confuse 'Homburger' with 'Hamburger,' and that he asked one of his sons for an alternative; being Erik's son he proposed 'Erikson'" (p. 98). Although such a procedure is a Scandinavian custom, it also connotes, intentionally or not, that Erikson is his own father, self-created. Observers have been both mystified and critical of the name change. Roazen (1976) concludes, "Whatever else this name change may have meant to him, it was also an act of repudiation of this German-Jewish stepfather, as well as the mother who had secured a legitimate name for her son" (p. 99). Erikson now claims that the name change was a family decision, taken with his stepfather's approval. He has also written that he "kept my stepfather's name as my middle name out of gratitude." But it is also relevant to note that Erikson, who was raised in a Jewish family, became a devout adherent of Christianity about the time of his name change (Dacey, 1982).

How Erikson's
Theory Differs From Freud's

Although Erikson's training and original theoretical orientation were in what is now called classical psychoanalysis, his evolving conception of the nature of personality reflects significant differences from Freud's view. Erikson is more positive in his orientation, placing his emphasis on understanding self-healing more than self-deception. He elevated the status of the ego, proposing that it has a psychic energy of its own. In keeping with Freud's original conception, Erikson believes the ego is largely unconscious, but unlike other post-Freudians, Erikson emphasizes that the ego has a unifying function, ensuring coherent behavior and conduct. Thus, as Roazen

(1976) observes, the job of the ego "is not just the negative one of avoiding anxieties but also the positive role of maintaining effective performance" (pp. 23-24). In a collection of articles (Schlein, 1987), Erikson asks, "If we know what can go wrong in each stage, can we say what should have gone and can go right?"

Erikson (1963), writing 50 years after Freud, also saw a different type of concern facing most of his patients. He has written, "The patient of today suffers most under the problem of what he should believe in and who he should—or indeed, might—be or become, while the patient of early psychoanalysis suffered most under inhibitions which prevented him from being what and who he thought he knew he was" (p. 279).

Third, Erikson objected to the heavy biological orientation of classical psychoanalysis. He believed that, more than biology, society "guides and narrows the individual's choice" (Roazen, 1976, p. 34). As we will see, the cultural environment has inputs into each of the life crises that serve as the guideposts in Erikson's developmental theory. For example, the "adolescent crisis of intimacy versus role refusal could be triggered by the sociological fact that during these years the adolescent is being asked to assume positions of role responsibility in the 'adult world' " (Smelser, 1980, p. 13).

Of course, Erikson's most apparent and influential difference from Freud was his extension of psychological development beyond childhood. Although his concept of the identity crisis, occurring in late adolescence, is his most widely known contribution, his theory contributed to recent investigations of the "midlife crisis" and similar issues in adulthood.

Erikson's Stage Theory

Erikson proposed that eight stages described the pattern of personality development from infancy through old age. (In the sexist language commonplace at the time, Erikson unfortunately christened these "the eight stages of man.") At each stage, a psychosocial "crisis" (Erikson's term) faced the individual; this crisis—really a choice point—led to subsequent development going in either one direction or another. A favorable resolution of the crisis leads to the acquisition of a virtue at that stage.

How the person adjusts to the crisis at each stage depends on what Erikson (1980a) labeled the *epigenetic principle,* which derives from the biological assumption that the development of the embryo follows a broad, designated plan (Chiriboga, 1989). Erikson hypothesized that "the success with which the demands of any stage are resolved lays the groundwork, good or bad, for resolution of any further crisis" (Chiriboga, 1989, p. 124). In this "ground plan," each part has its time of special ascendancy, until all the aspects have developed to form an integrated organism (Erikson, 1963, 1968a).

Thus, as indigenous to stage theories, Erikson saw these choices as building on previous ones. His epigenesis principle would ask, for example, if a person chooses isolation as a way of resolving the crisis at Stage 6, how can he or she develop generativity, instead of self-absorption, at Stage 7? We will illustrate the impact of the epigenetic principle as we explore each stage in sequence.

Stage 1: Trust Versus Mistrust

Erikson saw this stage as the foundation and hence by far the most important stage (Dacey, 1982). Trust, he viewed in a broad sense—learning what to expect in the world. Acquisition of trust meant not so much a belief that the world is safe as that it is orderly and predictable. Hence, trust involves negative as well as positive expectations. Acquisition of trust means learning that a dangerous person can be trusted to be dangerous, just as much as it means that a care giver can be "trusted" to reappear, to provide (Dacey, 1982). In an interview with psychologist Richard I. Evans (1967), Erikson states, "There is a correspondence between your needs and your world, this is what I mean by basic trust" (p. 15). In contrast, irregularity and inconsistent care can lead to the child experiencing anxiety and insecurity, and hence mistrust.

The columnist Ellen Goodman (1990), commenting on the film *Home Alone,* concluded that it was the surprise hit of the 1990 Christmas season because it "taps the most primal plot: the fears that kids have about being abandoned" (p. 5A). She goes on to state, "At some point, children become aware of their dependency on adults who aren't always reliable" (p. 5A). This is the essence of Erikson's first stage.

Regularity in one's early environment is desirable but so too is variation. Erikson felt that the development of a favorable ratio of trust to mistrust was ideal, leading to the acquisition of the virtue of hope. Complete regularity and predictability would not prepare the child for the vicissitudes of life, so a small amount of mistrust was desirable. In his interview with Richard I. Evans, Erikson said, "I use Mistrust in the sense of a readiness for danger and an anticipation of discomfort" (Evans, 1967, p. 15). Thus each of the eight life crises involves conflict between two opposing characteristics. By suggesting that the successful resolution of each crisis should favor the first of the two characteristics but still incorporate the second to some degree, Erikson proposed that the presence of some mistrust is healthy.

Stage 2: *Autonomy Versus Shame and Doubt*

The task of children 18 months to 3 years of age is to gain control and mastery over their bodies. As Dacey (1982) notes, "Erikson agrees with other psychoanalysts that toilet training has far more important consequences in one's life than just control of one's bowels" (p. 40). If children are encouraged to explore their bodies and their social and physical worlds, some degree of self-confidence develops (Dacey, 1982). If, on the other hand, they are consistently criticized for their inability to control their bowels, they feel ashamed and come to doubt themselves. They become reluctant to test themselves. Erikson has stated, "If in some respects you have relatively more shame than autonomy, then you feel or act inferior all your life—or consistently counteract that feeling" (quoted in Evans, 1967, p. 20). Again, at this stage are reflected three basic aspects of Erikson's conception:

1. At least at the early stages, the environment created by the care giver strongly influences the way the conflict is resolved.
2. The resolution is not "all-or-none"; some amount of the undesired choice—here shame and doubt—not only can occur, but has some healthy effects.
3. Following the principle of epigenesis, an undesirable resolution may negatively affect the choice at the next stage. For example, a child

possessing more shame and doubt than autonomy will be at a disadvantage at the next stage, when the task is to develop initiative.

Successful resolution of Stage 2 leads to accomplishment of the virtue of self-control and will.

Stage 3: Initiative Versus Guilt

Building on whatever degree of competence they have acquired in Stage 2 to control themselves, children ages 3 to 5 now discover that they can have some influence over others in the family and that they can be successful in manipulating their surroundings (Dacey, 1982). Children may ask questions in order to develop knowledge and skills; initiative results as they feel more comfortable in responding. But parents and others can make them feel inept, and hence guilt results. As opposed to shame in the earlier stage, guilt is an internally generated response to failure, and its importance at this stage, as a response, is that it denies the child the resources to deal with crisis at later ages.

It is this age that the superego emerges; family members serve as role models for the acceptable actions. Dacey (1982) notes, "If these role models are capable, effective people, the child will develop a sense of personal initiative" (p. 40).

For Erikson, acquisition of a sense of purpose is the ideal accomplishment at Stage 3. Children will have learned that they have to work to achieve goals.

Stage 4: Industry Versus Inferiority

Choices at Stage 4 occur during the elementary school years (ages 5-12). One interpretation of the task at this stage is how to go beyond models and learn the elementary technology of the culture (Dacey, 1982). Children begin to explore the neighborhood; they expand their horizons beyond their families. By "industry" as a desired resolution, Erikson, I think, means "industriousness," or learning to complete something. A sense of accomplishment in making and building should prevail. If not, the child may emerge with a life-long sense of inferiority. Once again, effects of an unfavorable resolution of earlier crises may appear. The child may not be able to be industrious because, in Erikson's words, he may "still want his mother more than he wants knowledge" (quoted by Dacey, 1982, p. 40). That is, children may consider their eager productivity merely as a device to please their teacher (i.e., a substitute mother) and not something desirable in its own right. Children may perform in order to be "good little helpers," rather than really achieving the ideal accomplishment of competence or workmanship (Dacey, 1982).

Stage 5: Identity Versus Role Confusion

Erikson invented the term *identity crisis* to signify the crucial importance of ego identity for entrance to adulthood. We are all aware that people strive for identity, for a coherent self-image or "persistent sameness within oneself" (Erikson, 1959, p. 102) in which beliefs and values are all of one piece. Identity is thus a structure, with an organized set of values and beliefs about oneself, expressed in views on occupation, politics, religion, and relationships.

But an integrated identity cannot occur before adolescence because the necessary ingredients from cognitive, physical, and social expectations have not formed until then (Marcia, 1992). Should the adolescent fail in this quest, the danger he or she faces is identity confusion.

This is not an easy task. Erikson saw the desirability of a moratorium period for at least part of the time between ages 12 and 18; during this "time-out" the adolescent has a chance to experiment with a variety of identities, without having to assume the responsibility of the consequences of any particular one (Dacey, 1982).

Repudiation of other identities is part of the successful resolution of this crisis. Previous identities such as "daddy's boy" or "mama's little girl" must be relinquished. But the endeavor may not go smoothly; for example, negative identities may have an impact. Erikson (1974) stated:

Every person and every group harbors a negative identity as the sum of all those identifications and identity fragments which the individual has to submerge in himself as undesirable or irreconcilable or which his group has taught him to perceive as the mark of fatal "difference" in sex role or race, in class or religion. (p. 20)

Sometimes teenagers actually choose to live their negative identities, at least for a while. Persons with negative identities adopt one pattern of behavior because they are rebelling against demands that they follow the opposite pattern. An example would be "a youth who joins a gang of shoplifters, not because he wants to steal, but because down deep he doubts his masculinity and seeks to prove through dangerous acts of theft that he is not a coward" (Dacey, 1982, p. 44).

The undesirable resolution, identity confusion, was seen by Erikson as an inability to make choices. The adolescent may see himself or herself as inconsistent, a trait not valued in our society. Erikson believed that gender identity was a central component of ego identity. By refusing to establish a clear sexual identity, the adolescent risks identity diffusion (Huyck & Hoyer, 1982, p. 213).

More extensive theorizing and research has emerged from this stage than any other in Erikson's theory. Roy Baumeister (1986) has identified two types of identity crisis: *identity deficit*, in which the self has not formed enough of an identity, and *identity conflict*, in which the self is over-defined and too many incompatible aspects of the self coexist. Furthermore, James Marcia (1966, 1980, 1992) has analyzed the process of identity development at this stage. He proposes that two discrete processes must be experienced before mature identity is attainable. First, the adolescent must experience a crisis, in the sense that treasured beliefs are questioned, threatened, reconsidered, perhaps abandoned, or reestablished with a firmer foundation. Such a crisis could occur with respect to one's religious beliefs, one's lifestyle, one's sexual preference, one's occupational plan, or other fundamental values. Second, the person must make a choice; that is, there must be commitment. Not all teenagers have experienced these factors. Building on these two qualities of crisis and commitment, Marcia generated four types of identity status in adolescents:

Status 1: Identity Confusion (or Diffusion). No crisis has been experienced and no commitment has been made.

Status 2: Identity Foreclosure. No crisis has been experienced, but the person has made a commitment to a certain identity, usually that of his or her parents, perhaps even forced on the adolescent by his or her parents. For example, we do not know if George Bush reflects foreclosure or identity achievement, but the dedication in his autobiography (Bush, with Gold, 1987)—To "my mother and father, whose values lit the way"—reflects the adoption of his parents' perspective on the world.

Status 3: Identity Moratorium. Considerable crisis is being experienced, but no commitments have as yet been made. Time is taken out to accomplish the task of psychological integration. A moratorium is a purposeful time-out from other social rules, not just a description of a person who is stalled or drifting (Swogger, 1989).

Status 4: Identity Achievement. The adolescent has explored several possible identities (lifestyles, collections of values, and so on) for himself or herself, one has been chosen, and a commitment has been made to it.

The last of these, Status 4, is clearly for Marcia, and for Erikson, the most desirable. It would produce the ideal accomplishment at this stage, the virtue of fidelity. Erikson is adamant about the validity of such a resolution; he has stated, "I would go further and claim that we have almost an instinct for fidelity—meaning that when you reach a certain age you can and must learn to be faithful to some ideological view" (quoted in Evans, 1967, p. 30). (See Box 4.1 for a summary of empirical research on Marcia's four identity statuses.)

A second type of theorizing and research generated by Erikson's identity stage is reflected in the work of Dan P. McAdams (1985, 1987). In contrast to Marcia's emphasis on the *process* of identity formation, McAdams examines the *outcome.* His main thesis is that "identity looks like a story and that, like all stories in literature and life, identity can be understood in terms of settings, scene, character, plot, and theme" (McAdams, 1987, p. 16). McAdams capitalizes on Erikson's (1959) conception that identity is a configuration of sorts; he proposes that this configuration takes the form of a narrative that integrates a number of identity elements, thus forming a life story.

BOX 4.1

**Testing Marcia's
Identity-Status Concept**

As Ellett (1986) notes, Marcia's identity-status conceptualization has generated a large body of research directed mainly at discovering correlates of each of the identity statuses (e.g., Dellas & Jernigan, 1988; Marcia, 1980). In the area of anxiety, Marcia (1967) found that persons in a moratorium status were the most anxious of the four statuses, caused, he speculated, by their "in-crisis" position. The same study revealed that persons in a foreclosure status were the least anxious of the four groups. In reviewing the literature on self-esteem and identity status, Marcia (1980) reports that among men, both achievement and moratorium status individuals generally scored higher on measures of self-esteem than did those in the foreclosure and diffusion statuses, but that persons in the foreclosure and diffusion statuses were more liable to change their evaluations of themselves, both positively or negatively, in response to external feedback than were those in the other two statuses. Among women, those in a foreclosure status scored higher in self-esteem, while those in the moratorium and diffusion statuses generally scored lower. Foreclosure individuals endorsed authoritarian values more often than did any of the other identity statuses (Marcia, 1966, 1967; Marcia & Friedman, 1970). Neuber and Genthner (1977) reported that men and women in the achievement and moratorium categories, especially when contrasted with those in the diffusion status, tended to take more personal

---

Stage 6: Intimacy and Solidarity Versus Isolation

Moving beyond identity, persons in their twenties face the task of developing intimate relationships with others. Erikson proposed that intimacy should include a sense of connectedness and a mutuality of orgasm with a loved partner of the other sex with whom one is able and willing to share a mutual trust and with whom one is able and willing to regulate the cycle of work, procreation, and recreation (Erikson, 1963, p. 266). That value judgments abound in Erikson's conception is apparent. But for Erikson, intimacy is more

---

BOX 4.1 (Continued)

---

responsibility for their own lives. Several studies have found no differences in intelligence among the identity statuses (e.g., Marcia, 1966; Marcia & Friedman, 1970). When cognitive styles were investigated, persons in the foreclosure and diffusion statuses were more impulsive, responding more quickly and making more errors, and those in the achievement and moratorium statuses were more reflective (Waterman & Waterman, 1974). In a study of the interpersonal style of each of the statuses, Donovan (1975) reported that individuals in the diffusion status were generally withdrawn, felt out of place in the world, and characterized their parents as distant and misunderstanding, while those in the foreclosure group appeared to be happy and described their homes as loving and affectionate. Persons in the moratorium status were volatile, seemed to thrive on intense relationships and exploration of their worlds, and appeared to have a stake in being attractive and visible people. Donovan found only two individuals in the achievement status in his study, and he described them as demonstrating nondefensive strength with a capability to care for others in a noncompulsive, nonbinding way. In discussing the outcomes of investigations on identity states and their correlates, Raskin (1984) points out that, in spite of the fact that the methods vary from study to study, most results support the hypotheses being tested, suggesting that identity status as a construct is rather robust. In addition, Bourne (1978) acknowledges that one of the major strengths of Marcia's approach is the abundance of research that it has stimulated.

---

than sexual closeness. In his interview with Richard I. Evans (1967) he provided a useful definition: "Intimacy is really the ability to fuse your identity with someone else's without the fear that you are going to lose something yourself" (p. 48). Persons who have achieved intimacy can accomplish the virtue of love, that is, they can commit themselves to a relationship and have the ethical strength to abide by such commitments even if sacrifices and compromises are called for. Erikson was fond of Freud's response to the question: "What should a normal person be able to do well?" "Lieben" and "arbeiten," or love and work.

The other resolution to the crisis at this stage, which Erikson sometimes called distantiation, is a readiness to isolate ourselves from others when we feel threatened by their behavior.

Erikson's distinction at this stage has been operationalized by Orlofsky, Marcia, and Lesser (1973), who identified five intimacy statuses: intimate, preintimate, stereotyped relationships, isolate, and pseudointimate. Whitbourne and Weinstock (1979) added a sixth status, merger, accounting for the situation in which individuals who have not achieved any individual identities form intimate relationships to compensate for their own lack of focus.

Stage 7: Generativity Versus Self-Absorption and Stagnation

Although Erikson proposed that the next stage spanned the broad range of ages of 25 to 65, the crisis would seem to occur in the thirties or forties. Once a person has achieved certain goals in life—marriage, seeing his or her children develop, establishing a niche in the occupational world—there is a temptation to become self-centered. The individual may become bored, self-indulgent, and unable to contribute to society's welfare, placing comfort and security over challenge and sacrifice. He or she falls prey to stagnation. In Erikson's words, such people often indulge themselves as though they were "their own only child."

In contrast, generativity is the ability to be useful to ourselves and society. Three aspects of generativity identified by Erikson are a preoccupation with caring for others, productivity, and an inner awareness of one's need to be needed (Stewart, Franz, & Layton, 1988).

A person's productivity, at this stage, means being helpful to others; generativity is driven by a voluntary feeling of obligation to care for others. In the broadest sense, it is a reaching out, transmitting a concern for the next generation. It goes beyond caring for one's own children; the issue is not that of taking responsibility in the adult world. For example, Diane Willis was the coanchor for the CBS affiliate TV station in Boston for 3 years, with a potential salary of $200,000. Although her job was "glamorous," it did not challenge her mind. She voluntarily resigned in order to teach journalism at Northeastern University, at a salary of $30,000/year, because teaching the art of writing the news is "nurturing instead of narcissistic" ("Movers & Shakers," 1987, p. 7).

Erikson later said he used the term *generativity* because "I mean everything that is generated from generation to generation: children, products, ideas, and works of art" (quoted in Evans, 1967, p. 51). The achievement of generativity leads to the virtue of care, which includes "the care to do" something, to "care for" somebody, to "take care of" that which needs protection and attention, and "to take care not to do something destructive" (quoted in Evans, 1967, p. 53). McAdams, Ruetzel, and Foley (1986) have proposed that generativity reflects a combination of needs for agency (expanding and asserting the self) and for communion (merging the self with a larger environment of which the self is a part) (Bakan, 1966). Generativity permits the mature adult to express power and intimacy at the same time (see also Box 4.2).

Thus, at the stage of generativity, the person's commitment has extended beyond the individual self (identity stage) and the significant other (intimacy stage) to a more generalized group, such as one's family, the community, or society in general. One conception of the Eriksonian approach sees identity development continuing in this stage through investing and committing oneself to the development of other individuals, collectively (Stewart et al., 1988).

Stage 8: Ego Integrity Versus Despair

The last crisis, according to Erikson, is coming to terms with one's own life. If integrity occurs, the person sees his or her life as well spent. The attainment of integrity is reflected in older persons who are reasonably satisfied with achievements they have attained.

On the other hand, if despair is the resolution of the crisis at this stage, the person feels that he or she has made many wrong decisions (or no decisions at all). Life has lacked integration. Despair is often associated with anger that the person will not have another chance. There may be disgust, and contempt for others that disguises contempt for oneself.

In the case of most people, we are not privy to their ruminations as they near death and come to terms with the meaning of their lives. But with Lee Atwater we were. The manager for George Bush's successful campaign for the U.S. presidency in 1988, Atwater had

BOX 4.2

Measuring Generativity

Erikson's conception of increased generativity during midlife sounds plausible, but little empirical support exists for the concept (Ryff & Heincke, 1983; Ryff & Migdal, 1984; Vaillant & Milofsky, 1980). After reviewing these and earlier attempts to operationalize the concept, de St. Aubin and McAdams (1991; McAdams & de St. Aubin, 1992) constructed the Loyola Generativity Scale in order to measure individual differences in generativity. The scale is composed of 20 statements (examples: "I have important skills that I try to teach others" and "I feel I have done nothing that will survive after I die.").

How does one validate a measure of generativity? The authors first administered the scale to 149 adults (ages 19 to 68) and 165 college students. The adult sample scored higher on generativity than the college sample, but the difference may have been a function of age alone. Scores on the Loyola Generativity Scale correlated positively with two shorter scales of generativity (Hawley, 1984; Ochse & Plug, 1986). But the major validation compared scale scores with two other instruments: first, self-reports on 49 acts chosen to represent generative behaviors; examples are "donated blood" and "produced a piece of art or craft," and, second, brief autobiographical reports.

Data from a sample of 79 adults (ages 25 to 74) found that different measures of generativity converge on the same construct; correlations were as follows:

Loyola Generativity Scale Score and Autobiographical Narratives	= .40
Loyola Generativity Scale Score and Number of Generative Behaviors Reported	= .59
Number of Generative Behaviors Reported and Autobiographical Narratives	= .45

All of these are self-report measures and may have been influenced by a social desirability response set, but the results offer support for efforts to measure individual differences in generativity among adults.

Further analysis by these authors (de St. Aubin & McAdams, 1992), using a larger sample of adults, concluded that generativity is a much more salient issue in the lives of middle-aged adults than it is for younger or older adults.

a reputation as a merciless and ugly campaigner; he was given credit for using the "Willie Horton issue" as a way of portraying Bush's opponent, Michael Dukakis, as a liberal soft on crime. But Atwater developed a brain tumor and died in early 1991 at the age of 40.

In the last year of his life, as he knew he was dying, Atwater reconsidered his philosophy and repented his ruthlessness. He told an interviewer that he regretted what he had done in 1988: "Mostly I am sorry for the way I thought of other people. Like a good general, I treated everyone who wasn't with me as against me" (quoted in Shogan, 1991, p. A-9). He also said, "My illness helped me to see that what was missing in a society is what was missing in me: a little heart, a lot of brotherhood" (quoted in Reynolds, 1991, p. 13-A).

To summarize: When Lee Atwater "was dying he made amends, publicly and privately, for all his affronts against political civility. It was as if his encounter with mortality had burned away his cynicism. He wished to leave something behind him besides the record of his campaigns. His legacy includes his regrets" (Blumenthal, 1991, p. 13; used with permission from *The New Republic*).

Erikson's Case Studies

As a clinician, Erikson sought to study individual lives. The ways that specific persons chose to resolve the crises of life provided opportunities to test his theory. (Furthermore, he wanted to demonstrate that the lives of great men and women cannot be explained on the basis of childhood traumas alone [Wright, 1982].) Erikson prepared detailed biographical analyses of two internationally known persons, Martin Luther and Mahatma Gandhi, who—he concluded—illustrated choice points at two important stages in adulthood. In examining these analyses at this point, we anticipate the approach of psychobiography, examined in more detail in Chapter 5.

Erikson on Luther

Martin Luther was born on November 10, 1483. His father, Hans Luther, was a coal miner, who gradually achieved a moderate degree of prosperity. However, Martin Luther's memories of his childhood were of poverty and an upbringing that was strict and perhaps even harsh.

In 1501, at the age of 17 or 18, he entered the university. He was obviously a brilliant student and his father hoped that he would become a wealthy lawyer.

In the middle of the spring semester of his first term in law school in Erfurt, on his way home, the 21-year-old Luther was caught in a tremendous thunderstorm and, in sudden fear of not surviving, made a vow to Saint Anne that if he survived he would become a monk (Spitz, 1973). Thus, despite his father's objections, he entered a monastery, took his vows, and was ordained as a priest in 1507. The following year he began to lecture at the recently founded university at Wittenberg.

Several years later he visited Rome on church business. Although he was overcome with emotion as he approached the center of Christendom, he much later was to talk about the upset and trauma at seeing how worldly and ostentatious Rome was. In a sense, Luther was a reactionary; even though he came to be a reformer, he wanted Christianity to return to the purity of the Apostles (Kolakowski, 1991). Despite his growing antagonism with the deviations of the Church, he progressed through the University hierarchy; in 1511, at age 28, he was appointed a professor at Wittenberg. But his frustrations with the Church came to a head in 1517 when, at the age of 33, he posted his 95 theses attacking the sale of indulgences by Church authorities. Word immediately spread throughout Europe of his action.

Luther refused to obey orders from the Church and began to attack the Pope, Leo X. The latter issued a statement condemning Luther's heresies; Luther publicly burned his copy of the message. Luther was henceforth excommunicated and the emperor of the Holy Roman Empire ordered him to appear for censure.

But Luther refused to recant. He spent the remaining 30 years of his life teaching, preaching, writing, and establishing what came to be called the Lutheran church. In his mature years, his productivity was immense. He wrote the equivalent of a pamphlet-length essay every 2 weeks; he traveled extensively, gave many lectures, and preached every week. In the Peasants War (1524-1525) he supported the princes against the rebellious peasants and thus lost much of the support he had had from the populace. At the age of

42, he married a former nun, Katherine von Bora; they had six children before Luther died on February 18, 1546, at the age of 62.

Erikson used Luther as an example of the place of a moratorium period in forming an identity. In his interpretation of Luther's life, *Young Man Luther: A Study of Psychoanalysis and History* (1958), Erikson focused first on Luther's abrupt religious conversion as a young man and his decision to become a monk, thus bringing his own potential career as a lawyer to a sudden halt. As Roazen (1976) observes, "His training as monk was a form of 'indoctrination'; yet only that discipline gave Luther the breathing space, in Erikson's view, to find himself" (p. 78).

Psychoanalysis—and Eriksonian analysis—puts emphasis on the importance of a single event in the formation of character. In his book on Luther, Erikson has chosen the so-called fit in the choir as the pivotal event. During his early or mid-20s, Luther supposedly fell to the floor of the choir loft in the monastery, raving, "Non sum! Non sum!," that is, "It isn't me" (or "I am not," depending on the translation one prefers). Crosby and Crosby (1981), in a critical evaluation of Erikson's book, note that:

> the occasion which set off this apparent fit may have been the reading of Mark 9:17 where a father offered his son to Jesus: "And one of the multitude answered and said, 'Master, I have brought unto thee my son, which hath a dumb spirit.' " To Erikson this event reveals a crisis in the development of Luther's identity—a protest by Luther of what he was not in order to break through to what he was to be. (p. 211)

Erikson sees the fit as "both unconscious obedience to the father and implied rebellion against the monastery" (p. 38). That is, at the point at which this fit occurred, Luther "was, in short, at the crossroads of obedience to his early father and to his heavenly father. It was, in Erikson's famous phrase, a crisis of identity" (Crosby & Crosby, 1981, p. 211).

Others have interpreted this event somewhat differently, while still seeing it as reflecting part of an identity crisis. Dacey (1982) concludes that:

> Luther's greatness as a leader, says Erikson, was built partly on the enormous anger and unresolved conflict he experienced in his late

teens. Luther's decision to become a monk was the assuming of a negative identity. The choice expressed his rejection of 15th century society rather than his devotion to Catholicism. (p. 45)

The earlier decision to become a monk was an example of negative identity, and for Dacey, the "fit in the choir" is an indication of how difficult it was for him to be who he was.

But did the "fit the choir" even occur? Luther never mentioned it. The only references to it were in publications that appeared after his death, and most of those were written by avowed enemies who might have been tempted to discredit Luther's stability (Stannard, 1980, p. 22).

For example, Spitz (1973) recounts that:

the story is told, however, by Luther's archenemy and dedicated de- famer, Johannes Cochlaeus, in his commentary on Luther's life and works published three years after Luther's death, or more than four decades after the event. It is told, moreover, to prove that Luther had secret commerce with a demon. Cochlaeus's whole book is so full of falsehoods that Cardinal Alexander warned against publication, fear- ing that the reaction would make it counter-productive. (p. 196)

Erikson recognizes the weakness of this evidence; at one place he calls it an "alleged event." But he also says the fact that Luther never mentioned it may be a result of his having amnesia for the event.

Recall that if the "fit in the choir" occurred, it took place when Martin Luther was around 22 to 25 years of age. It was not until a decade later, in 1517, that Luther nailed his 95 theses to the church door in Wittenberg. However, Erikson felt that it was characteristic of original thinkers to experience long delays in reacting. This decision to protest against the Church and offer a different theol- ogy—as well as Luther's greatness as a leader—is partly based on the enormous anger and unresolved conflict he experienced in adoles- cence. Roazen (1976) put it this way: "Then around the age of thirty—an important age for gifted people with a delayed identity crisis—Luther's distinctive theology emerges" (p. 79).

Monkhood provided an extended moratorium. As his identity evolved, Luther was able to devote himself unequivocally to God, and turn all his anger toward the Pope.

Why so much anger? Because of the harsh treatment he received as a child. Erikson claims that Luther's father was brutal, malicious, and tyrannical, that Hans Luther beat young Martin. Erikson even interprets Luther's "harsh" image of the Heavenly Father as a projection of his image of his earthly father. But Erikson also admits that there are almost no facts about Martin Luther's childhood. According to Stannard (1980), there are only two mentions of beatings that Martin Luther received as a child, one by his father and one by his mother. And Spitz (1973) responds that:

> the idea that Luther's father was harsh with him as a regular thing is based upon one saying in the *Tischreden* of May 1532. . . . "My father once whipped me so hard that I fled from him and felt ugly toward him [or, became sadly resentful toward him] until he gradually got me accustomed to him again." (p. 191)

Furthermore, Spitz concludes that "Hans Luther was not harsh, drunken, or tyrannous, but rather tender and pious as well as stern and ambitious for himself and his son" (pp. 193-194).

Why was Luther great? For Erikson, it was his struggle "to lift his individual patienthood to the level of a universal one and to try to solve for all what he could not solve for himself alone" (quoted in Roazen, 1976, p. 83). Erikson acknowledges that Luther was a gifted but troubled young man "who had to create his own 'cause' on which to focus his fidelity in the Roman Catholic world as it was then" (quoted in Evans, 1967, p. 42).

Erikson on Gandhi

For another of his book-length psychological analyses Erikson chose as his subject Gandhi, the advocate of nonviolent protest in India. But here the focus was on generativity rather than identity; Erikson sought to understand the development of Gandhi's protest as an "ideological innovation in the context of his middle age" (Roazen, 1976, p. 122). As indicated before, the characteristic crisis of midlife is that of generativity versus stagnation, with generativity defined as a concern for establishing and guiding the next generation. Central to generativity in *Gandhi's Truth,* Erikson (1969) reveals how it can be manifested in a bold, caring action:

From the moment in January of 1915 when Gandhi set forth on a pier
reserved for important arrivals in Bombay, he behaved like a man who
knew the nature and extent of India's calamity and that of his own
fundamental mission. A mature man of middle age has not only made
up his mind as to what, in the various compartments of his life, he
does and does not *care for,* he is also firm in his vision of what he *will*
and can take care of. He takes as his baseline what he irreducibly is
and reaches out for what only he can, and therefore, *must do.* (p. 255,
italics in original)

As the critical event in Gandhi's life, Erikson chose the textile
strike of March 1918, the Ahmedabad incident. It was the first time
that Gandhi fasted over a political issue, in order to publicize the
fact that the textile workers toiled long hours in the mills and were
pitifully underpaid. A year later, he led the first Indian nationwide
civil disobedience. Gandhi was about 50 years of age; he was "in
between things" in 1918. By fasting, his personal restraint became
a force in itself, and clearly fasting is the opposite of Erikson's negative choice, stagnation, which is defined as indulging oneself to
excess.

Gandhi's act of passive resistance was successful. Eventually the
mill owners acceded, and the workers' wages were increased.

Interestingly enough, Gandhi, in his own autobiography, mini-
mizes the importance of the Ahmedabad incident, as do most historians and biographers of Gandhi's life. If asked to pick the critical
event in the formation of his character, most experts would select
the shocking incident at Pietermaritzburg, South Africa, in 1893.
Gandhi was 24 at the time. He had just arrived in South Africa a
week before. After growing up in India, he had gone to England for
training as an attorney. Now dressed in a suit, London cravat, and
a stiff collar, he was traveling to his first job, seated in a first-class
railroad car going from Durban to Pretoria, South Africa. At this
time Gandhi was very conventional, very concerned about his
appearance and pleasing others. But apparently he did not know
about the rules about segregation of the races in South Africa. A
White man entered his railroad compartment, and demanded that
he leave. "Move your Black ass back to third class or I will have you
thrown off," he said. The police came, grabbed Gandhi, and rudely
deposited him on a railroad-station platform, where he spent a cold
night. This one act, Gandhi often said, changed his life. Gandhi

remained in South Africa for 21 years, organizing the citizens to combat racial prejudice.

Both the subjects of Erikson's case studies were men. Do women follow the same developmental path? Erikson himself (Erikson, 1968a; Evans, 1967; Strouse, 1974) and others (Chodorow, 1978; Franz & White, 1985; Gilligan, 1982; Stewart et al., 1988) have questioned whether women also follow a path from identity to intimacy to generativity; in fact, several varying interpretations of Erikson's position on gender similarities or differences can be supported (Franz & White, 1985). Chapters 6 and 7 will examine this issue in more detail, but at this point we note the criticism offered by Franz and White (1985), who argue that Erikson, in neglecting concern for the development of relationships, does not provide a framework for understanding how individuals move from the dependency of the trust versus mistrust stage to the mature interdependence of the successful resolution of the intimacy stage (Bar-Yam Hassan, 1989). Similarly, emphasis has been on the positive aspects of intimacy rather than a more realistic combinaton of both positive and negative aspects; in one empirical study, many adolescents of both genders expressed dissatisfaction and discomfort with their relationships, as well as positive aspects (Paul, 1989).

SUMMARY

Erikson's approach has the virtue of being comprehensive and life-span oriented. But it is not without its limitations. For example, is it a scientific theory or a philosophy of life? Is Erikson describing what *is* or what he hopes *should be* for good adjustment (Dacey, 1982)?

Critics have noted that desirable values are rife in his theory. For example, during adolescence, Erikson—and society in general—places a premium on independence, especially independence by males. This leads to a conclusion that adolescent identity is achieved only through turmoil and separateness. Recent research based on studies of normal populations (Kandel & Lesser, 1972; summarized in Montemayor, 1983, and Petersen, 1988) can be interpreted that conflict "is but one way, and a rare way at that, for getting through the teen-age years" (Tavris, 1990, p. 9). Most adolescents remain close to their parents and do not experience intense conflict with their parents. A recent book (Apter, 1990), reporting on lengthy interviews with 65 mother-daughter pairs, found that for most of the young women, the person they felt closest to and who offered them their greatest support was their mother.

Furthermore, concepts are seldom if ever defined precisely (Hudson, 1991, p. xviii; Huyck & Hoyer, 1982, p. 216), and it is difficult to translate the concepts into operational definitions. In fact, Erikson is inconsistent about the necessity of epigenesis and the time-bound resolution of conflicts. Smelser (1980) observes:

> Erikson's model of adult development is a complex mixture of determinancy and indeterminancy (Erikson, 1950). On the side of determinancy, he envisions a definitive sequence of stages which follow on and build on one another. In addition, he suggests definite age ranges for the various stages of the life from infancy to old age, though—on the side of indeterminancy—he does not fix exact or unvarying chronological ages for each stage or the transitions between them. His theory of development is also lent determinancy by its principle of epigenesis—the principle that for a given developmental process to transpire, others have to have transpired before it, and that the resolution of any given prior crisis is not fixed for all time but must develop further at all subsequent stages. Yet at the same time the principle of epigenesis is not a completely fixed one; each developmental stage has a measure of its own autonomous dynamics. (p. 19)

That is, issues can surface again later. Elkind (1982) comments that the problem of basic trust versus mistrust "arises again at each successive stage of development" (p. 15). Questions of identity, thought to be resolved in the late teens, may resurface in the 40-year-old faced with a divorce (see Box 4.3 for an example). In Chapter 10, we examine Hudson's (1991) conception that throughout life, we keep rearranging the same basic life issues—identity, achievement, intimacy, and search for meaning—around the changing conditions evoked by social conditions. (Hudson has also questioned whether age periods are the major determinants of personal change and development.)

One salient type of critique of Erikson's theory is to question whether further stages are necessary. Several stages (particularly Stages 7 and 8) cover broad age periods. Several elaborations of

---

BOX 4.3

The Recurrence of Crises

Are conflicts resolved once and for all? As Elkind (1982) reports, "A child who comes through infancy with a vital sense of trust can still have his sense of mistrust activated at a later stage if, say, his parents are divorced and separated under acrimonious circumstances" (p. 15).

Elkind notes that this point was brought home to him in a very direct way by a 4-year-old patient he saw in a court clinic:

> He was being seen at the court clinic because his adoptive parents, who had had him for 6 months, now wanted to give him back to the agency. They claimed that he was cold and unloving, took things, and could not be trusted. He was indeed a cold and apathetic boy, but with good reason. About a year after his illegitimate birth, he was taken away from his mother, who had a drinking problem, and was shunted back and forth among several foster homes. Initially he had tried to relate to the persons in his foster homes, but the relationships never had a chance to develop because he was moved at just the wrong times. In the end he gave up trying to reach out to others, because the inevitable separations hurt too much.
>
> Like the burned child who dreads the flame, this emotionally burned child shunned the pain of emotional involvement. He had trusted his mother, but now trusted no one. Only years of devoted care and patience could now undo the damage that had been done to this child's sense of trust. (p. 15)

Stage 7 issues are described in Chapters 6 and 7, on the newer stage theories of Roger Gould and Daniel Levinson. Related to this criticism is the question whether the current stages cover all the relevant issues in personality development. Ryff and Heincke (1983) identified complexity along with generativity as a key personality issue of middle age. Jane Loevinger's (1976) construct of ego development proposes that with the maturity of middle adulthood the person may establish a highly differentiated view of life's goals and issues.

Greatest scrutiny of the adequacy of Erikson's last stage has been carried out by Robert Peck (1968), who has suggested a modification of this stage.

Within the eighth stage Peck has elaborated two broad periods—middle age and old age—and within each, several "crises" (Troll, 1982, p. 19). Among middle-aged "crises," according to Peck, are:

1. learning an appreciation of wisdom versus an appreciation of physical powers;
2. learning to socialize human relationships rather than sexualize human relationships;
3. developing cathectic flexibility versus cathectic impoverishment (that is, Peck felt it was valuable to be able to shift emotional investments from one person to another and from one activity to another); and
4. maintaining mental flexibility versus mental rigidity.

In contrast, Peck saw other crises during old age:

1. ego differentiation versus work-role preoccupation (Here Peck is referring to the desirability that retired persons shift their value systems so as to redefine their self-worth in terms of something other than their occupation.);
2. body transcendence versus body preoccupation; and
3. ego transcendence versus ego preoccupation. As Peck (1968) puts it:

The constructive way of living the late years might be defined in this way: to live so generously and unselfishly that the prospect of personal death—the right of the ego, it might be called—looks and feels less important than the secure knowledge that one has built for a broader, longer future than any one ego could ever encompass. (p. 91)

Perhaps that is a fitting final word on Erikson's encompassing theory too; we can view it constructively as not only a final word but a building block for the theory and observations that follow.

5

Psychobiography and Personality Development in Adulthood

Biography helps me understand the lives of others in new ways, so that I can understand my own life better.

Steve Weinberg

Chapter 4 portrayed Erik Erikson's analysis of life-span personality development and employed his concept of crises, or choice points. Eriksonian theory assumes that our active choices can affect the evolving aspects of our lives and the adaptations we manifest. But how do other people, watching our struggles from the outside, conceptualize and explain our reactions to crises and our resultant choices? Biographers, writers of "personality profiles" in popular magazines, and even each of us who cares about our friends face this challenge to explain. Two provocative biographical works portray contrasting solutions to the dilemma faced by the person who must demarcate and describe the life of another individual.

Bearing the Cross (Garrow, 1986) is a long (800 pages), detailed, heavily researched biography of Martin Luther King, Jr., with emphasis on that part of King's life beginning with the Montgomery,

Alabama, bus boycott and ending with his murder in April 1968. The author, David Garrow, took 7 years to write the book, and in the process interviewed 200 people and incorporated into his narrative the contents of 500 interviews carried out by others. A recipient of a Pulitzer Prize, *Bearing the Cross* is a valuable, chronologically based description of the activities in the last 12 years of King's life.

But critics have consistently concluded that a much-needed integrative view of King is lost in the mass of detail provided by this book. Martin Luther King, Jr., was—even more than most of us—a frustratingly complex person whose life choices insisted on explanation. On the one hand, he was a man with vision, with the courage and character to combat immoral laws, and with the galvanizing oratorical skills to rally others behind him. At the same time he was a risk-taking philanderer whose sexual promiscuity placed the achievement of his goals in great jeopardy. At periods during the height of his effectiveness he drank heavily. How do we explain the psychological development and behavior of this complicated man? One of the book's reviewers notes that:

> Mr. Garrow presents the reader with the most complete dossier yet published on the life King led in hotel rooms and in his hideaway apartment in Atlanta. Yet he seems reluctant to integrate this material into a deeper understanding of why King continued his libertine pursuits even when it became clear that they might be used to destroy him. (Raines, 1986, p. 34; Copyright © by The New York Times Company. Reprinted by permission.)

This all-too-vulnerable human being deserves some theory-based explanation of his behavior.

The Definition of Psychohistory and Psychobiography

Psychohistory seeks to fill the deficits in the above analysis. Erikson (1974) defined this approach as "the study of individual and collective life with the combined methods of psychoanalysis and history" (p. 13). In a valuable review that serves as a structure for this chapter, Crosby and Crosby (1981) state, "We define psychohistory as a form of history which explicitly uses the concepts, principles, and theories of psychology to enhance our understanding of particular people and events in the past" (p. 196). Technically, *psychohistory* refers to the analysis of some historical or contemporary event or phenomenon (such as the Salem witchcraft trials in Colonial New England, or the rise of Nazism in Germany) or the explanation of a particular culture or nationality. In contrast, *psychobiography* is usually reserved for the psychological exploration of a given individual's life, such as Martin Luther King, Jr., or—as we saw in Chapter 4—Martin Luther. Dan McAdams (1988) defines *psychobiography* as "the systematic use of psychological (especially personality) theory to transform a life into a coherent and illuminating story" (p. 3). (But, just to complicate things, "psychohistory" occasionally is used as a generic label for either the focus on events or the focus on an individual's life.)

Because psychobiography's mission is in keeping with the thrust of this book—and because the first and most influential psychobiographical analyses were constructed by Freud and by Erikson—this chapter is directed toward illustrating the benefits and limitations of such an approach.

Although some analysts of an individual's life, like author David Garrow, may be faulted for not supplying a structure for explaining their subject's life, other biographers have the opposite limitation, in that they go overboard in providing explanations that rest more on speculation and assumption than on data and observation. At least for some reviewers, a second book generates such an example.

Bernhard Goetz received instant, nationwide publicity as the "subway vigilante" when he shot four Black youths in New York City a few days before Christmas 1984. Two years later, a San Francisco Bay area psychotherapist and sociologist, Lillian B. Rubin (1986), offered a book-length biography and diagnosis of Goetz. Here are some excerpts from her book:

> As he struggled, as all adolescent boys must, with his developing sense of himself and his maleness, the issues of sexuality and identity would have been even more difficult for him than for the ordinary teenager. (p. 140)

> Unquestionably, Bernie's continuing problems with authority were born in childhood when he had to fight so hard to maintain some sense of his own integrity, his own autonomy. (p. 141)

The validity of these interpretations rests on their sources. And these are limited because the author never interviewed Bernhard Goetz (who refused the invitation), nor his former wife. (The author did talk to Goetz's sisters.) It is true that some reviewers have been tolerant of Rubin's sweeping interpretations; Wray Herbert (1987) wrote, "Like all psychohistories it is somewhat conjectural, relying heavily on distant memories of secondary sources" (p. 80). But others have been quite critical: "Rubin sometimes writes as if she had gotten inside his head" (Foreman, 1986, p. 3C), and "Some of it seems plausible and some of it is silly" (Johnson, 1986, p. 31). The latter reviewer observes:

> For example, she speculates that there might have been a connection between the $5 that one of the teenagers asked Mr. Goetz for just before the shootings and the $5 that Mr. Goetz's father was alleged to have paid to fondle two young boys in a sordid scandal when his son was an impressionable 12-year-old. (Johnson, 1986, p. 31)

We do not know for sure. But how often does psychobiography, in its quest for an explanation, let speculations and selective evidence override scholarship and a balanced review of the facts? We will see.

Causal Explanations of Individuals

The introduction to this chapter has implied that psychobiography seeks to capture the essence of an individual's personality development. Crosby and Crosby (1981) classify psychobiographies as reflecting two types of explanations: *Causal* and *coherent whole*. Causal explanations are "those explanations which seek to account for adult behavior in terms of childhood experiences" (p. 199), as Rubin has done with Bernhard Goetz. In contrast, coherent whole explanations "aim to create a unified whole out of apparently divergent bits of data as they relate to the actions of persons or groups" (p. 199). To a limited degree, Garrow tried to do the latter in his biography of Martin Luther King, Jr.; at least he provided those "divergent bits of data" from which a composite portrait might be painted.

Generating either type of explanation is a challenging task but the development of a causal explanation is more so, because it asks *why* is the person the way he or she is or was? In seeking to establish links between childhood experiences and adult behavior—a fundamental assumption of psychoanalytic theory described in Chapter 2—the quest for causal explanations faces several kinds of difficulties, particularly if the subject of the psychobiography lived in earlier times (Weinberg, 1992). Especially with these circumstances, psychobiographers are forced to rely on letters, diaries, autobiographies, memoirs, and similar personal documents. (The use of these in understanding personality development in adulthood is further described in Volume 2 of this book.) And such materials usually devote scant attention to childhood. But even when the subject is alive, those people who were relevant to the subject's early years may no longer be.

Without access to direct evidence about the purportedly vital childhood experiences, psychobiographers have sometimes capitalized on what Crosby and Crosby (1981) justifiably label as two questionable devices. First, "they often substitute generalized clinical studies for the emotional states of their specific subjects. In so doing, they misapply the legitimate use made by analysts of clinical studies as supplementary guides to the therapeutic dialogue" (Crosby & Crosby, 1981, p. 200). Second, psychobiographers have relied too heavily on the psychoanalytic concept of the unconscious in explaining the sources of personality development. The following sections provide illustrations of these excesses, by examining psychobiographies of Adolf Hitler and Richard Nixon, before evaluating works written by Freud and Erikson.

Adolf Hitler and Causal Explanations

His evil regime caused the death of 6 million Jews and a devastating world war. Not surprisingly, Adolf Hitler has been one of the most frequently analyzed subjects by psychobiographers; one of the most comprehensive is a book by R. G. L. Waite (1977). In summary,

Waite concludes that Hitler's adult behavior—his speeches, his late-night monologues—reflect an oral fixation, strongly lacerated with aggression. But, he proposes, Hitler also possessed anal character traits, including a compulsion for cleanliness and an obsessive concern about time.

But Waite then reasons backward in time, from the oral behaviors of Hitler's adulthood, suggesting that there may have been serious interference in the feeding process when Hitler was an infant. And because of the anal character trait, Waite claims, it "may be assumed" that Hitler's mother was "particularly rigorous" in toilet training her children. But—regrettably—we do not know anything about Hitler's toilet training. Waite's interpretation remains unproved.

Furthermore, Waite relies heavily on the unconscious as an explanation of Hitler's behavior. As Crosby and Crosby (1981) conclude, "Of course, Hitler's behavior may well have been unconsciously motivated. But we simply have no way of knowing; we lack the vital evidence" (pp. 202-203).

As observers seek to understand Hitler's orientation, a major question centers on the source of his anti-Semitic feelings. In Waite's explanation, the family doctor, Edward Bloch, plays a prominent role. Dr. Bloch, a Jew, tried to treat the breast cancer that developed in Hitler's mother, but he failed, and she died. Hitler was a teenager at the time; he developed feelings of ambivalence toward the doctor, who also had begun to serve as a kind of father substitute for Hitler. The youth, according to Waite, appreciated the doctor's efforts but resented his failure. Perhaps also, what the young Hitler perceived as the doctor's "intimacies" with his mother—the frequent examination of her breasts—may have stimulated Oedipal feelings in her son. Waite concludes that he came to see Dr. Bloch as a "brutal mutilator" of his mother after the doctor performed a mastectomy. (Dr. Bloch had also tried to treat her with iodoform, which caused her to experience a severe and painful burning sensation.) But all this is speculation, and not very parsimonious speculation, at that. It could be just as plausibly argued that the function of Hitler's anti-Semitism was to manipulate and mobilize the feelings of the German populace and solidify Hitler's Nazi political party.

The criticism of Waite's approach does not mean that the search for understanding of Hitler's development should be forsaken—only that more sophisticated analyses are necessary. As Cocks and Crosby (1987) conclude, "Historians have turned away from the early easy conviction that Hitler could be understood in crude psychopathological terms alone; they have become increasingly sophisticated about the fascinating mixture of the rational and irrational, the conscious and unconscious within Hitler" (p. xi).

The "Why" of Richard Nixon

Richard Nixon continues to fascinate the American news media, despite the fact that his presidency abruptly terminated 20 years ago. A *Newsweek* cover in 1986 proclaimed, "He's back!" and 5 years later the distinguished journalist Tom Wicker (1991) of *The New York Times* provided a 700-page book concentrating on the key events and characters in the development of Nixon's personality.

Nixon has been the subject of close to a dozen book-length biographies, as well as innumerable chapters and articles. As the topic for psychological analysis, Nixon possesses the virtue of being a contemporary figure, long visible to the public eye, and hence the focus of much written material, including observations and reminiscences by his associates and family. Nixon himself has written three books of memoirs, plus several other books. And, of course, we have increasing access to all kinds of official records, including even the White House tapes!

Alan Elms, a judicious exponent of the psychobiographical approach, calls President Nixon's informal farewell to his staff, upon his resignation in August 1974, "a psychobiographer's dream." Elms (1976) observes:

> With sweat and tears streaming down his face, Nixon praised the staff for not having robbed the public till and pitied himself for having to "find a way to pay my taxes." He remembered "my old man" who moved from job to job and who sold "the poorest lemon ranch in California . . . before they found oil on it" but who was nonetheless "a great man, because he did his job and every job counts up to the hilt regardless of what happens." (p. 103)

Nixon said the following about his mother in that speech:

Nobody will ever write a book probably about my mother. Well, I
guess all of you would say this about your mother; my mother was a
saint. And I think of her two boys dying of tuberculosis, nursing four
others in order that she could take care of my older brother for three
years in Arizona and seeing each of them die. Yes, she will have no
books written about her. But she was a saint. (pp. 103-104)

Elms (1976) points out that this was followed by "an odd combination of self-deprecation and implied self-praise" (p. 104) and then
finally a set of "concluding homilies" by Nixon:

Because the greatness comes not only when things go always good for
you, but the greatness comes when you're really tested, when you take
some knocks and disappointments, when sadness comes. . . . Always
give your best. Never get discouraged. Never be petty. Always remem-
ber, others may hate you, but those who hate you don't win unless
you hate them. And then you destroy yourself.

An ironic message, coming as it does from Richard Nixon, we
would all probably conclude. Elms proposes that:

if a skilled psychobiographer had sat down to write a farewell speech
for Nixon that would incorporate in dramatic form the major psychological themes of Nixon's life, he [or she] would have written just such
a speech. That Nixon did it himself, apparently with little advance
preparation and under great emotional stress, makes it one of the prize
psychobiographical documents of modern times. (p. 104)

Whence came these themes? Psychobiographers looking for causal
explanations concentrate on Nixon's childhood. Richard Nixon was
the second son of a hard-working but frequently unsuccessful father
and a Quaker mother. The latter, Hannah Nixon, everyone agrees,
was the major influence on his life.

The death of children is a recurrent theme in Nixon's own childhood. He was almost killed in a wagon accident when he was 3,
and a serious illness almost led to his death at age of 4. Again, during
his senior year in high school, he was quite ill. (Yet as President he
claimed that he had never been sick a day in his life.) His younger
brother Arthur died suddenly of tubercular encephalitis when Richard Nixon was 12. Furthermore, Harold, his older brother, also died

of tuberculosis when Richard was 19, after a long struggle in which his mother, hoping for a recovery, took Harold to Arizona for 2 years (not 3, as President Nixon said in his farewell speech).

Nixon grew up in a small town in Southern California, and remained there to go to Whittier College, a small Quaker school. He once noted that Whittier "did not offer a course in political science in the years I spent there." (He added that he had received a good education, but that if he *had* been "exposed" to a political science course, he might have defeated John Kennedy in the 1960 presidential election.) But Fawn Brodie (1981), one of his psychobiographers, examined his college transcript and discovered that he had completed courses titled "Government," "The American Constitution," and "International Relations and International Law."

Richard Nixon worked hard in college, and continued to do so at Duke University Law School, where he graduated 3rd in a class of 25. But his career as a lawyer began with disappointment. Denied jobs with the Federal Bureau of Investigation or with any prominent New York City law firm, he was forced to return, shamefaced, to his hometown. There, his family persuaded an old friend to take him into a local law firm (Elms, 1976).

After practicing law for 5 years in Whittier, Nixon migrated to the East Coast again, in 1942, shortly after World War II began. After struggling for 8 unhappy months as a low-level government bureaucrat, he joined the wartime navy and served as a supply officer in the South Pacific. Returning to Southern California at the end of World War II, he was persuaded to run for the U.S. Congress, thus initiating his 30-year political career.

The psychobiographers who seek to explain the "why" of Nixon's personality development range from fairly conventional to exceedingly negative interpretations. One of the most substantial is that by Bruce Mazlish (1973), a historian trained in psychoanalysis. As we would expect, Mazlish chooses to emphasize the influence from Nixon's early family life, by noting that Richard adopted one set of characteristics from his mother, and one set from his father—with a resulting clash between them. His "Protestant ethic" traits—emphasis on planning, hard work, and persistence—came from his mother, but Mazlish also describes the young Nixon as identifying with his father in a number of ways, including his love of argument, his interest in politics, his being a "loner," and his fear of failure.

Mazlish hypothesized that Nixon "sought to redeem his father by being successful" (p. 27) and used his mother's admirable traits in the service of that goal. He also identified more with his father's fundamentalist version of Quakerism than with his mother's pacifist and relatively liberal version. But the conflict between these led him to feel ambivalent about peace and war throughout his life.

In Mazlish's interpretation, Richard Nixon's brothers played important developmental roles in negative ways, because they aroused the "natural emotions of sibling rivalry" (p. 25). Each took their mother away from Richard, in one way or another. The deaths of two of his brothers must have generated powerful emotional responses; Mazlish speculates that these were fear of getting tuberculosis and of dying, along with strong guilt feelings over having survived them after experiencing the resentment toward them while they were alive.

Mazlish went on to speculate that Nixon's later pattern of seeking out crises—or at least basking in the glory of having coped with each crisis—was "partly motivated by the need to confront his death fears, repeatedly and constantly" (p. 26). Nixon's own childhood illnesses presumably intensified this fear of death. As a child he not only was severely ill, but he was clumsy and socially inept; he also apparently developed the notion that he was not terribly bright.

Mazlish concludes that Nixon reflects an almost classic case of compensation for inferiority. Nixon is a man with "an insecurely held self" (p. 86), driven to succeed and possessed by a need to "create crises, as a means of testing himself and assuring himself greater personal support" (p. 87).

Mazlish's conclusions might appear to some to be overgeneralized, but the other psychobiographers of Nixon have generated interpretations that are even more extreme. Eli Chesen (1973), a Phoenix psychiatrist, was aware of Mazlish's book and criticized it as too much of a classical psychoanalytic interpretation for the available data to support (p. 21). He also was critical of Mazlish's "tenuous theories of sibling rivalry followed by sibling guilt" (p. 69).

But Chesen had his own opinions; he diagnosed Richard Nixon as a standard obsessive-compulsive neurotic whose every action was fueled by anxiety and fears about his own weakness. He described Nixon's father as a quite violent man who frightened Richard by his wrathful and authoritarian ways. Chesen (1973) portrayed Nixon's mother Hannah as loving but with an iron will and a sense of ambition. Richard Nixon, in this view, identified more with his mother than with his father, and her nature as a domineering matriarch led to "significant feelings of uncertainty about himself as a male" (p. 77), and an exaggerated concern with the task of proving himself manly. Chesen concluded that Nixon moved to "shut the world out" (p. 91) and seek total control over every situation because unconsciously he was helpless, dominated, and weak but did not want anyone to know it.

Hostility is the key concept in the explanation of Nixon's personality development offered by David Abrahamsen (1977), a psychoanalyst who has also written extensively on the criminal mind. Nixon's unhappy childhood left him with such a reservoir of anger, bitterness, and repressed hostilities, and he was so guilt-ridden because of his unresolved Oedipal feelings toward his mother, that "ultimately he willed his own destruction in the Watergate affair" (quoted by Anderson, 1977, p. 5; Copyright © by The New York Times Company. Reprinted by permission). Abrahamsen believes that Nixon feared his father (described in his book as an angry, impulsive man who failed at almost everything he undertook); he also "was ashamed of his hand-me-down clothing, felt deprived of both love and material goods, and began to imitate the secretive and manipulative behavior that his mother used to deal with her troublesome husband" (quoted by Anderson, 1977, p. 5).

But Abrahamsen (1977) goes on to conclude:

Although he was unaware of it, the real poverty of his life was not economic; it was emotional. He covered up the lack of love and affection particularly from his father—a lack which was reflected in Nixon's later personal and professional life. This attitude toward his childhood is an important character structure. As an adult he wanted to give the impression that his home life was simple, even poor, difficult at times, but good, because the emotional involvement was too powerful for him to deal with. To protect himself from these memories, he needed to construct an image of an orderly and harmonious home. When a person says his home is good when in fact it is not, he is distorting the truth to give a false impression. It is this need to push painful situations out of his mind which became a vaunted

---

BOX 5.1

A Letter Written by Richard Nixon at Age 10

My Dear Master:

The two boys that you left me with are very bad to me. Their dog, Jim, is very old and he will never talk or play with me.

One Saturday the boys went hunting. Jim and myself went with them. While going through the woods one of the boys triped [*sic*] and fell on me. I lost my temper and bit him. He kiked [*sic*] me in the side and we started in. While we were walking I saw a black round thing in a tree. I hit it with my paw. A swarm of black thing [*sic*] came out of it. I felt pain all over, I started to run and as both my eys [*sic*] were swelled shut I fell into a pond. When I got home I was very sore. I wish you would come home right now.

Your good dog,

Richard

Nixon quality. It was his way of rearranging reality so that he did not have to face up to and cope with his repressed anger and emotional stress of his early years. (p. 5)

Abrahamsen, describing it as a pathetic document, reprints Nixon's "My Dear Master" letter (see Box 5.1) written at age 10, in which a terribly unhappy child portrays himself as a victim of a hostile world.

The "faithful dog" metaphor is prolonged in Richard Nixon's stubborn courtship of Pat Ryan, during which, when she insisted on seeing other men, he would drop her off on dates and pick her up afterward. Abrahamsen thinks that Nixon was attracted to Pat primarily because she reminded him of his mother; she was a strong woman who could sustain him, as Hannah had.

Our fourth, and final, book-length psychobiography of Nixon's character development, by the late historian Fawn Brodie (1981), moves away from psychoanalytic concepts. Brodie concludes that

Nixon manifested a lifelong habit of deception. As a youth, Nixon was portrayed by Brodie as rigid and unable to make true friendships with members of either sex. He became addicted early to the habit of manipulating the truth, according to Brodie. He was compulsively driven to seek almost any elective success to compensate for his own sense of worthlessness.

Brodie's (1981) description of Nixon's parents was somewhat similar to previously described ones. Frank Nixon was portrayed as punitive and occasionally violent, a man who made scapegoats of his sons to palliate his own sense of missed opportunity. She speculated on whether his father ever kicked Richard, because "the theme of kicking, and being kicked, appears early in Richard Nixon's life and surfaces repeatedly" (p. 44). She documented nine references that Richard Nixon made to kicking over a period of 50 years and an actual kick he delivered to a protester in Peru. Brodie described his mother as saintly but somewhat less than truthful. She was frequently absent, she withheld affection, and she apparently never communicated an Eriksonian sense of trust and self-esteem to her son.

The viciousness of Nixon's often blatantly dishonest attacks on political opponents Brodie (1981) attributed to the "sinister theme of fratricide, running like a lethal shadow through Nixon's life" (p. 506). According to Brodie (1981), Nixon saw himself in fierce competition with Harold, his much adored older brother who died of tuberculosis when Richard Nixon was a freshman in college. She wrote:

> One thing Richard Nixon could not do after his older brother contracted tuberculosis was to challenge him, since the threat of death had removed him as a natural antagonist. But he did challenge scores of other brothers, seeking . . . to defeat his opponents "without annihilation." . . . Later he would embrace a more dangerous object than winning—the irreparable destruction of an opponent. (pp. 105-106)

Freud's Venture Into Psychobiography as an Explanation

Although these analyses of Nixon's psychological development contain some plausibility along with their similar interpretations, they also reflect some of the problems in seeking causal explanations within the psychobiographical approach. These limitations extend back to the very first psychobiographical analysis, Sigmund Freud's attempt in 1910 to explain the character of Leonardo da Vinci (Freud, 1910/1957).

Despite what he wrote in his book, *Leonardo da Vinci and A Memory of His Childhood,* Freud was an admirer of Leonardo (Coles, 1987); he had no desire to harm the reputation of a great man. But Freud was perplexed by the inconsistencies in Leonardo's behavior; for example, he was known to possess a "feminine delicacy of feelings" (Stannard, 1980, p. 4) (he was a vegetarian, and he had a habit of buying caged birds at the market and freeing them), but he also designed "the cruellest offensive weapons" of war. Likewise, he maintained an "insatiable and indefatigable thirst for knowledge" (Stannard, 1980, p. 4) while showing a "frigidity" and a "cool repudiation of sexuality" (Stannard, 1980, p. 8). In one of his letters to Jung, Freud noted his insights into "the riddle of Leonardo da Vinci's character" (A. C. Elms, 1988, p. 21), and what started as a peripheral issue became a major work.

Freud proposed that Leonardo had engaged in the defense mechanism of sublimation; his persistent investigative orientation constituted an outlet for his repressed sexuality. But, wrote Freud (1910/1957), to substantiate this hypothesis we would "need some picture of his mental development in the first years of his childhood" (p. 17). The problem is that very little is definitely known about Leonardo's early life. (Freud acknowledged that.) Leonardo was apparently born in 1452, the illegitimate son of a notary and probably a young peasant woman. Freud quotes Leonardo's "earliest memory" from his scientific notes on the flight of birds:

> It seems that I was always destined to be so deeply concerned with vultures; for I recall one of my very earliest memories, that while I was in the cradle a vulture came down to me, and opened my mouth with its tail, and struck me many times with its tail against my lips. (Freud, 1910/1957, quoted by Coles, 1987, p. 85)

For Freud, this was a very diagnostic memory, or dream, because the tail of a vulture can be interpreted as a "substitute expression" for a penis. To Freud, this was illustrative of a "passive" homosexual experience. The desire to suck on a penis may be traced to a reminiscence of sucking at his mother's breast.

Freud attributed the purported homosexual orientation to Leonardo's having spent life alone with his mother. He concluded that Leonardo was "emotionally homosexual." But the actual evidence for Leonardo's homosexuality is very thin; at the age of 24 he was anonymously accused, with three other young men, of homosexuality. The accusation was investigated and the charges were dismissed. No evidence exists that Leonardo had any adult sexual life of any kind. Freud seemed to rely heavily on an 1895 biography of Leonardo da Vinci that contained an incorrect translation; the word "vulture" in the above quotation should have been "kite" (a small bird). As A. C. Elms (1988) observes, "In retrospect, we can say that Freud should have exercised extra care concerning the translation's accuracy" (p. 24), but he did not.

Ironically, Freud's biography failed to follow a number of the sensible guidelines he advocated in this self-same book. These include:

1. Avoid arguments based on a single clue.
2. Avoid "pathographizing" the psychobiographical subject (i.e., avoid the mean-spirited interpretations such as found in some of the psychobiographies of Nixon).
3. Avoid idealizing the psychobiographical subject.
4. Avoid drawing strong conclusions from inadequate data (summarized by A. C. Elms, 1988, pp. 29-31, who adds a final admonition).
5. Avoid assuming that you are less susceptible to psychobiographical error than Freud was.

Erikson as a Psychobiographer

Chapter 4 reflected the centrality of the psychobiographical method in the testing by Erik Erikson of his theory of development. Crosby and Crosby (1981) note that Erikson is generally considered to be the most effective exponent of psychohistory. He would seem to be ideally qualified to be a psychobiographer. Is he? Erikson (1958), in *Young Man Luther*, followed the common psychobiographical assumption, linking childhood experiences to adult behavior. Crosby and Crosby conclude that even though few facts are available on Luther's childhood, "Erikson believes he overcomes this disadvantage by using his clinical training which allows him to recognize major trends 'even when all the facts are not available' (Erikson, 1958, p. 50)" (Crosby & Crosby, 1981, p. 211). Erikson (1958) had delved into Luther's early life in order to substantiate his conclusion that Luther experienced a crisis of identity. He concluded that Luther's childhood was "somber and harsh" (p. 47) and "intensely unhappy" (p. 53). Erikson portrayed Luther's father as brutal and stern and yet ambitious for his son; the relationship between father and son was crucial in Luther's analysis. But his sources were from Luther's later writings and reminiscences—not guaranteed to be accurate.

Criteria for Causal Explanations

The search for causal explanations dominates psychobiography. How can we tell whether a psychobiography presents a legitimate or convincing explanation for the life choices and accomplishments of its subjects? Crosby and Crosby (1981) emphasize two criteria: proper evidence and sound inference. Furthermore, they state, "The psychohistorian should also be able to convince us that the temporally antecedent events are likely causative agents for the documented effects" (p. 214). Also, competing explanations should be refuted.

In a masterful act of evaluative scholarship, Crosby and Crosby (1981) reviewed approximately 50 books and articles that provided causal explanations of the personality of individuals. Two thirds of these used psychoanalysis as their theoretical reference point. Crosby and Crosby conclude that, as a group, these did a rather effective job of expressing principles clearly, but they were less successful in demonstrating "cause." They rarely offered alternative explanations. Only 9 of the 50 studies—less than 20%—received a positive evaluation.

Coherent-Whole Explanations

Not all psychobiographies seek to detect the reasons why some subject behaves in characteristic ways. Using the valuable structure provided by Crosby and Crosby, we note that some psychobiographies aim to create a unified whole out of the divergent bits of data from a person's life. These psychobiographers have an advantage over those offering causal explanations, because they do not necessarily delve into the subject's childhood and thus have less of a problem regarding the scarce childhood information.

One strategy in developing a coherent-whole explanation is—like the life script approach—to look for repetitive patterns—that is, to determine whether, in the person's life, distinctive modes of behavior recur in certain types of contexts. If so, the psychobiographer may introduce a construct or constructs that make sense of the person's behaviors (Crosby & Crosby, 1981, p. 219). Any hypotheses offered by the psychobiographer should be specific enough that they can be refuted. As in the case of the earlier causal explanations, the psychobiographer should consider plausible alternative constructs.

An Example of the Coherent-Whole Approach

Woodrow Wilson is a case in point. Numerous analysts (e.g., Friedman, 1990; Hargrove, 1966; Tucker, 1977) have noted that Wilson, throughout his career as Princeton University president, governor of the state of New Jersey, and U.S. president, would turn disputes over policies into personal fights. He refused to compromise in matters in which he had an emotional stake if the conflict was with another man whom he saw as a rival. George and George (1956) conclude that when the rivalry was with a strong male authority figure, Wilson had a tendency to become self-destructive and rigid. When Wilson was president of Princeton University, he fought with the dean of the graduate school, Andrew West, over the construction of a new graduate center. Wilson, having been offered a compromise with West that would have met his terms for the financing and location of the center, refused. He behaved similarly when the U.S. Senate balked at his request that it ratify a peace treaty and his plan for U.S. participation in the League of Nations (a forerunner of the United Nations) after World War I. Hargrove (1966) writes:

Historians agree that Wilson blundered in his fight with the Senate and finally killed his own idea of the League. It was a fight with West all over again. He translated a substantive fight into a personal one and so structured the situation that he would have to lose unless his opponents would bend their wills to him completely. . . . He had never been able to work well with men of the same stature as himself, and he saw this mission as peculiarly his own. (p. 51)

The psychobiography of Wilson by George and George (1956) is propelled by Harold Lasswell's (1930) claim that individuals seek power in order to overcome poor estimates of themselves. George and George "piece together, in an intelligible psychological whole, Wilson's love of constitutional writing, his desire for strong leadership, his constant need for reassurance, and his stubborn refusal to compromise in certain situations to show that, for Wilson, power compensated for low self-esteem" (Crosby & Crosby, 1981, p. 220).

Another example of the coherent-whole approach is described in Box 5.2.

Evaluation of Coherent-Whole Explanations

Coherent-whole explanations seek to answer the question "What is this person like?" Crosby and Crosby (1981) suggest the following criteria in evaluating the accuracy of these explanations:

1. How well does the psychobiographer document the behaviors he or she seeks to explain?
2. How well does the psychobiographer demonstrate that the behaviors documented were an expression of the subject's own adjustment or personality and not simply the response to a situation or a role the person is playing?
3. How appropriately and effectively are psychological constructs and theories used?
4. Are alternative explanations explored?

Crosby and Crosby apply these criteria to 56 books and articles that offer coherent-whole explanations of individuals' lives; all the subjects were political figures. Some 60% of these works used psychoanalysis as the theory-based explanation. Exactly half of these (28 of 56) were rated favorably by Crosby and Crosby on these criteria, as compared with only 20% of the causal explanations. Most

---

BOX 5.2

Bushman on Benjamin Franklin

Crosby and Crosby (1981) conclude that perhaps the most promising example of any of the coherent-whole explanations is R. L. Bushman's (1966) article that deals with Benjamin Franklin's widely recognized tendency to be conciliatory. In doing so, Bushman completely avoids references to Franklin's unconscious or to events in his childhood. Instead, he focuses on the correlation between Franklin's personal traits and his political behavior.

For example, Franklin (1961) writes in his autobiography:

> When about sixteen years of age, I happened to meet with a book written by one Tryon, recommending a vegetable diet. I determined to go into it. My brother, being yet unmarried, did not keep house but boarded himself and his apprentices in another family. My refusing to eat flesh occasioned an inconvenience, and I was frequently chided for my singularity.
>
> I made myself acquainted with Tryon's manner of preparing some of his dishes, such as boiling potatoes or rice, making hasty pudding, and a few others; and then proposed to my brother that he would give me weekly half the money he paid for my board, and I would board myself. He instantly agreed to it, and I presently found that I could save half of what he paid me. This was an additional fund for buying books. But I had another advantage in it. My brother and the rest going from the printing house to their meals, I remained there alone, and dispatching presently my light repast (which often was not more than a biscuit or slice of bread, a handful of raisins or a tart from the pastry cook's, and a glass of water) had the rest of the time till their return for study, in which I made the greater progress from that greater clearness of head and quicker apprehension which generally attend temperance in eating and drinking. (pp. 29-30)

Bushman notes that this was an advantageous arrangement for all concerned. A similar pattern can be found in Franklin's behavior as a diplomat and public servant; he was an expert negotiator and reconciler of conflicting viewpoints. Numerous examples abound, both in his role during the Constitutional Convention and his representation of the United States as an emissary to France.

Bushman concludes that Franklin's personal desire to avoid hostility motivated him to select negotiating roles throughout life.

psychobiographers who use coherent-whole explanations show that the subject behaved consistently and many demonstrate that the behaviors are distinctive and not inevitable. But these usually did not consider plausible alternative explanations; they are refuted in only about 10% of the studies.

Attempts to Explain a Specific
Event or Pattern in a Person's Life

More limited than the previous approaches is the effort to explain a particular action or event in an individual's life. An example is Robert Sears's (1979a) analysis of Mark Twain's letters and stories.

Like all writers of fiction, Mark Twain may be assumed to reflect personal issues in his stories and other fiction. But these personal fears and misfortunes may or may not be heavily disguised. Binion (1978) offers the example of Henrik Ibsen:

> Inquiry on him would almost have to begin with his impregnating a servant girl when he was eighteen. This misadventure looms even larger behind his later dramas than the two unsettling circumstances of his childhood: his rumored illegitimacy and his father's financial ruin. All three come into *The Wild Duck* practically undistorted in the back drop of the sorry menage of a photographer and dreamer (read: naturalist and poet). Tragedy ensues when an idealistic illusion-destroyer (Ibsen again) drags the old misadvantage upstage center. Ibsen took his own hint here and returned to distinguishing his experience of the unwanted child again and again until his last heroine went mad from reliving it again and again in disguise. Here, in *When We Dead Awaken,* the child is a statue for which she had posed in the nude. Traumatized by the sculptor's mere thanks for the chaste episode, she relives it in reverse as a nude artist who teases men to despair. (p. 315)

Sears attempted to demonstrate the effects of an early experience of loss of love on the letters and novels written by Mark Twain. Sears was aware of many facts in Samuel Clemens's boyhood that could lead to the development of separation anxiety; the presence of a mother who mixed love and rejection; the deaths of a brother and a sister before he was 10 years old; and his father's death when he was 12 years old. Later, when Samuel Clemens (Mark Twain) was an adult, his first-born son died at the age of 18 months.

Sears has content-analyzed those letters written by Mark Twain between 1868 and 1904 as well as the novels he composed over that period. Thus Sears (1979a) was able "to match the peaks and valleys of (Twain's) suppressed feelings with the events of his adult life" (p. 100). Sears concludes that the analysis of letters in combination with fiction writings provides additional understanding of a long-standing fear, "because fictional expression is under less conscious control than are direct communications such as letters" (pp. 102, 104).

Similarly, William McKinley Runyan (1982) chooses one dramatic event in the life of painter Vincent Van Gogh—his cutting off of part of his ear—and illustrates various explanations for the motive behind this act.

Criticisms of Psychobiography

Throughout this chapter we have alluded to criticisms of the psychobiographical approach. It is appropriate now to systematize and evaluate these criticisms. The following structure relies on Stannard's (1980) exceedingly critical review of psychobiography.

Errors of Fact

Psychobiographers sometimes create "facts" to fill gaps in the historical record. Erik Erikson's use of Martin Luther's "fit in the choir" (see Chapter 4) is a highly questionable "fact," the importance of which is compounded by the central role that Erikson gives it in explaining Luther's midlife crisis. Freud's use of a mistranslation of "vulture" also qualifies here.

Another type of error is to take an actual fact but overinterpret its meaning or importance. On the issue of the causes of the numerous suicides from people leaping off San Francisco's Golden Gate Bridge, one commentator noted that "virtually every person jumps . . . from the side facing land, and people" (quoted by Koenig, 1991, p. 34). But, as Joseph Koenig (1991) notes, the reason for this fact is not some mystical need to relate interpersonally but simply that the pedestrian footpath runs along that side of the span. He writes, "No one with his heart set seriously on a high dive into the frigid waters of San Francisco Bay would be so foolhardy as to risk a dash across six lanes of high-speed traffic" (p. 34).

Errors of Theory

Previously we described some of the theory-related exaggerations in causal explanations. One example, again from Waite (1977), will suffice: "Because Hitler's hatred of Jews was monumental, his feelings of guilt and self-loathing must have been great indeed" (p. 424). Does the mechanism of projection exist, as this statement assumes? A detailed review of empirical evidence by David Holmes (1972, 1974) questions the broad applicability of projection as an explanation.

Errors of Culture

Psychobiographers sometimes reflect what we may call "psychological imperiousness" or psychological overdetermination; that is, they explain an individual's behavior on the basis of the person's unique internal qualities and experiences—such as the individual's personality, talents, and childhood experiences. A more parsimonious explanation may stem from the culture or society in which the person has lived. Freud took as evidence of Leonardo da Vinci's gentleness his habit of buying and freeing caged birds. But this procedure was a very old and popular folk custom that was believed to bring good luck.

Similarly, Fawn Brodie (1981), in *Thomas Jefferson: An Intimate History,* makes much of Jefferson's involvement with a young slave, Sally Hemings. Brodie notes as evidence of his preoccupation that on a trip through Holland, Jefferson makes eight references to the land as "mulatto." But "mulatto" was commonly used in the 18th century America to describe the color of the soil.

But explanation is not "either/or." Inner personality and outer society interact and integrate. The philosopher of history Hans Meyerhoff (1987) observes, "The fate of the libido is always decided in a concrete historical situation. This does not mean that the psychological processes do not have their own 'inner logic'; what it does mean is that outside conditions, both social and ideological, are built into the psychological structure of man" (p. 26).

Errors of Reasoning or Logic

Stannard (1980) claims that psychobiographers frequently fall victim to a "common error" in historical writing: post hoc, ergo propter hoc. That is, if event B followed event A, then B must have happened because of A. But he proposes that psychobiographers go even further: "So long as B is found to exist, it is *assumed* that A *must have happened* since B is a psychoanalytically posited consequence of A" (p. 24, italics in original). Examples of Waite's analysis of Hitler, reported under Causal Explanations of Individuals in this chapter, reflect this type of circular reasoning.

Further Criticisms

Noting that "up to now, psychohistory has put its worst foot forward" (p. 243), the excellent review of Crosby and Crosby (1981) notes other kinds of criticisms, including methodological flaws, vagueness of definition, and simplistic approaches in a different sense from the earlier criticisms in that a handful of early determinants may be relied on for a "complete" explanation.

One of the personally most aggravating tendencies in many psychobiographical analyses is the emphasis they place on pathological explanations for the individual's behavior (Weinberg, 1992). The novelist and reviewer Joyce Carol Oates (1988) coined the term "pathography" for this kind of biography, preoccupied with "dysfunction and disaster." Even altruistic or socially beneficial acts by successful people are portrayed as the result of personality malfunctions or deviations. As Coles (1987) observes, psychopathological labeling can become a device for moral condemnation or clumsy debunking. The reader legitimately asks, are there not any well-adjusted people out there? Are all significant actions in history (Lincoln's freeing of the slaves, Florence Nightingale's work with hospitalized soldiers) explained only by relying on failures of healthy childhood experiences to occur?

An extreme example of the tendency to provide negative explanations is Freud and Bullitt's (1967) posthumous psychobiography of Woodrow Wilson. In the book, President Wilson's virtues are portrayed as weaknesses and his visions as the fruits of compulsion. His idealization of the League of Nations is interpreted by Freud and Bullitt as evidence of a passive feminine relationship between Wilson and his father (Brown, 1967).

Resuscitating Psychobiography

The general stance of this chapter has been one of criticism toward psychobiography. That is regrettable if it becomes a final verdict, for the approach holds promise if it is carefully applied. Concerned critics like Cocks, Crosby, and Elms have made a number of suggestions for strengthening the procedure:

1. Recognize the limits of the approach (Cocks & Crosby, 1987, p. x).
2. Pay attention to the suitability of their subjects for investigation. For example, in analyzing Martin Luther's life, there is little information available about his childhood. As Elms (1976) puts it, "Don't move very far out in front of your data" (p. 94).
3. Reexamine reliance on classical psychoanalytic theory. As exemplified by object-relations theory, revisions have focused more on the mother-child relationships than on the role of the id and the fixations of psychosexual stages emphasized by Freud originally. Cocks and Crosby (1987) conclude that:

The evolution within the various schools of depth psychology in the 1920s and 1930s toward a greater emphasis on ego functions, character, and object-relations operating throughout an individual's life, rather than on id impulses buried deep within the psyche and childhood, has offered the psychologically attuned historian greater interpretive flexibility. (p. xi)

4. Preconceptions and biases of psychobiographers need to be acknowledged. Occasionally, these works clearly are motivated by the authors' hostility and vindictiveness toward their subject (Elms, 1976, p. 95).

But even when these do not exist, psychobiographers should be explicit about their methods. For example, Erikson employs the method of "disciplined subjectivity," and he develops this concept in

Young Man Luther and *Gandhi's Truth,* as well as more theoretical articles. But as Strozier (1976) concludes, Erikson never precisely defines what he means by "discipline." He does state that psychobiographers must be "reasonably clear about" the stage and conditions of their own lives when they involve themselves in the historical lives of others (Erikson, 1968b).

Despite these qualms, much can be learned from psychobiography. J. W. Anderson (1981) reflects my view eloquently: "It seems to me that if psychology has anything to say about people—their complexities and their accustomed patterns and motivations—then biography is an area to which understanding should be applied" (p. 265). Psychologists should not neglect this avenue as a means to help us make sense of the development of individual lives.

6

Contemporary Stage Theories

HAVIGHURST AND GOULD

*As we grow and change, we take steps away from child-
hood and toward adulthood—steps such as marriage, work,
consciously developing a talent or buying a home. With
each step, the unfinished business of childhood intrudes,
disturbing our emotions and requiring psychological work.*

Roger L. Gould

As Chapters 4 and 5 demonstrate in detail, Erik Erikson's stage
theory has served as a foundation for systematic thinking about
personality development in adulthood. This chapter and the next
illustrate how the Eriksonian influence is an indirect one also; the
more recent theories—described in these chapters—are, in a sense,
laboratories of Erikson's ideas. The systematic writings of Robert
Havighurst, Roger Gould, and Daniel Levinson contribute to the
intensive investigation of adult development that has surfaced in
the last 20 years; empirical tests of their theories are beginning to
appear.

110

The theories presented in this chapter maintain the age-based definitions of transitions reflected in Erikson's conception. They also reflect how society's expectations help determine what tasks capture our attention.

Chapter 7, by focusing on the theorizing of Daniel Levinson, illustrates a shift toward a mixture of a stage-theory approach with a dialectical one.

Robert Havighurst:
An Emphasis on Life Tasks

Robert Havighurst (1972), an educational psychologist, was struck by the notion that every society seems to generate a rather explicit timetable for the accomplishment of various life tasks (Huyck & Hoyer, 1982). Building on Erikson's approach, he identified what he called specific developmental tasks (see Box 6.1). As an educational psychologist, Havighurst was particularly interested in helping the schools prepare individual students to deal with developmental tasks, but he extended his analysis through adulthood, also.

According to Havighurst, a developmental task arises at a certain period of life because of a combination of physical maturation and cultural pressure. He identified six to eight tasks for each period in life; Havighurst's system resembles Erikson's in that it is age-graded; that is, one in which people expect particular life events to occur at specific ages. Whether age should be used as such a precise indicator is controversial; the issue will be faced later in this chapter and the next one.

A further similarity with Erikson's approach is that Havighurst maintained that these tasks, once accomplished, made development firm and secure (Huyck & Hoyer, 1982). As noted by Chiriboga (1989), one of Havighurst's most helpful contributions is the idea that certain tasks confront the lives of each and every one of us. Rather than focusing on "crises," Havighurst's optimistic view has the individual facing clear-cut and expectable tasks (Chiriboga, 1989).

Havighurst's conception is, of course, very simplified (Huyck & Hoyer, 1982). In addition, like Erikson's it often seems to blend

BOX 6.1

Havighurst's Proposed Developmental Tasks
(Adult Periods Only)

Ages 18-30:

1. getting started in an occupation
2. selecting a mate
3. learning to live with a marriage partner
4. starting a family
5. rearing children
6. managing a home
7. taking on civic responsibilities
8. finding a congenial social group

Ages 30-60:

1. assisting teenage children to become responsible and happy adults
2. achieving adult social and civic responsibility
3. reaching and maintaining satisfactory performance in one's occupational career
4. developing adult leisure-time activities
5. relating to one's spouse as a person
6. accepting and adjusting to the physiological changes of middle age
7. adjusting to aging parents

Ages 60 to end of life:

1. adjusting to decreasing physical strength and health
2. adjusting to retirement and reduced income
3. adjusting to death of one's spouse
4. establishing an explicit affiliation with one's age group
5. adopting and adapting social roles in a flexible way (such as expansion in family, community, or hobbies, or a slowdown of all activities)
6. establishing satisfactory physical living arrangements

SOURCE: Adapted from Havighurst, 1972.

"typicality" with "normality"; it assumes that all people marry and have children. Furthermore, there is no recognition that the consequences of being "out of phase" may be beneficial rather than harmful (Huyck & Hoyer, 1982, p. 219), as in the case of a woman delaying her first child until after establishing a professional career, or a man in his fifties, divorced, remarried, and starting a second family.

The term *out of phase* implies that there is a "right time" for achievement of these tasks. Increasingly the effort to peg development to specific ages is being criticized. Bernice Neugarten (1979; Neugarten & Neugarten, 1987), a leading authority on adult development, has argued that our society is becoming an age-irrelevant one, in which chronological age is not and should not be used as a criterion for expecting a particular kind of behavior. The schedules of our lives are so varied that, according to Neugarten, a single timetable is impossible to specify. As just one example of variation, different cohorts (a *cohort* is a group of people born in the same years or time period) move through the life course on different schedules (Rosenfeld & Stark, 1987).

Roger Gould and
Rejecting the Myths of Earlier Ages

That people move through stages during adulthood generated its greatest impact on the public through the publication of Gail Sheehy's *Passages* in the mid-1970s. Sheehy, a professional journalist, used the work of Roger Gould and Daniel Levinson as support for her conclusions. These two theorists may be considered the "gold dust twins" of contemporary stage-theorizing, for they started collecting data at about the same time (the late 1960s)—one on the East coast and one on the West coast—and they both published influential books reporting their findings and theories in the late 1970s. Although each classifies adults into age-graded periods and each sees qualitative differences in the relevant issues at different periods during childhood, Gould and Levinson also have different contributions to make to theorizing. And each has ideas worthy of further investigation. Thus we devote the major portion of two chapters to their work.

Gould's Theoretical
Background and Major Thesis

Roger Gould is a psychiatrist trained in a psychoanalytic perspective. His writings reflect a combination of classical psychoanalytic theory, with its reliance on biological determinants, and object-relations theory (see Box 2.2), placing emphasis on the child's interaction with his or her mother. Every child is born with an insatiable biological drive to have what it cannot have, the total attention and love of its mother, states Gould (1978). Consciousness in childhood, replete with a strong residue of anger, grows out of this "basic fact of biological helplessness and immaturity" (Gould, 1978, p. 18).

This unfinished business of childhood provides the basis for adult development. McCrae and Costa (1990) portray Gould's approach eloquently:

> As children we are fundamentally helpless in the face of both danger and inner passions of lust, rage, and greed. We depend wholly on our parents to control both of these threats, and we analyze a series of false assumptions, illusions that allow us to believe that we are perfectly safe. Maintaining these beliefs has the benefit of preserving our sense of security, but it also has a cost: We are confined by the rules that bound us as children. We cannot get free of these confining inhibitions without facing the illusory nature of some of our most fundamental beliefs and without giving up the security they provide. But when we do get free, we come to see reality more clearly and thus stop the unexpected shocks that must repeatedly occur when our illusions collide with life. And . . . we also gain from this process real freedom to be our own persons, in touch with our inner needs and passions, living vital and meaningful lives. (p. 144)

Thus, for Gould, the person's basic developmental task—recurring throughout life—is to shed major *false assumptions* in order to achieve further levels of adult maturity. These illusions of safety, like Freudian defense mechanisms, are unconscious. Different myths are predominant topics for renunciation at different ages; thus does Gould structure growth around developmental periods, or stages.

Gould's Developmental Periods

Gould organizes adult development through five major periods, spanning from the ages of 16 to 60 (see Box 6.2 for elaboration). Age, in and of itself, is an important marker for Gould; he states:

> My data suggest that not only does adulthood consist of a series of tasks to be performed, but there exists an actual clock that is thoroughly universal and thoroughly regular, which defines the task at hand. The fact that you're 40 or 43 years old, for example, really does affect the way you view life and the decisions you make. When you reach 50, your perspective changes. (Gould, quoted by Walker, 1974, p. 20)

Thus major life events—the death of a parent, divorce, failure at work, or disappointment over one's child—have different meanings at different periods during adulthood.

What are the myths, that, for Gould, the developing person must shed? For ages 16 to 22, the developmental task is "leaving our parents' world" and the major false assumption to be renounced is that "I'll always belong to my parents and believe in their world." Young people want autonomy; yet this autonomy is precarious because young people also want safety and belonging and "the comforting assurance that parents will always be there to help and guide" (McCrae & Costa, 1990, p. 145). They possess "condensed energy looking for a direction" but they fear that if they express their true feelings, they will not be loved. They have not as yet internalized the belief that people can love each other despite being different. Any disagreement by a friend has the potential for being seen as a betrayal.

The task identified by Gould for this period is reminiscent of Erikson's concept of identity crisis (see Chapter 4). Those young people who are unable to move away from the myth that "I'll always belong to my parents and believe in their world" are condemned to play out, in their lives, their parents' values, perspectives, and styles of adapting. Failure to shed this false assumption would, for Gould, be equivalent to James Marcia's identity status of foreclosure (see Chapter 4). Gould (1978) quotes a young man, age 19, who says,

---

BOX 6.2

**The Myths in Each Age Period,
According to Gould**

Ages 18-22: "I will always belong to my parents and believe in their world."

Five component false assumptions:
1. If I get any more independent, it will be a disaster.
2. I can see the world only through my parents' assumptions.
3. Only my parents can guarantee my safety.
4. I don't own my body.
5. My parents will be my only family.

Ages 22-28: "Doing things my parents' way, with will power and perseverance, will bring results. But when I become too frustrated, confused, or tired, or I'm simply unable to cope, they'll step in and show me the way."

Four component assumptions:
1. Rewards will come automatically if we do what we are supposed to do.
2. There is only one right way to do things.
3. Those in a special relationship with us can do for us what we have not been able to do for ourselves.

"Sometimes I wish my father was dead so I could be free to be what I want to be" (p. 49).

But liberation does not come easily during this period. Consider, for example, the dilemma when a 18-year-old, in the first year of college, brings her boyfriend home for dinner for the first time. "Will my parents like him? Will they approve of him? What if they don't?" An anticipated disagreement over something (or someone) important leads to a fear that the result will be rejection by one's parents, as we do not feel prepared to contest the worldview of our parents.

BOX 6.2 (Continued)

---

4. Rationality, commitment, and effort will always prevail over other forces.

Late twenties to early thirties: "Life is simple and controllable. There are no significant coexisting or contradictory forces within me."

Four component assumptions:
1. What I know intellectually, I know emotionally.
2. I am not like my parents in ways I do not want to be.
3. I can see the reality of those close to me quite clearly.
4. Threats to my security are not real.

Late thirties to early forties: "There is no evil or death in the world. The sinister has been destroyed."

Five component assumptions:
1. The illusion of safety can last forever.
2. Death cannot happen to me or my loved ones.
3. It is impossible to live without a protector (women).
4. I am innocent.

Beyond Midlife: "The life of inner-directedness finally prevails; I own myself."

SOURCE: Adapted from Gould, 1978.

Gould states that the doubt is less a function of realistic self-assessment than an uncertainty about our *right* to take care of ourselves, because until the age of 16 or 18, we have only been the lowly actors in our lives—others have been the producers, directors, and screenwriters.

Gould's second period occurs at ages 22 to 28, a period Gould tags with the slogan "I'm Nobody's Baby Now." The major false assumption at this time is: "Doing things my parents' way, with will power and perseverance, will bring results. But if I become too frustrated, confused, or tired, or am simply unable to cope, they will step in and show me the right way."

Gould proposes that the young "twentysomethings" who are carving out a career and founding a family have joined the establishment—with a vengeance. They adopt their new roles without question because they are inexperienced actors in these roles (McCrae & Costa, 1990).

The difference from the first period is that previously the young person was moving away from his or her parents' view. Now, the person is moving toward her or his own unique perspective. But the freedom to mess up your own life is frightening. When we are able to reject the major false assumption of this period, we "add to our identity a new sense of fundamental strength and independence built on the solid rock of proven competence" (Gould, 1978, p. 40).

Two issues dominate this period. Even though they may portray themselves as autonomous and self-reliant, people in their twenties must still deal with the strong ties to their parents. They must internalize the realization that "This is it—I'm on my own." They must move toward their own independent views; mastering their own environment becomes vital.

Gould (1978) even proposes that many people who marry at this age pick the partner they do because they cannot deal adequately with the relationships with their parents. He writes, "Each and every one of us pick partners that, in subtle ways at least, recreate a parent-child relationship that has not yet been mastered" (p. 145). Or, conversely, we may choose a companion who possesses a strong quality we lack; "initially we marry in the effort to achieve wholeness" (p. 113). In summary, Gould concludes that the separateness from our parents that we proudly portray in our twenties is just a fiction.

The second major thrust of the ages 22 to 28 is rampant optimism. Determination and self-confidence are high; making a million dollars by age 30 is considered attainable. Careers are pursued without much introspection; young adults assume that rewards will come to them automatically "if I do what I'm supposed to do." Even commitments to a relationship are not analyzed deeply; "love will conquer all." These beliefs become false assumptions, ready for rejection, during the next stage.

The third period, salient at ages 28 to 34, Gould titles "Opening Up to What's Inside." Two major false assumptions exist now: first, that life is simple and controllable, and second, that there are "no significant coexisting contradictory forces within me."

Gould portrays the period of the late twenties and early thirties as one of disillusionment and soul searching. Life is seen as much more difficult than it was in one's twenties; self-confidence wavers; the world becomes one that is complicated and unfair. Simple rules—"work hard" or "be nice" or "love will conquer all"—may prove ineffectual in the complicated real world. People at this age are more likely to say "Life is a struggle; life is unfair."

What is more frustrating is that we relied on these admonitions to lead to a good outcome. The television actress Rue McClanahan, commenting on her life, says, "I think one of the main reasons that my marriage . . . didn't last is that I had this naive notion that everything always just sort of worked out" (quoted by Esterly, 1987, p. 21). Gould (1978) puts it this way: "During our twenties, we agree to do what is necessary to pursue our dreams. When we accept that contract, we agree to a series of obligations—to be a certain kind of person, to act a certain way, to see the world in a certain way" (p. 159). It hurts to see that life is not what it is supposed to be.

Why this change around age 30? One reason is that we feel we are not accomplishing our dreams or even if we have, our life is now on a downhill slide. Dissatisfaction with one's position in the world increases; people at these ages are more likely to say, "I don't have enough money to do what I want."

Second, pressures to play a role become more difficult to fulfill. People become weary of trying to be what others expect them to be; yet they reluctantly persist. They poignantly ask, "Why can't I be accepted for what I am, not for what others (the boss, one's spouse, one's family) expect me to be?" These people, compared to younger ones, are less likely to agree that "for me, marriage has been a good thing." According to Gould, divorce increases during this age period, as people cannot adjust to each other's developing values.

In Gould's view, a major cause of the incipient distress is parenthood. Dacey (1982), commenting on Gould's perspective, concludes, "As we attempt to explain to children what their values ought to be, we are often forced to see how unsure we are of our own values." Furthermore, the task of instilling values in children conflicts with the parent's emerging need to be accepted for "what I am."

To adapt, people at this age must develop a new view of life and recognize that if they want to satisfy a need or desire, they will have to work on it *directly*. Also, they must come to realize, and accept, how like their parents they are, especially in ways they do not want to be.

This is a difficult task. Probably many parents aspire to be better at the task than their parents were; "I'm not going to make the mistakes that my folks made with me," they say. But Gould (1978) asserts that "we essentially become our own parents when parenting our child" (p. 185).

Problems and challenges increase during the fourth stage, called by Gould the midlife decade and applicable to persons ages 34-45. Here the major false assumption is that "there is no evil or death in the world; the sinister has been destroyed." Not only do the unresolved problems of the early thirties create tumult, but the latter is exacerbated by the first emotional awareness that time is shrinking, or even running out, and death will inexorably come. Whatever must be done, must be done now.

Gould's (1978) description of the nature of this period borders on the melodramatic:

> Time, the messenger of finality, is the ultimate limitation of life. It strips away our last remaining illusion of safety and makes existentialists of us all. We stand naked and exposed, toe to toe with life. Our naivete is lost forever. The illusion of our immortality is dying; in a crunch, no all-powerful hand is going to save us. (p. 218)

Life seems to constrict. There is little time left to shape the behavior of one's adolescent children and even less time to "make it" in one's own career. One must hurry if one's dreams are to be made to come true.

An intensive in-depth study of successful middle-aged professional persons by Neugarten (1968) confirmed the feelings of dissatisfaction and anxiety. Consistent was a recognition that career options, with increasing age, were increasingly limited.

Gould portrays the early forties as an unstable and uncomfortable age. Regrets compound for "my mistakes in raising my children."

On top of everything else, the decline of parents creates a problem; no longer can they save us from danger. Elderly parents may turn to their middle-aged offspring for support, thus reversing the roles of dependence and independence. A recent book by Elaine M. Brody (1990) documents the enormous stress on people in midlife (usually women more than men) who must care for a dependent parent, especially if they must do so in a shared household. Also the death of one's parents may come quickly, leaving unresolved issues and conflicts.

During midlife, people, according to Gould, have to "dig deeper" to examine the deepest strata of their own "demonic badness" or worthlessness. The ugly side of our lives can no longer be ignored. Neugarten (1976) refers to this process of turning inward for self-assessment as *interiority*.

Beyond midlife, things get better, according to Gould. The ages 43-53 are characterized by the feeling that "the die is cast," that we are whoever we are going to be. "The life of inner directiveness finally prevails" (Gould, 1978, p. 310). People become less competitive and more inner directed. At the same time, they may come to seek sympathy and affection from their spouses in a way that resembles a much earlier dependence on their parents.

Gould has less to say about later middle age and old age. He proposes that as persons reach the ages of 53-60, the negative feelings they experienced in their forties diminish even further. Relationships with their friends, their children, and their parents, if the latter are still alive, become warmer and more mellow. The spouse becomes a valuable companion and less a parent.

Gould sees no major changes after age 50, but—as McCrae and Costa (1990) observe—he did not survey any subjects of those ages.

The Empirical
Basis for Gould's Theory

Roger Gould has painted a provocative but depressing picture of development during adulthood. On what basis does he draw his conclusions?

His original data were based on statements made by persons who were outpatients in therapy sessions at the University of California at Los Angeles. Gould had eight medical students listen to the tape recordings of these group therapy sessions and then list the statements about personal feelings that seemed to stand out.

Then other people—not patients—were given questionnaires listing these feelings and were asked to indicate how applicable each statement was to their lives. A total of 524 white, middle-class males and females responded; they ranged in age from 16 to 60. Gould (1972) then determined the number of people in each age category who reported each statement; the age groupings were 16-17, 18-21, 22-28, 29-36, 37-43, 44-50, and 51-60. Men and women were not separated in this data analysis, even though the percentage of subjects who were women was higher in the over-40 groups.

In reporting his results, Gould prepared figures showing the relative incidence of statements by age groups. But his use of rank-ordering creates the illusion of greater differences than may really exist. His failure to do any tests of statistical significance between groups means that we cannot say whether any apparent differences are real ones or not.

Also, it is apparent that these are cross-sectional data; that is, they are drawn from people who were at different ages at the same time. There is no direct evidence that these differences would apply to the *same people* at different times in their own lives. For such a conclusion to be a firm one, it would have to be based on a longitudinal study, one that measures and remeasures the same individuals throughout their lives. Longitudinal methods are, by definition, time consuming and hence are seldom feasible.

SUMMARY

An Evaluation of Gould's Approach

In his book, his articles, and his interviews, Gould has a tendency to make extreme pronouncements that he applies to all individuals. Probably it is a myth that life is that simple and binding. A major theme in this book is that no one theory "fits all." Also, posed against the standards for rigorous social science methodology, Gould's procedures fail. Although his observations may be applicable to many of us, their universal validity—recall his "universal time clock"—is not proven on the basis of his data.

The variability in response to midlife challenges—as one example—is reflected in the results of a study by Farrell and Rosenberg (1981) who surveyed 200 men ages 38-48 years. They categorized those subjects who were dissatisfied with their lives and who denied any stress as in a *punitive-disenchanted* category; only 30% were in this group.

But 20 years before we confront any midlife crises, different responses to developmental challenges result. We are all aware that more young people are having a difficult time moving from adolescence to adulthood. One of three unmarried men ages 25-29 and one of four unmarried women in that age group lives with their parents (Usdansky, 1993). As Vobejda (1991) observes, "Young people increasingly loop in and out of their parents' homes, trade in one career for another and delay major commitments, including marriage, children, and homeownership" (p. 9). Nearly 40% of American men of age 29 have failed to obtain a stable job, and "life as an independent adult remains an elusive destination" (p. 9).

In the past 30 years the median age of first marriage increased by approximately 3 years. In 1960 the average age for men was 22.8 years; in 1992, 26.5 years; for women, the figures were 20.3 years and 24.24 years (Usdansky, 1993).

Even after marriage, regression in development of independence occurs. Among women married in the 10 years prior to 1985, 20% returned home within 10 years of the marriage, compared to only 11% who married in the 1950s. And the financial support reflected in returning to one's home and family of origin carries an emotional price. Kutner (1990) observes that "in many families, money is rife with symbolism. It can be an unconscious substitute for affection or as a measure of general competence and worthiness. That symbolism is often unspoken, but is generally understood within each family" (p. B7; Copyright © 1990 by The New York Times Company. Reprinted by permission).

Such contemporary trends reflect just one reason why I prefer to treat Gould's ideas as hypotheses worth pursuing in later studies. I consider as provocative and plausible his idea that, as we develop during adulthood, we must forsake beliefs that previously were useful to our adaptation. Similarly attractive is his thesis that the person has "an ever-increasing need to win permission from oneself to continue developing" (Gould, 1975, p. 74).

Finally, it is hard to dispute Gould's (1975) view that "the direction of change is toward becoming more tolerant of oneself, and more appreciative of the complexity of both the surrounding world and of the mental milieu, but there are many things that can block, slow down, or divert that process" (p. 74). Such a broad statement covers everyone, but by the same stroke it lays bare Gould's lack of exploration of individual differences and their determinants.

Plausibility also stems from similarities in Gould's conclusions and those of theorists both previously described (Erikson) and reviewed subsequently (Levinson). Although Gould's theory has more periods in adulthood than does Erikson's, they agree on the dangers of premature identity determination in adolescence and the need for young people to develop independent values. And like Levinson, Gould finds that the early forties is a tumultuous age.

7

Contemporary Stage Theories

DANIEL LEVINSON

At 46, I wanted to study the transition into middle age in order to understand what I had been going through myself.

Daniel Levinson

Daniel Levinson's theory of changes in development in midlife, which appeared about the same time as Gould's, reflects differences in theoretical background, methodology, and conclusions (Levinson, Darrow, Klein, Levinson, & McKee, 1978). Unlike Freud, Erikson, or Gould, Daniel Levinson is not a psychiatrist; he was trained in social psychology and participated in the research leading to the publication of the book *The Authoritarian Personality* (Adorno, Frenkel-Brunswik, Levinson, & Sanford, 1950), one of the classic works of social psychology. Levinson candidly acknowledges that his study of adult development was motivated by his desire to understand himself better.

Levinson's Theoretical Orientation

Levinson's major theoretical contribution—an important one—is his ability to combine influences from vastly different perspectives. Among contemporary theorists, he best reflects a synthesis of Eriksonian stage theory, Carl Jung's concept of individuation, and dialectical ideas (the latter to be discussed more thoroughly in Chapter 8). For Levinson, the major task for a man in midlife is to come to terms with four polarities, or choices in self-image, that face him. We will review these in an subsequent section, after outlining Levinson's conception of stages in adulthood.

The Seasons of a Man's Life

Levinson's initial goal was to blueprint the structure in men's development. (He is currently preparing a book on women's development; an early report may be found in Levinson [1990].) Like previous stage theorists, he pegs his *periods* (a term he prefers to *stages,* for these qualitatively different eras) to ages. For each period, he provides a title for the major task. They are as follows:

Ages 16-24: leaving the family (titled the Early Adult Transition)

Ages 24-28: getting into the adult world (though Levinson [1985] later preferred the title Forming a Life Structure)

Ages 29-34: settling down (or, his later term, Developing a Culminating Life Structure)

Ages 35-40 or 42: Becoming One's Own Man (Levinson [1985] has defended the use of *man* rather than a nonsexist term because the achievement of masculinity—however defined by each man—is central.)

Early forties: Midlife Transition

Age 45 on: restabilization, into Late Adulthood

Universality in the underlying sequence of periods is central to Levinson's (1986) approach. He writes:

It is abundantly evident that, at the level of events, roles, or personality, lives unfold in myriad ways. I make no claim for order in the concrete individual life course. . . . I do propose, however, that there is an *underlying* order in the human life course, an order shaped by . . . the periods in life structure development. Personality, social structure, culture, social roles, major life events, biology—these and other influences exert a powerful effect on the actual character of the individual life structure at a given time. . . . It is my hypothesis, however, that the basic nature and timing of life structure development are given in the life cycle at this time in human evolution. (p. 11, italics in original)

Levinson views adulthood as a set of shifting periods from "structure-building" periods of stability to "structure-changing" periods of transition and back again. Transition periods are important in his theory; each is about three-quarters the duration of a stable period (5 years versus 7 or 8), and they are the places where change takes place—a reappraisal of past experiences and of shifting to new goals.

Levinson (1979) conceptualizes the resulting changes as structural ones, and, in fact, he presents his theory as one of the formation of life structures, not as a theory of personality development. He is adamant on the latter point; in a letter replying to a critic, he states, "It is not [a study of personality development]. It is a study of the development of individual life structure. . . . We find age-linked periods in life structure development. Periods in adult personality development have not been demonstrated by anyone, and I certainly am not positing them" (p. 727).

"Life structure" is a rather elusive concept (Sears, 1979b, p. 98); for instance, at one point Levinson (1980) defines it as the individual's conception of his life at the time. He elaborated, "The life structure is the pattern or design of a person's life, a meshing of self-in-world. Its primary components are one's relationships, with self; with other persons, groups, and institutions; with all aspects of the external world that have significance in one's life" (p. 278). (See also Box 7.1.)

"Where do I invest my energy? What is important? What is missing in my life?" Such questions are relevant to one's life structure.

For Levinson (personal communication, July 8, 1985), no life structure is permanent; "I've never seen one last beyond seven or eight years," he has stated. A transition period thus reflects a shift from one life structure to another, requiring that now different aspects of one's life have become central. Transitions do not always

---

BOX 7.1

Levinson on Life Structure

Further elaboration of the life-structure concept by Levinson:

The life structure as a whole, and every component in it, has both external and internal aspects. The external aspects have to do with the persons, social systems, and other outside realities with which the person is involved. The internal aspects are values, desires, conflicts, skills—multiple parts of the self that are lived out in one's relationships . . . .

The life structure stems from the engagement of self with the world. To be truly engaged with the world, one must invest important parts of the self in it and, equally, must take the world into the self and be enriched, depleted, and corrupted by it. . . .

One or two components (rarely as many as three) have a central place in the life structure. Others are more peripheral, and still others are completely detached from the center. . . . We found that occupation and marriage-family are usually the central components, though there are significant variations in their relative weight and in the importance of other components.

SOURCE: Levinson, 1980, p. 278.

---

demand turmoil or conscious questioning, but everyone goes through them, concludes Levinson (personal communication, July 8, 1985; 1986). They may include the termination of certain values or self-labels (Levinson's equivalent to Gould's rejection of prior assumptions) and they lead to the initiation of new structures. Parkes (1971) concluded that a psychosocial transition required "the abandonment of one set of assumptions and the development of a fresh set to enable the individual to cope with the new altered life space" (p. 103). In using transitions as a central feature of his theory, Levinson reflects Erikson's conception of a crisis as a transition period marked by personal vulnerability and capacity for change.

Polarities in Midlife

As noted earlier, Levinson devotes special analysis to the midlife transition. He concludes that the early forties comprise a crisis period for many men, leading some of them to adolescent-like periods of doubt and confusion. He reports that 80% of the men he studied experienced a tumultuous period here.

One of the tasks of midlife is to resolve discrepancies in one's self-image. The dialectical approach, which Levinson uses, conceptualizes adjustments as constantly striving to respond to competing needs. These needs act as end points that tug the individual first toward one, then toward the other. Closure can never be achieved because whichever need is currently unfulfilled is actively seeking satisfaction.

Levinson, like only some of the dialectical theorists, believes that integration of these competing needs or self-images is possible (see Chapter 8 for elaboration). He proposed that four issues (he calls them "polarities") face a man at midlife. These are:

attachment/separateness
destruction/creation
masculine/feminine
young/old

He writes, "Each of these pairs forms a polarity in the sense that the two terms represent opposing tendencies or conditions. . . . Both sides of each polarity coexist within every self" (Levinson, 1978, p. 197). Each of the polarities provides a perspective on the dilemmas of midlife.

Attachment/Separateness

We all need to be close to others and yet we need our own identity. Levinson defines attachment in the broadest sense; "to be attached is to be engaged, involved, needy, plugged in, seeking, rooted" (Levinson et al., 1978, p. 239).

Similarly, separateness is not the same thing as isolation or loneliness. "A person is separate when he is primarily involved in his inner world—a world of imagination, fantasy, play. His main interest is not adapting to the 'real' world outside, but in constructing and exploring an imagined world, the enclosed world of his inner self" (Levinson et al., 1978, p. 239). The child absorbed in play reflects separateness, as does the novelist or composer.

In childhood, attachment is vital for survival. In adolescence, we seek separateness, not only from parents but sometimes from society. But in young adulthood, attachment is likely to again tug and pull, not only romantic attachment but the attachment to others in his field of work. In midlife, a new type of separateness may emerge; the man begins to look inside himself. He may decide to divorce, or may make a stronger commitment to an existing marriage. In the latter sense, Levinson uses "separateness" to refer to an increased concern with one's inner world.

He and his colleagues observe, "During the mid-life transition, a man needs to reduce his heavy involvement in the external world. To do work of reappraisal and de-illusionment, he must turn inward . . . he needs to become more engaged with himself" (Levinson et al., 1978, p. 241). He enjoys solitude more; he places less value on possessions, rewards, and social approval; he lives more in the present.

How can a man achieve a greater integration of attachment and separateness?

> A man who attends more to the self, who becomes less tyrannized by his ambitions, dependencies, and passions, can be involved with other individuals and perform his social roles in a more responsible way than ever before. He can respond more to the developmental needs of his offspring and other young adults if he is more in touch with his own self and responding to its needs. (Levinson et al., 1978, p. 242)

Destruction/Creation

Some of the most creative people in the world can also be the most destructive, at least with respect to their relationships with others. Pablo Picasso is an example (Gilot & Lake, 1964; Huffington, 1988).

The midlife transition activates a man's concern with death and destruction. Levinson (1980) proposes that here a man recognizes the evil within himself, including his own power to hurt or destroy others or himself. "He becomes more aware of the many ways in which other persons, even his loved ones, have acted destructively toward him. . . . What is worse, he realizes he has done irrevocably hurtful things to his parents, lovers, wife, children, friends, rivals" (p. 286).

But there is a positive aspect to this recognition of the capacity to be destructive. By recognizing his power to tear down things, he begins to realize how truly powerful he can be in creating new and useful forms of life. For example, he can create new products that have value to himself and others, or participate in collective enterprises that advance human welfare, or contribute more extensively to future generations (Levinson, 1980).

Thus in middle adulthood a man can come to realize—at least more than ever before—that "powerful forces of destructiveness and of creativity coexist in the human soul and can be integrated in many ways—though never entirely" (Levinson, 1980, p. 286).

Masculine/Feminine

With regard to this polarity, Levinson capitalizes on Carl Jung's distinction between the animus and the anima (see Chapter 2). Jung proposed that each of us possessed both a masculine and a feminine part to our personality. The emphasis on expressing only one side costs us greatly, and he believed that a rich adulthood can be achieved only by compensating that part of us that was denied during childhood. For Levinson, midlife is the period when this deficiency must be reconciled. In defining masculinity, Levinson includes conceptions of oneself as possessing toughness, achievement and ambition, power, and a thinking orientation (as opposed to the feminine feeling orientation). A man must feel secure enough in his masculinity to enjoy his ability to feel, to nurture, to be dependent. Here men can become mentors; they can ease away from competing with others and devote more energy to transmitting their values to younger associates.

Young/Old

We are terribly interested in maintaining our youth, if only to avoid the ultimate consequence of our mortality, our death. At about 40, a man is confronted with evidence of his aging appearance and declining powers, from lines in his face to sags and spreading seemingly everywhere. His eyesight may deteriorate, he may lack stamina or previous physical skills, he may start to forget things. Friends may become ill; his parents may die. Realization that he may die takes on a more personal focus.

Yet he may strive to recapture his youth. Mark Spitz won seven gold medals for swimming in the 1972 Olympics. In 1992, at the age of 42, he sought to repeat—but failed. George Foreman continued his heavyweight boxing career through the age of 44. At the age of 45, baseball pitching legend Jim Palmer tried out with the Baltimore Orioles, nearly 7 years after his last big-league pitch.

Levinson (1980) comments:

> At mid-life a man feels young in many respects, but he also has a sense of being old. He feels older than the youth, but not ready to join the generation defined as "middle-aged." He feels alternatively young, old, and "in-between." If he clings too strongly to the youthfulness of his twenties, he will find no place for himself in middle adulthood. If he gives up on the young, he will become dry and rigid. His developmental task is to become young-old in a new way. (p. 286)

How to reconcile the young/old discrepancy? Levinson suggests that each identity possesses some positive aspects; we associate youth with enthusiasm, energy, curiosity, and spontaneity, while we associate the elderly with maturity, wisdom, and tolerance. One resolution is to combine the best of both perspectives in a new young/old identity.

Levinson's Method

The procedure used by Levinson and his colleagues to generate conclusions is a rather atypical one. He chose 40 men, ages 35-45, and carried out what has been called a "briefly longitudinal" study of them. Data collection began in 1968 with in-depth interviews and ended in 1971 with detailed follow-ups. The men were from four diverse occupations—they were biologists, novelists, factory workers, and business executives. Levinson and his staff interviewed and reinterviewed these men about their lives; interviews, spread over several days, accumulated 15-20 hours of responses from each man. The men also completed the Thematic Apperception Test and other personality measures. Biographies were prepared for each man. Then Levinson and his staff read and reread all the material, discussed it extensively, and extracted common themes. As Sears (1979b) notes, "In the classical clinical tradition, Levinson uses biographical case material to illustrate the stages of personality development that he sees men as going through" (p. 97). The book resulting from this extensive project is rich in sensitive conclusions, but almost completely lacking in quantified results and statistical tests (Maas, 1979).

Evaluation of Levinson's Theory

The findings and theory presented by Levinson and his associates are provocative and could be very important, but they suffer from some important problems and limitations.

The theory is impressionistically derived from the data without any expressed criteria for determining what stage the subject was in, whether he encountered the themes and stages as hypothesized, and whether his passage was rough or smooth. Furthermore, our curiosity about the processes by which change comes about is not satisfied (Sears, 1979b, p. 98). *Why* do people change when they do, when equivalent others do not?

In a different area, no statements are provided about the degree of reliability between coders, and thus no indication of the agreement between staff members in the ratings they gave.

There are other major limitations. The data collection stopped at age 45; the interview procedure had a psychoanalytic orientation but the interviews did not go into enough depth to use this theory as an explanation of choices (Sears, 1979b). And, of course, the sample was limited to males.

Perhaps the most serious criticism derives from the discrepancy between findings and conclusions (Maas, 1979). Levinson's concept of mentoring provides an example. The authors claim that mentoring is crucial in the transition period of "becoming one's own man." Prior to this period, a man felt that no matter what he had accomplished, he was not sufficiently on his own. Now he must cut the ties with his mentor; in fact, he must reinterpret the character of the mentor. The mentor, according to Levinson, could be a teacher, a boss, an editor, or an experienced co-worker who takes the younger man into confidence, imparts wisdom, sponsors, criticizes, and bestows a blessing. This person is ordinarily 8 to 15 years older than the protégé. The final relinquishing of a mentor should occur during this transition period, between the ages of 35 to 40. Levinson and his colleagues (1977) state that, "One does not have mentors after [the age of] 40" (p. 55). But does one have them *before* the age of 40? As Sears (1979b) notes, late in Levinson's book "we discover that among the 40 men in this study, the mentoring experience rarely occurred in any effective way" (p. 98). The concept appears to be given much more prominence in Levinson's theory than his data so far would seem to warrant. (In a rejoinder, Levinson, 1979, states that half his subjects received little or no mentoring, but that does not mean that good mentoring is unimportant.)

Can other sources of data, via personal documents, clarify this ambiguity? Perhaps. Additional support for lack of mention of mentors comes from a content analysis of psychologists' autobiographies, carried out by David H. Mack and myself. We selected Volume 5 from the collection *A History of Psychology in Autobiography* (Boring, Langfeld, Werner, & Yerkes, 1952; Boring & Lindzey, 1967; Lindzey, 1974; Murchison, 1930, 1932, 1936). Mack and I selected this series for content analysis because we assumed that if anyone would discuss the impact of a mentor on his own youthful career development, it would be an academic person, and particularly a psychologist. Yet a careful reading of Volume 5 by two independent content analysts reveals virtually no mention of mentoring in any of its 15 autobiographies. Although former teachers, professors, and more advanced colleagues are frequently mentioned, there is almost no detailed indication of a protégé role nor an expression of a close relationship. Gordon Allport's autobiography (1967) probably provides the most detailed and personal description of a mentor; he devotes an entire paragraph to Richard Cabot, a professor of cardiology and social ethics at Harvard in the 1920s. Not only does Allport detail Cabot's contributions to his own development, but he also writes about how he admires Cabot's qualities as a mentor. In contrast to Allport's evocation and to the total neglect by the other autobiographers, Carl Rogers's (1967) autobiography is characterized by a rejection of mentors and a self-concept of a "lone wolf in . . . professional activities" (p. 343) who followed his own course and was not even considered to be a psychologist by his colleagues during the Rochester years (1928-1940). A common theme in Rogers's autobiography is his nature as a rebel—he rejected his parents' anti-intellectual and fundamentalist religious beliefs; he rejected traditional psychotherapeutic assumptions and procedures; and while at the University of Wisconsin, he rejected participation in doctoral training that emphasized "rigorous" examinations and the failing of large proportions of graduate students.

There may be quite plausible reasons why these collections of autobiographies by prominent psychologists fail to mention the mentoring process in detail. The absence may be a function of the setting; it is not necessarily an indication that mentoring did not occur. In fact, the concept of mentoring may be an important one. The lack of a mentor has been proposed by Epstein (1970) as a major obstacle in the professional development of women. Counseling psychologists are beginning to investigate the impact of the concept.

Although these criticisms are critical, they do not exhaust the questions about the validity of Levinson's conclusions. A perspective that emphasizes consistency in personality development (detailed in Chapter 9), reflected in the work of Robert R. McCrae and Paul T. Costa (1990), raises other concerns, listed in Box 7.2.

Empirical Evidence for Stage Theories

For each of the stage theories described in the previous chapters and this one we have noted certain logical or methodological limitations. The theorists' own procedures that led to their theoretical contributions are not in keeping with the standards of sophisticated social science methodology. Given these qualms, how much empirical evidence exists for them? Is the "midlife crisis" truly prevalent in American society? Is there more turmoil for men in their early forties than in, say, their early fifties? Can the theories be applied to women as well as to men?

BOX 7.2

Further Questions and Levinson's Conclusions

McCrae and Costa (1990), operating from a perspective emphasizing stability in personality, ask the following questions about Levinson's body of work:

1. Are Levinson's findings universal?

As noted in this chapter, Levinson concludes that the sequence in stages described earlier is predominant in his sample. In contrast, McCrae and Costa (1990) conclude, "But reading the cases even as he presents them leaves doubts. Some people had ostensibly smooth transition periods; some tried to break out of their life structure when they should have been settling down (of course, they paid the penalty later for that transgression)" (p. 141).

2. Is it intrinsically age-related?

McCrae and Costa question Levinson's emphasis on chronological age as the basis for his stages; they claim that most other developmental theorists break up the life cycle with marker events such as marriage, birth of children, and retirement. In Chapter 1 of this book the work of Lowenthal and her colleagues illustrated the use of such events as does, in Chapter 6, Havighurst's use of tasks. Lowenthal and her colleagues believe that experience, rather than age in and of itself, may be the determinant of stage shift.

Related to this—and of special relevance to Levinson's choice of four different occupational samples—is Tamir's (1989) review of research studies that show social-class differences between working-class groups and professional groups with regard to the perceived

---

Beyond these commonalities, the empirical evidence lends support to the theories in regard to their broadest conclusions. In a review, Whitbourne and Weinstock (1979) note:

> There is surprising consistency in the findings of these studies, despite differences in the composition of samples and the methods used to collect information . . . the pattern of the "average" adult life that these findings portray suggests: a tentativeness and vigor in early adulthood,

---

BOX 7.2 (Continued)

---

onset of midlife. A blue-collar worker may consider himself to be middle-aged by 40, while a man in a higher level position often does not consider himself entering middle age until his early fifties (Hunter & Sundel, 1989).

3. Is it discontinuous?

The third question posed by McCrae and Costa (1990) reflects the kind of fundamental ideological difference that drives this volume. McCrae and Costa portray the changes proposed by Levinson as occurring "in quantum leaps" (p. 141). They do acknowledge that our conceptions of ourselves do not change at a continuous rate. "We tend to think we are as we have always been until something confronts us with our age and forces us to acknowledge the change. But it seems unlikely that this occurs in discrete, age-related changes" (McCrae & Costa, 1990, p. 142).

4. Is it personality change?

Again, this is a difficult question to answer, particularly because different approaches use different levels of concepts (see also Box 10.1). McCrae and Costa (1990) conclude:

> When children leave home, when aged parents require care, when one retires from a life long occupation, there are profound changes in the daily routines that constitute the bulk of behavior, but these changes do not amount to changes in personality, and they come about in response to external necessity rather than internal development. (pp. 142-143)

---

greater assumption of adult roles and responsibility in an early portion of middle adulthood, followed by a questioning in the latter portion of middlehood. (p. 124)

Some specific studies are illustrative:

1. Tamir (1980) reported a cross-sectional survey from a large sample of men ages 20-60. Men in their late forties, especially the

most highly educated ones, reported more stress and lower self-esteem than men in other age groups, verifying the existence of a "midlife crisis." These men drank more, were more depressed, and were more immobilized than men of any other age group.

2. Lowenthal et al. (1975), comparing men of differing ages who were anticipating a major life transition, found that the preretirement men (average age of 61 years) differed from the middle-aged sample (average age 52 years): They showed a decline on a "masculinity index," placed higher weight on "interpersonal-expressive" goals, claimed less stress from dealing with other people, and were less preoccupied with their jobs or worried about finances. In general, they were more comfortable and relaxed, reflecting Whitbourne and Weinstock's (1979) conclusion from a literature review that the late fifties are a quieter, mellower time of life.

3. With regard to occupational achievement, outstanding creative contributions are more frequent in the thirties (Lehman, 1953, 1962). Like quality of work, quantity of output varies from one occupation to another, but tends to peak in the forties (Dennis, 1968). Career drive apparently diminishes in many men after these ages.

Stage Theories
and Women's Development

Clearly, these stage theories possess a male bias. They were developed by males, with applicability to males in mind (either explicitly or unconsciously). Gilligan (1980) has noted that women seemingly reflect incomplete and inferior development when judged by developmental standards formulated on, for, and by males. (Volume 2 elaborates this point.)

The differences have recently become apparent in adolescence. Compared with boys of the same age, girls experience greater drops in resilience and self-esteem and greater increases in emotional distress and depression. Brown and Gilligan (1992) conclude that as girls enter adolescence, they struggle with the image of the "perfect girl"—who is nice and kind and does not get angry. They are treated differently in classrooms; rather than being encouraged to speak their minds, they are graded on how neat their papers are

(Brown, 1993). In summary, in the opinion of these researchers, society stifles adolescent girls by instilling in them the value of relationships rather than accomplishments.

Several differences and omissions emerge. First, there are value differences. In most theories of adult development, autonomy and achievement, rather than attachment and relationships, are the valued developmental milestones. Yet women often define their identities in the context of relationships as well as a context of personal achievement.

However, what is most consistent is that women, compared to men, have more choice in their development in early adulthood. Based on their longitudinal survey of Mills College graduates from the classes of 1958 and 1960, Ravenna Helson and her colleagues (Helson, Mitchell, & Moane, 1984) used the concept of "social clock" to distinguish between two types of goals and graduates. During the late twenties, some alumnae followed a "masculine occupational clock" (or a career that required extensive training and a clear ladder to occupational eminence), while others listened to the ticking of a "feminine social clock," reflecting the goals of marriage plus motherhood. In early adulthood, these goals were mutually exclusive for these women who completed college around 1960. Adoption of a particular social clock project in the twenties was consequential for the woman's later development, as it was in the follow-up study of the Radcliffe graduating class of 1964, studied by Stewart and Vandewater (1992). The latter authors suspect that in more recent cohorts of female college graduates, a higher percentage would be committed to both "social clocks" (only a small proportion of their 1964 graduates were). For example, Baber and Monaghan (1986) report results indicating that, even compared to results of similar research published a few years before, women are perceiving more options and expanding their career choices—for example, more are choosing business careers and fewer teaching or nursing.

Regardless, comparisons of older women who were mothers and those who were not find similarities in the timing of major life transitions but vast differences in the nature of those transitions. Mercer, Nichols, and Doyle (1989) collected life histories from 80 white women ages 60 to 95. Fifty were mothers; their transitions usually revolved around events in the lives of their children, while the nonmothers organized their lives and the changes around their employment. But even for the latter group, embeddedness in relationships (including work relationships) is the content of their life structure rather than a career per se (Mercer et al., 1989, p. 177), and for many of the nonmothers motivation to move ahead in a career came from a desire to be of assistance to their family rather than from their own individual ambition (Deutsch, 1991).

Levinson concluded that four tasks fill the agenda in the early adulthood of men: forming a dream, identifying occupation, finding a mentor, and forming a love attachment. Barnett and Baruch (1980), who interviewed women ages 35 to 55 about what had been their expectations for adulthood when they were age 16 or 17, found that only the last of these four goals was retrospectively relevant to those respondents.

Further support for this point is found in a longitudinal study by Josselson (1987), who measured the identity status of 60 women when they were seniors in college and then resurveyed 34 of them 12 years later, when they were in their early thirties. She concluded that developmental theories that emphasize constructs of independence and adulthood overlook the aspects most important to women's identity development, specifically communion, connectedness, relationships, and spirituality. Josselson also found impressive evidence for the power of the identity status during late adolescence. All of the women who had a foreclosure identity status when assessed in college still did 12 years later; they were all family-centered women who reflected a need to be loved and cared for. Josselson calls these "purveyors of the heritage" because they carry forward childhood conceptions about life, career, and marriage without going through crisis and self-examination. Their development has employed the concept of identification rather than individuation.

Similar, at least in their consistency over time, were those who were earlier classified in the identity-achievement status, or "pavers of the way." Twelve years later all but one of these reflected the same status.

Women who earlier were in the identity diffusion status were, as a group, more likely to have moved more frequently and held more jobs than women originally in the other identity-status groups.

A second difference occurs at midlife. It may well be that women, in contrast to men, *increase* their desire for autonomy and achievement in middle adulthood (Reinke, 1982). Judith Bardwick (1980) states this as follows:

> The sexes begin adulthood at opposite ends of the psychodynamic continuum; as men are enabled by success in achievement to give up their egocentric preoccupation, and as women succeed within relationships and become more autonomous, both become more interdependent. This implies that men will become more involved with internal psychological needs and states and be more sensitive to their dependence upon affirmation within relationships. Women will be better able to engage the world, experiencing themselves as initiators, having gratifications as individuals. (pp. 49-50)

Third, the above theories, never much for recognizing individual differences even in men's lives, fail to account for the vast diversity even among those women following the same "social clock" (Reinke, 1982). A woman may not enter the workforce until she is 30 or 40, she may work part time, and she seldom has a mentor (Josselson, 1987). It is clear that as a group, women possess more varied combinations of work and family involvement.

Given these differences, how well do the findings on men extend to women's lives? One review concluded that the *timing* of developmental periods and tasks for women was similar to those of men (Roberts & Newton, 1987). But, as indicated, the content may be more differentiated. The above review reported that women's autobiographies indicated that their life dreams were more complex than men's life dreams; the latter focused on particular occupational roles.

Some evidence exists that, compared to males, females increase the complexity of their lifestyles over the course of adulthood. Lowenthal et al. (1975) interviewed 216 males and females who were facing one of four major life transitions: graduating from high school, starting married life, anticipating one's children leaving the home, or anticipating retirement. (The researchers labeled the first two "incremental transitions" and the last two "decremental" ones.) High-school females were more simplistic and diffuse than males, but a shift occurred at the transition points of starting marriage and anticipating retirement.

Regardless of the transition, men facing it had more positive self-concepts, as a group, than did the equivalent women. Particularly discrepant were the middle-aged group (men averaging 52 years; women, 48 years). The women of middle age were the most preoccupied with stress of all the groups. Lowenthal et al. noted they possessed many signs of desperation—with themselves, their husbands, and their marriages. In contrast, men of this age cohort had generally positive outlooks. This difference seems to confirm Gail Sheehy's (1976) speculation that men and women are more dissimilar at midlife. Lowenthal et al. (1975) found that men's and women's lifestyles were, indeed, most discrepant at middle age, with middle-aged women having few activities beyond homemaking and family care, while their husbands were most heavily involved in occupational roles at this time.

Similarly, Thurnher (1983) found that as women grew older, they became more assertive, but men decreased in assertiveness, a conclusion consistent with the results of Reinke's (1985) interviews with women in four different age groups.

Reinke (1982) reviews several dissertations of relevance to these points. In an early study, W. A. Stewart (1977) tested the validity of Levinson's "age thirty transition" to women by administering a retrospective interview to 11 middle-class women, ages 31-39. For those women who had pursued a career beginning in their early twenties, the theory fit; for them, beginning around age 28, an increased sense of urgency to create a marriage and family emerged. The transition usually took 4 to 5 years—as Levinson found for men's transitions—and led to drastic changes in some of these women. But for the women who committed to a relationship rather than a career early on, the marriage-family adult life structure remained stable for a longer time, although dissatisfaction with it did begin to appear around age 30. The transition usually took the form of an increase in dissatisfaction with marriage and a desire for a more egalitarian relationship with her husband.

Farmer (1979), in another dissertation concentrating on a small number of women, focused on women in their forties. Most of these had begun adulthood in traditional roles; in midlife they became more autonomous in their attitudes about themselves and less concerned about gaining the approval of others. Jackson (1975), based on interviews with 25 women in their forties, reported that 64% of them had experienced periods of disruption and change in their late thirties.

A comprehensive survey based on Roger Gould's concepts and using a modified version of his questionnaire was completed by Desjardins (1978), who questioned 10 women at each age from 21 through age 59. However, all the subjects were former homemakers who were now attempting to reenter school or the workforce. Desjardins noticed a trend that has been verified in subsequent research; periods of change were more associated with those ages near decade markers (i.e., ages 29, 30, 39, 40) than the middle years, where stability predominated. Women of ages 28 to 32 showed the greatest personal change; the ages 38 to 45 also reflected a major transition period. Of all the women, those at age 40 had the most negative self-concepts. Although this is a cross-sectional study that possesses the previously mentioned limitations of that approach, its systematic surveying of every age point over a 29-year span, among other reasons, qualifies it as an improvement over Gould's original study.

Empirical findings on women's development reflect a shift away from firm age-based determinants, in keeping with the greater diversity of roles held by women. The phases of the family life cycle were found in Ellicott's (1985) study to determine transitions. See also Box 7.3 for a summary of a retrospective study of elderly women.

Similarly, with regard to the shift from traditional female roles to greater assertiveness and career aspirations, the time at which children are "on their own" seems to be a greater determinant than the woman's age per se (Rubin, 1979). Also, Neugarten (1968) found that women tend to define such terms as "middle age" on the basis of events in their families, or the phase in their families' life cycle.

The most sophisticated empirical studies of women's development include two cross-sectional studies that interviewed women of the ages 30 to 60 (Harris, Ellicott, & Holmes, 1986; Reinke, Holmes, & Harris, 1985). All the subjects lived in middle-class neighborhoods in the same medium-sized midwestern city. The subjects in the first study, 60 women who were either 30, 35, 40, or 45, completed a thorough interview, averaging more than 2 hours in length, that sought to detail how and when they had changed

---

BOX 7.3

Elderly Women View Their Lives

Mercer, Nichols, and Doyle (1989) obtained life histories from 80 women ages 60 to 95 (average age 73.5). Overall, their subjects reported experiencing developmental periods at later ages than did Levinson's men; also, their sequences were much more varied and erratic than those of the men.

Of particular value in this study is its focus on older respondents. The authors conclude:

> The age from 76 to 80 represented a transition to an age of wisdom, as women who were challenged to adapt to the loss of their health, in addition to loss of friends and family members through death, faced life with equanimity. As a counter balance to life's destructive forces, a surge of creativity was evident as women found pleasurable ways to fulfill their lives. An additional developmental challenge was preparing for the end of their own life course. (pp. 182-183)

---

during adulthood. For this goal, the women were asked to trace retrospectively their lives since leaving high school and to describe events, thoughts, feelings, plans, and goals over the years (Reinke, Holmes, & Harris, 1985). In addition to assessing differences from one age group to others on many specific answers, the research team rated each woman with respect to global life change on the basis of the interview as a whole.

The ages 27 to 30 reflected dramatic change for most of these women. Overall, 80% of the 30-year-olds, 83% of the 40-year-olds, and 60% of the 45-year-olds seemed to have undergone a major reorientation in the way they lived their lives or the way they thought about themselves, beginning between ages 27 and 30. Although change was manifested in different ways by different women, the researchers detected three common phases to the change process:

1. The initial phase, which usually began between 26 and 30, was characterized by a feeling of *personal disruption*. Specifically,

"women perceived themselves as reassessing their lives and seeking some unknown change; they identified life changes and personality changes as commencing at this point; and the incidence of professional counseling (and extramarital affairs) peaked at this period" (Reinke, personal communication, August 1, 1981).

2. The second phase, which usually began between the ages of 28 and 31, generated a *focus on the self* and *self-development*. At this age, respondents described themselves as having been less oriented to others, seeking something for themselves and setting personal goals (often for the first time). For some of these women, satisfaction with childbearing declined during this period, and separations or divorces became more frequent. Some also reported a new emphasis on physical fitness.

3. The third period, between the ages of 30 and 35, reflected a *new sense of well-being*. Women stated that "they felt periods of seeking and introspection were generally over by this time and that they started feeling a great deal of life satisfaction, self-confident about their direction and personal competence, and experienced fewer self-doubts" (Reinke, personal communication, August 1, 1981). Remarriages occurred in this period for a few subjects. Preliminary findings from Daniel Levinson's study of women (Levinson, 1985) indicate that for a sample of career women, around age 33 the "age thirty transition" begins to end and women initiate the formation of a "culminating life structure" for early adulthood.

In Reinke, Harris, and Holmes's sample, the late twenties also reflected a peaking of other life events, such as moves across the country, death of family members, and personal illnesses; the incidence of such events declined during the next 15 years. Relationships with their parents seemed to improve when the respondents were in their late twenties and again about age 40. Although family cycle was a powerful explanation of many of the changes, especially with regard to work, childbearing, and marriage, the preponderance of change at ages 27-30 was independent of family cycle phase.

Why this "age 30 crisis" in women? It is possible that "the age 30 marker has been imbued with societal significance for women" (Reinke, Holmes, & Harris, 1985, p. 1361)? In this study, such reevaluation and transition occurred more frequently in women working outside the home at age 26 than in those who were homemakers. (Only 63% of those who experienced changes worked outside the home, whereas only 31% of those who experienced no crisis at these ages worked outside the home.) But whether this difference resulted from biological urgency to start a family or increased independence or other factors, we cannot say (Reinke, Holmes, & Harris, 1985).

Although the first of these articles by the same team of investigators finds age *and* family cycle phase both to be related to significant psychosocial changes, the second study—concentrating on women ages 45 to 60—concludes that family cycle phase is more influential at these older ages (Harris et al., 1986). A total of 64 women, 16 each from age cohorts of 45, 50, 55, and 60, completed a comprehensive interview like the one in the previous study.

Again, a majority of the women (actually, 74%) were rated as having experienced at least one major transition in status and self-concept between the ages of 36 and 60. Harris et al. (1986) used a stringent criterion for a transition; an example is provided in Box 7.4.

Phases of the family cycle contributed to these; 80% of the women experienced at least one major transition during one of the phases of the family cycle. Most frequent changes were during the preschool, launching, and postparental phases, whereas there were fewer transitions during the no-children, school-age, and adolescent phases of the family cycle.

These women, ages 45 to 60 at the time of the interview, did not report any major transition around the age of 40, as men appear to do. Instead, "the women experienced changes somewhat later [during their late forties and fifties]. At that time, the women experienced increases in life and marital satisfaction and positive personality changes such as increased mellowing, patience, assertiveness, and expressivity" (Harris et al., 1986, p. 415). Another interview study of women ages 45 to 60, by Goodman (1980), generated the same conclusions.

SUMMARY

Levinson proposed that adulthood in men can be characterized by alternating periods of stability and change, or specifically by

---

BOX 7.4

A Midlife Transition

Harris, Ellicott, and Holmes (1986) report the following as an example of one of their interview subjects who experienced a midlife transition:

> This woman earned an RN degree in her early 20s and then married a man who was beginning a military career. During her 20s and 30s she raised four children and worked part-time, but she never fully developed her own career because of their frequent geographical moves and their family responsibilities. When she was 44, her husband had to retire unexpectedly, and his difficulty adjusting to retirement began to create marital problems. The woman began to feel an increasing need for challenge and stimulation, which was precipitated by the marital problems and her children's departure from home. When she was 45 she revised her occupational goals and subsequently returned to college to pursue a BA degree. The return to school was associated with increasing feelings of self-confidence, self-reliance, and autonomy. At this time, the woman's marital problems escalated, and after briefly considering a separation, she and her husband entered marital counseling. During the next 3 years, they resolved their marital problems and adjusted to their new roles. The woman entered the work force, began building her new career, and entered a period of greater stability and satisfaction. This woman was rated as undergoing a major psychosocial transition between the ages of 44 and 48. (p. 411)

shifting from "structure building" to "structure changing" periods. He based his theory on extensive interviews and other psychological data from 40 men, ages 35-45.

Perhaps his most useful contribution is the identification of four polarities operating on men in midlife: attachment/separateness, destruction/creation, masculine/feminine, and young/old. In describing these, Levinson's approach serves as a bridge between stage theories and a dialectical approach to personality development.

The theories of Levinson and others previously described in this book are less successful when explaining the lives of women, because (a) the genders differ in what the valued developmental milestones are, and (b) women reflect greater diversity in lifestyles than do men.

8

The Dialectical Approach

The whole content of my being shrieks in contradiction against itself.

Kierkegaard

The pattern of personality development through adulthood does not go smoothly. All the conceptions reviewed in Chapters 4, 6, and 7 capitalize on labels like *crises, conflict, transition,* and *turmoil.* But do issues ever get stabilized? Are there points in one's life at which one says, "I've got this major task under control; I can move to something else"?

Erikson's theory, described in Chapter 4, is often portrayed as one that sees choices resolved, as decisions are made at the choice points that demarcate each stage. But it seems to me that Erikson wavers. Although the above interpretation follows from his writings, he also states that conflicts can resurface at a later point. Even the initial issue of trust versus mistrust may be triggered again much later by a set of experiences in adulthood, say, for example, exposure to an unpredictable boss or companion. Even more explicitly does Daniel Levinson's conception capture the flavor of a struggle and a never-complete resolution of developmental issues. Regarding "polarities," Levinson (1978) proposed that they "exist during the entire life cycle. They can never be fully resolved or transcended" (p. 198).

The dialectical approach to personality development brings to the forefront this assumption that no significant issues are ever put to rest throughout adulthood. It views Levinson's stability and crisis periods as mutually dependent, and proposes that it is the mix of the two that makes mature development possible. This chapter examines this conception, both because of its importance and also because of its relevance to an underlying controversy in personality development: Whether one's personality remains consistent or changes during adulthood.

Basics of the Dialectical Approach

The idea of dialectics comes from Plato's analysis of the dialogues of Socrates. In Socrates' questioning of his students, thought was clarified and enriched by challenge, and thus moved toward truth (Smith, 1977). The interplay of ideas, and the resulting challenge, are central concepts in a dialectical approach. Although the term has various meanings throughout the humanities and the social sciences, I consider the approach to include three major points:

1. the idea of opposing forces, or polarities
2. the unity of opposites, in the sense that opposites define each other, or lend meaning to each other (Without hate there can be no love.)
3. the dynamic relationship between opposites, or their struggle for control, hence necessitating constant change

Dialectical Approaches
to Personality Development

How might these abstract ideas be applied to the understanding of personality? In this approach, personality can be described as reflecting opposition within pairs of characteristics, within the individual. Personality development reflects a striving toward fulfillment or achievement of each of these forces, separate from the other. These characteristics can be thought of as needs to be met. They do not reflect simply a presence versus an absence; rather each is an explicit need that has a substantive nature of its own. The tug is between two different poles representing, for example, belongingness and individuality, rather than a state of being awake versus sleepy (Altman et al., 1981). See, for illustration, one life's analysis in Box 8.1.

For example, an article about the dancer Rudolf Nureyev (Kaye, 1991) describes him as follows:

> Nureyev has never liked to be alone. Nighttime visitors to his home have always noted the book-strewn canopied bed, assorted volumes set out like provisions to nourish him through the long night ahead. And though he has come to cherish solitude, he often desires whatever he does not have: Alone, he is apt to crave company; in company, he may crave seclusion. And there are no patches of gray; only the irreconcilable tension of black and white. (p. 124)

These contending needs create a state of constant tension in the individual (*tension* like the tension on an extended rubber band, rather than necessarily *tension* in the sense of emotional stress). As one need is effective in pulling the person toward its achievement— that is, as the person devotes more energy to responding to that need—the pull from the other need becomes even more insistent. Thus, in contrast to Erikson, the dialectical approach views *disequilibrium* as a normal state.

Thus, as noted in Chapter 1, in a dialectical view, the characteristic nature of the system is a never-ending struggle. Klaus Riegel, a radical dialectician, believed that developmental tasks are never completed; "At the very moment when completion seems to be achieved, new doubts arise in the individual" (Riegel, 1976, p. 697). In a dialectical analysis, the concept of balance or homeostasis has no permanent applicability, because it is the nature of behavior always to be changing. This approach considers this experience of disequilibrium to be healthy, for it induces change, in contrast to a theory that assumes that closure or resolution is possible. A dialectical analysis would propose (to paraphrase Gail Sheehy, 1976) that the whole idea behind the nature of psychosocial development in adulthood is that issues can (and should) never be settled with

---

BOX 8.1

Dialectical Analysis of a Life

W. E. B. Du Bois is, arguably, the father of the Black studies movement in the United States, as well as the NAACP in this country and Pan-Africanism abroad (Woodward, 1987). The re-publication of his collected writings (Du Bois, 1987) led the distinguished historian C. Vann Woodward to remind us of the duality of personality for members of minority groups.

"One ever feels his two-ness—an American, a Negro; two souls, two thoughts, two unreconciled strivings; two warring ideals in one dark body, whose dogged strength alone keeps it from being torn asunder" (Du Bois, quoted in Woodward, 1987, p. 32).

Woodward notes that the concept of "two-ness" also serves to characterize other aspects of Du Bois's personality beyond his racial identity. For example, with respect to contradictions in his intellectual life, he was a humanist schooled in the scientific approach. "The two-ness did not end there; it was found also in the young Puritan who would be a libertarian, the man of thought who would be a man of action, the populist who was fundamentally an elitist, and the traditionalist who became a professed revolutionary" (Woodward, 1987, p. 32).

NOTE: Quotes from Woodward, 1987, are used with permission from *The New Republic*.

---

finality. At the end of the play *Broadway Bound,* the playwright Neil Simon has the main character Eugene Jerome say, "Contrary to popular belief, everything in life doesn't come to a clear-cut conclusion" (quoted in Henry, 1986, p. 74). Furthermore, conflict is natural and inevitable and contradictions facilitate development.

Does Synthesis Lead to a
Higher Level of Adaptation?

In a dialectical framework, change sometimes is assumed to be a cumulative process. That is, the long-term effects of oppositional forces lead to a synthesis of these in the form of a new structural integration (Altman et al., 1981). For example, the philosopher Hegel spoke of a progression of, first, thesis; then antithesis, or opposition; and third, synthesis, or an integrating of these competing forces. Some dialectical theorists consider this integration to be of a higher level or more mature than the forces contributing to it. Recall in Chapter 7 that Levinson, in speaking of the four polarities facing a man at midlife, described the man's task as, for example, blending his needs for both destructiveness and creation into a higher level of responding. That is, the contradictions within the person may cause the person to feel uncomfortable and motivate him or her to resolve the disequilibrium, leading to a higher level of development.

But as noted in Chapter 1, there is a more pessimistic view held by some dialecticians that the struggle does not lead to assimilation or integration; rather, that the person cycles back and forth, responding to first one need and then another. Levinson, trying to come to terms with the middle-aged man who failed at an attempt at a higher level integration of conflicting identities, speculated that he would form inner contradictions that would be reflected in the flaws of his next life structure.

Typical Dialectical Issues in Adulthood

It is impossible to provide a checklist of "typical dialectical issues of the average American adult," for if we really subscribe to George Kelly's (1955) personal construct approach (see Chapter 1), we believe that each of us generates our own labels for these never-ending struggles. But it can be argued that growing up in contemporary society causes many of us to face similar choices.

Some would even argue that the commonplace nature of our existence generates an inevitable dialectic. In the book *Waiting for the Weekend* (1991), Witold Rybczynski concludes that the repetitive weekly pattern of work and leisure must reflect some "ancient inclination, buried deep in the human psyche" to experience "the world in two distinct ways corresponding to two discontinuous modes of being: the sacred and the profane." Monday through Friday at work are profane. Saturday and Sunday at home are sacred.

Continuity Versus Change

There is an attraction in continuing to do what you have been doing, because it is nice (to a point) for life to be predictable, especially if one has a need to be in control. Yet the need for change also has a pull, not only because consistency can become stagnating, but because change offers novelty and the opportunity for growth. (Another person might offer a similar dialectical struggle, but label it as between order and creativity.)

Achievement Versus Relationships

As we saw in Chapters 6 and 7, the workplace exerts a mighty tug on people, especially those in their twenties, toward achievement. But men in their forties may feel the need to relinquish this quest for success and supplant it with a sense of sharing, of exploration of feelings, or community with another.

Filling a Role Versus Being an Individual

We are socialized to fill roles, and we know what behaviors are expected of the dutiful son or the solicitous mother. Often we are comfortable playing our designated role, for our predictable behavior makes the recipients of it happy and reassured. By telling us how to behave, the role relieves some of our anxieties. But at the same time, our need for individuality may be clawing for recognition and expression. We may demand to be recognized for our uniqueness, and tugs toward spontaneity and candor may overcome the conforming and superficial nature of rule-dominated behavior.

Immediate Gratification Versus Deferment of Pleasure

This is offered as a dialectical issue not only because it reflects the everyday conflicts of many adults (especially those who need to diet or those who have work assignments with short-term deadlines), but also because it makes the point that Freud's conceptualization of the structure of personality in the young child (see Chapter 2) can be reformulated as a dialectical choice. In fact, Freud has been described as a "reluctant dialectician," in that these systems—in his theory—are in a continuing unresolvable struggle for control.

Freedom Versus Security

There is nothing as appealing to many workaholics as an occasional day with no structure—no deadlines, no requirements, no agenda—a day to do whatever one wants, or if one wants, a day to do nothing. But freedom can become seen as empty unless it operates within some limits or within a broader structure that gives it focus and direction (Aldridge, 1984; Karl, 1984).

In *Escape From Freedom* (1941), Erich Fromm, a psychoanalyst but also a critic of Freud, states that freedom is seen as antithetical to our needs for security and identification. He proposed that even though we have greater freedom than any society in the past, this also leads to a greater sense of alienation and need for security.

But these are only examples. A little thought should generate those dialectical issues most appropriate to you or to a particular individual whom you know well.

A Case History Using a Dialectical Analysis

A dialectical analysis may provide a new understanding of development throughout adulthood, if it is applied to the analysis of materials that reflect the person's state of mind at differing points in his or her life. Jenny Masterson, a widow with one son, lived from the late 1860s to 1937. She was no celebrity; in one sense she was just an average person. Most of her adult life was spent as a telegraph operator. Her husband died one month before her son was born; she was 29 at the time. Between the ages of 58 and 70 Jenny Gove Masterson wrote 301 letters to two young friends, a married couple, who were living in a nearby Eastern college town. The friendship traced back to the time when the husband had been a college roommate of Jenny's son Ross; this was about 10 years before the beginning of the correspondence. The exchange of letters began in March 1926 and continued without interruption—an average of a letter exchanged every 2 weeks—for $11\frac{1}{2}$ years, until Jenny's death in October, 1937.

The prominent psychologist of personality, Gordon Allport (1965), collected these letters and after reprinting the contents of most of the letters, he analyzed Jenny's personality development from three theoretical perspectives: A psychoanalytic approach (like that of Chapter 2), an existential approach focusing on self-meanings, and a structural-dynamic approach that sought to identify the basic traits descriptive of Jenny's character.

In publishing the letters, first when he was editor of the *Journal of Abnormal and Social Psychology* (Anonymous, 1946) and later in his 1965 book, Allport identified the couple as Glenn and Isabel, "a married couple living and teaching in an eastern college town" (Anonymous, 1946, p. 318). For years it has been speculated that they were actually Allport and his wife, though Allport repeatedly denied this. But now, David G. Winter (1993) has persuasively proved that the speculation was correct, and that Jenny's son Ross and Allport were roommates at Harvard. This revelation does not affect the interpretation in this section but it reminds us that Allport "was not a detached editorial observer, but rather a participant in a demanding and difficult relationship" (Winter, 1993, p. 151). (See Box 8.2 for a further analysis of Allport's role in personality analysis.)

Allport carried out his interpretations before a dialectical approach had generated much impact on personality development. This is unfortunate because this conception provides a rich and meaningful focus on Jenny's life.

What is missing from the ingredients in the other theoretical interpretations is a procedure for characterizing the dynamic, changing relationship between Jenny and her son, who is certainly the most important person or object in her worldview. But a dialectical analysis provides this; it notes how Jenny's feelings toward Ross shift from rejection to trust and love to distrust and revulsion to, after his death, almost idolization. At an early point in her correspondence with the young couple she expresses the feeling that Ross is lying to her, that he has abandoned her. In March 1926 she wrote, "How impossible it would be for me to ever again believe one word that left his lips" (Allport, 1965, p. 14). At this point she envies his woman friends and calls them "prostitutes."

Later, there is a reconciliation. Ross returns, responds to her, and a mother-son romance of sort ensues. For her, Ross becomes an

BOX 8.2

**Theorists' Lives and Their Theories:
More on Allport**

Chapter 3 argued that personality theorists' specific lives contributed to what they emphasized in their theories, and Gordon Allport was offered as one example. Thanks to David G. Winter's (1993) analysis of Allport's relationship to *Letters From Jenny,* we can further apply Chapter 3's thesis to Allport.

Allport believed that Freudian theory had only limited usefulness. Although he saw the bitter dilemma between Ross and Jenny as reflecting an Oedipal conflict, he also proposed that "Freudian interpretations seemed to fit well if and when the family situation in early life was disturbed" (1968, p. 181) as in the Masterson family. Allport (1968) wrote:

> When the father was absent or ineffectual [Ross's father died before he was born], when the mother was notably aggressive, when there was deliberate sex stimulation within the family—in such cases, it seems that the Oedipal formula provides a good fit, together with all its theoretical accoutrements of identification, superego conflict, defense mechanisms, castration threats, and all the rest. When, on the other hand, the family life is reasonably normal and secure, a Freudian conceptualization seems forced and artificial. (p. 181)

Second, Allport, in contrast to Freudians, had doubts about the effectiveness of psychotherapy to alter basic character. As Winter (1993) notes, his theory of personality leads to a limited number of explicit therapeutic implications. And in Allport's discussion of the role of the married couple (i.e., Allport and his wife) in Jenny's life, we can see "a sense of personal powerlessness about the possibility of intervention" (Winter, 1993, p. 154).

Third, Allport's personality theory made a sharp distinction between normal and abnormal. "His views on the role of unconscious defense mechanisms, the importance of early experience, and the usefulness of projective techniques all follow from this fundamental distinction" (Winter, 1993, pp. 155-156). Consistent with this is the rejection of unconscious processes as central; Elms (1972) has described Allport's view of human nature as "the clean personality . . . reject[ing] psychological data on such unsavory creatures as rats,

(Continued)

BOX 8.2 (Continued)

---

children, and neurotics as being largely irrelevant to the understanding of the mature personality" (pp. 630-631). As Winter (1993) concludes, Allport felt that unconscious wishes could operate in certain situations but he sought to limit their application and "segregate" the normal from the abnormal. With regard to Jenny, Allport (1965) wrote:

> We shall have to admit that in her personality neurotic processes took the upper hand. Narrowness, rigidity, inappropriateness marked her behavior. Compulsively she expressed her anger, having little tolerance for frustration. Almost always she dwelt on the past, rigidly and regressively. . . . If character neurosis is "inflexible self-centeredness" . . . then Jenny stands diagnosed. . . . Toward the end of her life . . . from the neurosis an actual psychosis seems to be developing. (p. 221)

---

object of love. He takes her to dinner, kisses her good night on a rooftop. But subsequently Ross comes to "betray" her again, and she describes her own son as a "contemptible cur." As a final twist, Ross dies at a rather young age, and Jenny's feelings then shift toward acceptance and even veneration of him.

What's the major dialectical issue operating within Jenny? Trust versus distrust of Ross? Of people in general? Financial independence versus dependence on Ross? Each of us, on reading this collection of letters, might generate a different label. But we would agree that the crisis of their relationship, the absence of equilibrium in it, was central to her personality development during this long span of time.

SUMMARY

Among the approaches to personality development in adulthood, the dialectical one is, at best, a stepchild. It is not as well developed a theory as are the other approaches (and even they lack sufficient precision to satisfy most philosophers of science). It is probably best seen as a point of view rather than a testable theory (at least testable through traditional methods).

In teaching courses on the topic of this book, I have found that students have more difficulty grasping the essence of the dialectical approach, compared to early formation and stage theories. From talking about the approach with a variety of people, including students, therapists, and psychology professors, I sense that some people are enthusiastic advocates while most others react to the approach with indifference if not hostility.

This chapter has sought to identify the basic principles of the dialectical approach and to illustrate these principles through reference to autobiographical and biographical writings. For example, in a collection of intellectual autobiographies by leaders in the environment-and-behavior movement (Altman & Christensen, 1990), many of the contributors describe their efforts to resolve their own professional dialectical challenges. Among these are finding connections between disparate concepts and the need to combine viewpoints that others see as disparate. It is this expectation of achieving a synthesis between oppositional forces, leading to a higher level of integration, that is the greatest promise of the dialectical approach.

9

Consistency Versus Change
in Personality Development

Continuity is the exception in 20th century life and adjusting to discontinuity is . . . the emerging problem of our era.

Mary Catherine Bateson

For the dialectician, instability is a way of life. But even this perspective recognizes the legitimacy of the quest for stability, at least on a short-term basis. The issue of consistency or changeability has run through all the conceptions so far discussed in this book. As we age, we ask ourselves: Am I the same person I was? If so, is that good or bad? Psychologists of an empirical bent, over the past 50 years, have asked similar questions about people in general. They have not always agreed about the correct answers.

The Early Emphasis on Personality Traits

For many years the dominant view in psychology was that one's personality remained the same throughout life; this assumed stability was a result of the emphasis on traits as the building blocks of personality. Traits are usually defined as consistent, generalized qualities of personality that endure over time and that influence behavior. Examples of personality traits include introversion, optimism, hostility, dominance, shyness, and competitiveness.

Criticisms of Trait-Based Consistency

But about 30 years ago there began a questioning of this belief in consistency; three different theoretical perspectives gave thrust to the revisionist view. First, a highly influential review, published by psychologist Walter Mischel (1968), concluded that traits showed very little consistency across behaviors; that is, a quality such as honesty, usually considered a trait, could not be generalized across situations. It is important to understand the procedures that tested these ideas; an early example—a series of studies by Hartshorne and May (1928)—will suffice. Children in elementary-school classes were given opportunities to act in dishonest ways in a variety of situations. On one day, the teacher left some coins unattended while a child was in the schoolroom; on another day, each child scored his or her own true/false test so each child had an opportunity to change the score; on other days children were asked questions that tempted them to lie about themselves. Hartshorne and May found very low correlations (average of .23) between different manifestations of dishonesty; that is, the child who stole money was not likely to be the child who lied; the child who cheated was not necessarily the child who falsified records of his or her athletic performance. Mischel interpreted these results, along with newer studies testing the generalizability of other traits, to indicate that the situation had a greater influence on the person's behavior than did any internalized personality disposition, a conclusion in keeping with Mischel's Skinnerian or behaviorist orientation. It is not an exaggeration to say that Mischel and his followers were concluding that "personality is largely an illusion" (Helson, 1992a, p. 1). (Allport, 1937, countered the Hartshorne-and-May findings by pointing out that inconsistent behaviors may reflect a consistent underlying trait.)

A second criticism of the importance of trait stability emerged from the rise of humanistic psychology in the 1960s. Spurred by the writings of Carl Rogers, Abraham Maslow, Rollo May, and others, humanistic psychology reflected the philosophical belief in the possibility of change. Not only did it reject a Skinnerian view of people automatically responding to external stimuli, but it also denied the implied predictability of behavior stemming from trait theory's emphasis on stability of personality. In the humanistic viewpoint, people possess a virtually limitless capacity for change. As we have seen in previous chapters, it is now fashionable to believe that change exists—in physical abilities and perceptual skills but also in lifestyle and religious outlook—and the humanistic perspective has contributed to this perspective.

Stage theory, the topic of Chapters 4, 6, and 7, also contributed to questioning of consistency. The popularity of *Passages* (Sheehy, 1976) implanted the expectations of growth and change in the American consciousness. The "Santa Fe experience"—to be described in Volume 2—captured the increasing tendency for people in middle age to shift their careers to entirely new and different types of work.

Just one manifestation of stage-related change is Bernice Neugarten's (1968) concept of increased "interiority" with middle age, characterized by greater separation of the person from his or her environment and a decreased complexity or "simplifying" of life.

Behavior Change: Does It Denote Personality Change?

Certainly we can think of highly publicized persons whose *behavior* has changed dramatically over the years. Box 9.1, describing the changes in Bernadine Dohrn, provides just one example. Similarly in the late 1960s, Jerry Rubin was the personification of protest against the Establishment, a member of the Chicago Seven who provoked the police brutality at the 1968 Democratic national convention in Chicago. As psychologist Zick Rubin (1981) has noted, "Jerry Rubin enters the 1970's as a screaming, war-painted Yippie and emerges as a sedate Wall Street [stock] analyst wearing a suit and tie" (p. 18).

Another highly visible *behavior* change noted by Zick Rubin is that of Richard Alpert, "an ambitious assistant professor of psychology at Harvard, [who] tunes into drugs, heads for India, and returns

---

BOX 9.1

Bernadine Dohrn: Consistent or Changed?

Bernadine Dohrn spent 11 years as a fugitive from justice. Back in the early 1970s, she was virtually a household name; as one of the leaders of the Weatherman faction of the SDS (Students for a Democratic Society), she was wanted for conspiracy to bomb several places throughout the United States. The core of the Weatherman philosophy was "Kill all the rich people. Break up their cars and apartments. Bring the revolution home, kill your parents, that's where it's really at" (quoted by TRB, 1985, p. 40).

In 1980, Bernadine Dohrn surfaced, surrendering to authorities to face other charges. (The bombing conspiracy charges had been dismissed because of illicit federal surveillance.) Dohrn was given 3 years probationary sentence. But by 1985, she was married, the mother of three, and had passed the New York State bar exam and was employed by the Manhattan office of Sidley & Austin, a Chicago law firm. (She had graduated from the University of Chicago Law School back in 1967.) One of her bosses describes her as "very mature, hardworking, and quiet"; a colleague says, "She acts like a perfectly typical lawyer in a big firm"; another claimed "She's so conservative she's dull" (quoted by TRB, 1985, pp. 4, 41).

NOTE: Quotes from TRB, 1985, are used with permission from *The New Republic*.

---

as Baba Ram Dass, a long-bearded mystic in a flowing white robe who teaches people to 'be here now' " (Rubin, 1981, p. 18).

But do these changes in appearance reflect *personality* change? Rubin (1981) quotes psychologist David McClelland, who was a colleague of Richard Alpert at Harvard and who, two decades later, spent time with Baba Ram Dass; McClelland (1981) says:

When I first saw Ram Dass again in the early 1970s he seemed like a completely transformed person. His appearance was totally different from what it had been. He was wearing long Indian style clothes with beads around his neck; he was nearly bald but had grown a long bushy beard. He had given away all his possessions, refusing his father's inheritance, carried no money on his person, and for a time lived as a nomad in a van which was all he had in the world. He had given up drugs, abandoned his career as a psychologist, no longer wanted even to save the world and talked all the time as if he were "nobody special," although previously it had been clear to himself and others that he was somebody special. . . . Yet after spending some time with him, I found myself saying over and over again, "It's the same old Dick." . . . He was still very intelligent . . . he was still verbally fluent. . . . And he was still charming. . . . At a somewhat less obvious level, Alpert was very much involved in high drama, just as he had always been. . . . I would certainly conclude that he continues to have a strong interest in power. . . . Furthermore, he still feels guilty about being so interested in power. (pp. 89-91)

Sometimes, dramatic changes in behavior and valued activities may disguise *consistent* values and personality style. Charles Colson was one of the most dedicated staff members in Richard Nixon's White House; he supervised a number of illegal and immoral activities on behalf of President Nixon and was once quoted as saying that he would run down his own grandmother if that was what it took to get President Nixon reelected. After his conviction for Watergate-related crimes and during his prison time, Colson became a born-again Christian. Upon release, he devoted his life to prison reform, and a reading of his books (Colson, 1976, 1979) convinces at least this reader of Colson's dedication. More importantly, in 1993 he was awarded the Templeton Prize for Progress in Religion, previously granted to Billy Graham and Mother Teresa and carrying a one-million-dollar stipend. But Colson, though "born again," still describes others in "macho" terms; Colson's brothers-in-Christ are invariably "tall," "rugged," "tough," or "jut-jawed."

The "Big Five" of Personality Traits

Almost a decade ago, Marvin Zuckerman (1986) stated:

If we are to ever agree on a paradigm for a science of personality, we must begin with agreement on what constitutes the basic dimensions of personality. It is difficult to imagine a physics which studies matter without some classification of particles; a science of astronomy that studies "heavenly bodies" without distinction between moons, planets, stars, and galaxies; or a science of biology without a taxonomy of living creatures. Yet much of personality today [in 1986] consists of studies of ad hoc traits applicable only to limited areas of situation-person interaction. (p. 1)

One of the problems with an approach that emphasized personality traits was that, until recently, little agreement existed between psychometric psychologists as to what the basic traits were (John, 1990). But in the past decade, some degree of agreement has emerged regarding the basic trait structure of personality (Digman, 1990; Goldberg, 1993; McCrae & Costa, 1985). Although factor analyses of different inventories (Costa & McCrae, 1985a, 1989; Digman, 1988; Hogan, 1986; Lorr, 1986, for example) provide somewhat different labels, general agreement exists that five factors encompass major aspects of personality (Digman, 1990). These "Big Five" factors may be labeled as follows:

1. extroversion (also labeled surgency or assertiveness or interpersonal involvement in some analyses)
2. agreeableness (also called conformity or sociability)
3. conscientiousness (dependability, self-control)
4. neuroticism (or emotionality or chronic anxiety)
5. openness to experience (or enquiring intellect or culture)

(The first terms are the one used in Costa and McCrae's 1985a analysis.) These are tentative. As Digman (1990) notes, there is less agreement over their meaning than their number. But still the emergence of the "Big Five" reflects a scientific breakthrough that provides us a useful set of dimensions by which to characterize individual differences in personality (McCrae, 1989) and by which to determine if personality does remain stable over time.

What Does Consistency of Personality Mean?

The foregoing paragraphs should alert us that *change* can be a broad term and controversies over "personality change" can reflect different meanings. Caspi and Bem (1990, p. 549) provide us the example of the boy who has daily temper tantrums when he is 2 but weekly temper tantrums when he is 9; he has increased his

---

BOX 9.2

An Example of Absolute Consistency

Person	Extroversion Score at Age 20	Extroversion Score at Age 40	Extroversion Score at Age 60
A	55	55	55
B	45	45	45
C	35	35	35
D	25	25	25
E	15	15	15

---

level of emotional control in absolute terms, but he ranks highest in frequency of temper tantrums among his peers at both ages. He has not changed, relative to others.

This section examines different conceptions of personality change. Psychologists, when discussing the issue, have at least three meanings:

1. On a given personality trait, people who are high at say, age 25, are also highest at age 45 or 75. In psychometric terms, this reflects a high test-retest coefficient; it is graphed in Box 9.2. (A longitudinal study would be necessary to generate such data.)

We may label this *absolute* consistency, because each person maintains the exact score from ages 20 to 40, and 40 to 60. Given the exact consistency in the scores of each individual, it is inevitable that each person maintains his or her position relative to the others. Although this may reflect what some people think of when "consistency of personality" is mentioned, it is too severe a definition of consistency for psychologists of personality.

2. A second meaning: As different people age, their personalities change in a consistent direction. (See graphic representation in Box 9.3.)

BOX 9.3

An Example of Relative Consistency

Person	Extroversion Score at Age 20	Extroversion Score at Age 40	Extroversion Score at Age 60
A	55	50	45
B	45	40	35
C	35	30	25
D	25	20	15
E	15	10	5

We may label these results as reflecting *relative consistency*. Note that although the patterns in Box 9.2 and Box 9.3 are somewhat different, the correlation coefficients—as a measure of personality consistency—would be the same, 1.00. That is, the method of quantifying the degree of personality consistency is not able to distinguish between absolute consistency and relative consistency.

3. Now consider a third pattern, graphed in Box 9.4. Like the data in Box 9.3, these results reflect a general decline in extroversion from the ages of 20 to 60. Looking at these results, you may be tempted to conclude that personality is not consistent over time. After all, Person A has dropped from a score of 55 at age 20 to only 25 at age 60. Every one of the five people has a lower extroversion score at age 60 than at age 20. Is this not an indication of *change* in personality?

It is not an indication of change to the personality trait theorist; in fact, such advocates would define even this state of affairs as an indication of *consistency,* because each person has maintained his or her relative position from age 20 to age 40 to age 60. Even though each person's level of extroversion has declined and even though some people's scores have declined more than others, at age 60, Person E is still the least extroverted and Person A is still the most extroverted, compared to the others.

BOX 9.4

Another Representation of Relative Consistency

Person	Extroversion Score at Age 20	Extroversion Score at Age 40	Extroversion Score at Age 60
A	55	50	25
B	45	32	20
C	35	20	15
D	25	17	10
E	15	10	5

Longitudinal Studies of Adolescent and Adult Personality

One of the criteria of a science is the use of research methods that permit the testing of scientific hypotheses. As the science of psychology progresses into its second century, the use of longitudinal studies is increasingly feasible. Psychologists who advocate the consistency of personality and who use correlation to assess the degree of consistency have done a number of such studies; in fact, a recent book (Phelps, Savola, & Young, 1991) provides a listing of 200 investigations that meet a definition of longitudinal study.

The studies used to offer support on the issue of consistency of personality are summarized in this section.

The Institute of Human Development at Berkeley, California

Jack Block (1971), a psychologist at the Institute of Human Development at the University of California, Berkeley, has studied the consistency of personality for almost 40 years. Several hundred residents of Oakland and Berkeley, California, first measured in the 1930s when they were in junior high school, have been reexamined several times: When they were in their late teens, in their mid-thirties, again in their mid-forties (this latter testing took place in the 1960s). Data collected on them were very extensive—from attitude checklists and interviews to interviews with their parents and teachers, to later interviews with their spouse. Clinical psychologists rated the persons on a variety of personality characteristics, keeping separate the information from each of the four testing periods listed above. No psychologist rated the materials for the same subject at more than one time period.

The results of this massive study, coordinated by Jack Block (1971), generated a level of consistency within themselves. On virtually every one of the 90 rating scales, there emerged a statistically significant correlation between the subjects' ratings when they were in junior high school and their ratings 30 years later, when they were in their forties. Almost 30% of the 114 personality variables had correlations of .35 or greater from the senior high school testing to age 30 and above. Some correlations were as high as .61. That is, the most self-defeating adolescents tended to be the most self-defeating adults. Cheerful teenagers tended to be cheerful 40-year-olds.

In another project as part of the Berkeley study, Norma Haan and her colleagues (Haan, Millsap, & Hartka, 1986) found consistency in ratings over a 50-year period, from childhood to post-middle-age. (These ratings generally produced correlations of .24 to .37.) These results are even more impressive, because they are not simply based on a re-administration of single personality inventories (as is done in the next study to be described) but they reflect composites based on ratings drawn from a variety of measures and observations.

The Baltimore and Boston Studies

Paul Costa and Robert R. McCrae (1976, 1977, 1980, 1985b) administered two personality inventories, the 16 PF and the Guilford-Zimmerman Temperament Survey, to a sample of adult males who ranged from the ages of 25 to 82 when they were initially tested. Then these subjects were tested on these same inventories 10 years later.

Very high consistency was found for extroversion; various measures of extroversion, including gregariousness, warmth, and assertiveness, had test-retest correlations of .70 to .84; these are very impressive when one considers the 10-year interval. Anxiety and neuroticism measures also reflected consistency; their correlations were from .58 to .68. Similarly, a tender-mindedness measure showed a correlation of .63, whereas an imaginativeness measure correlated .44. Like Block, Costa and McCrae conclude that neurotic persons are likely to be complainers all their lives. They may complain about different matters, but they persist in complaining.

Also, Costa and McCrae did 6-year and 12-year follow-ups of another group of 200 men, age 20-76. These produced high correlations leading Costa to claim that "the assertive 19-year-old is the assertive 40-year-old is the assertive 80 year-old" (quoted by Rubin, 1981, p. 20). The average 12-year test-retest coefficient for all scales on the Guilford-Zimmerman inventory was an impressive .73 (Costa, McCrae, & Arenberg, 1980).

These researchers also used retrospective methods to look at changes. They interviewed a sample of adult men, asking them to describe in their own words if and when they had changed in the past 10 years. Costa and McCrae (1978) conclude that a great majority perceived no changes worth mentioning, a conclusion in sharp contrast to those of Levinson and other stage-theory approaches reviewed in Chapters 6 and 7. In support of the latter interpretation, Epstein (in a personal communication to Costa and McCrae, May 1979) has argued that old people may retain and report an image of their personalities that they had at younger ages, and thus appear more stable than they really are.

What do these results mean? Let us apply these differing meanings of consistency, presented in Boxes 9.2 through 9.4, and ask if there is any evidence that age has a dampening effect, that is, that individual differences are reduced with increasing age. The research of the trait theorists finds strong evidence for relative consistency, but is there an indication even of absolute consistency?

The short answer is: more absolute consistency than many of us would expect. Even with regard to social introversion—certainly the stereotype of elderly life—the increase in reported introversion is only 0.3 of a standard deviation over 30 years, from ages 50 to 80. Leon, Gillum, Gillum, and Gouze (1979) used 71 men, first tested in 1947 and then retested in 1977. They found significant correlations on all 13 of the MMPI scales. The Baltimore study by Costa and McCrae found *slight drops* over the course of adulthood in people's levels of excitement-seeking activity, hostility, and impulsiveness. No real changes occurred in gregariousness, warmth, assertiveness, depression, or anxiety.

If personality does "stabilize" as the above results imply, how early does it occur? Bachman, O'Malley, and Johnston (1978) tested 1,628 tenth-grade boys and retested them after 6 years. The general pattern, they felt, was stability, not inconsistency, even though there were increases over the 6 years in self-esteem, increases in reported drug use, and decreases in aggressive behavior.

The Mills College Study

Helson and Moane (1987) tested and interviewed 132 women who graduated from Mills College (in Oakland, California) between 1958 and 1960. They were contacted again when they were around age 27 and again when they were about 43. Scores on the California Personality Inventory stayed generally consistent, especially from ages 21 to 27; for the 22-year interval, the degree of consistency was, as expected, somewhat less. However, the Self-Control and the Dominance scale scores on the CPI correlated .50 and .58, respectively, on the 22-year retest.

Traits Versus States and the Midlife Crisis

Consistency theorists such as Jack Block or Costa and McCrae are very dubious that midlife crises have any permanent effect in the sense of "changing" one's personality. The latter researchers specifically attacked this question in an undergraduate honors thesis, by M. W. Cooper (1977), that they supervised. Cooper developed an inventory of items in order to measure the midlife crisis (MLC scale); 10 characteristics were included:

1. inner turmoil
2. inner orientation
3. change in time perspective
4. sense of failing power
5. rise in repressed parts of oneself
6. marital dissatisfaction

7. job dissatisfaction
8. life viewed as tedious, boring
9. disharmony with one's children
10. a sense of separation from one's parents.

As we saw in Chapters 6 and 7, Roger Gould portrayed the midlife crisis as cresting in persons ages 37-43, whereas Daniel Levinson concluded that it occurred between ages 40 and 45. Cooper gave his scale to 233 men ages 35 through 79. Average scores were then computed for different age groups, from the mid-thirties to the mid-fifties; groups spanning 5 years in age and also groups spanning 10 years were composed. Cooper found that there were no age-group differences on the midlife crisis scale; that is, those men who were 40 to 45 years of age did not, as a group, subscribe to these characteristics to any greater degree than did men in other age groups.

Cooper repeated this procedure with a different group of 315 men, ages 33 to 79. Again, there were no significant differences between age groups. If there is a midlife crisis, according to Cooper it is not confined to midlife.

Furthermore, Cooper reports data that lead him to conclude that high scores on the midlife crisis scale reflect a consistent trait rather than a transitory state, as purported by the stage theorists. By correlating subjects' midlife-crisis-scale scores with their scores on Eysenck's neuroticism scale, Cooper found a relatively high correlation of .51. Even more impressive was the fact that Cooper had available the scores of these men on a measure of neuroticism that they had completed 10 years before. For different groups, the correlations between the neuroticism score from a decade before and midlife crisis scores were from .19 to .35, indicating that a long-term tendency toward self-described neuroticism was related to reporting of crisis-related responses.

Consistency Among
"The Best and the Brightest"

One of the major longitudinal studies of personality change in adulthood was done for another purpose, to identify those characteristics that caused some of the freshmen men at Harvard University to excel over their peers. Despite the limitation that its sample was restricted to Harvard freshmen—and only an elite sample of those—the variety of materials it collected about these men and the fact that it systematically followed them up for 30 years makes it worthy of extended review in this chapter.

Originally called the Grant study of adult development, it was initiated in 1937 through the financial support of William Grant, a variety-store millionaire and philanthropist. Grant and the director of the Harvard University health service agreed to carry out a study that would select a small but healthy sample of several consecutive college classes for intensive medical and psychological study. They used men from the Harvard freshman classes of 1939 through 1944; originally, 268 young men were selected, although 10 of these dropped out of the study during college, mostly because of the wishes of their parents.

The directors of the project were fascinated by what Freud had called "the psychopathology of everyday life"; that is, problems are always with us and good mental health resides in the ways of reacting to problems, not an absence of problems. The quality of one's adjustment becomes most visible only when one faces difficult problems. Some adaptations are better than others, and the original purpose of the project was to identify the ways of adaptation to problems used by the most capable young men. Specifically, the researchers wished to identify the defense mechanisms, or ways of adaptation, used by these young men, to determine which were most effective, and to see how consistent they were. The directors of the study selected those freshmen who were superior in physical and mental health and ability. Preference was given to ambitious, success-oriented persons, rather than rebels or easygoing types.

These young men completed 20 hours of tests—physical, mental, and psychological. They were even given measures of body type and they provided urine samples. Each had eight interviews with a psychiatrist. While they were still freshmen, an interviewer visited their parents (wherever they lived) and completed a family history, including information about child rearing.

Furthermore, from the time of their graduation from Harvard college until 1955, these men answered questionnaires annually about their employment, family situation, hobbies, sports interests, vacations, political views, and drinking practices. From 1955 on, these questionnaires were administered in alternate years. During the years 1950 to 1952, when these men were in their thirties, an anthropologist intensively interviewed each of them, and they were re-administered a projective test of personality, the Thematic Apperception Test. At that time, the research staff even classified their children's adjustment to life.

Raters, blind to the identity of each subject, rated each subject on the basis of the defense mechanisms he used. When the subjects' responses were divided into three age periods (freshman age, ages 20-35, and over 35), it was found that with aging, there was an increase in the use of mature defense mechanisms and a decrease in use of immature devices, especially from the freshman year to age 35.

George Vaillant, a professor of psychiatry at Harvard Medical School, joined this long-term project in 1967 and personally interviewed a sample of 94 men from the original group, between 1967 and 1969 (the men were then in their late forties). These men included best-selling novelists, members of the U.S. President's cabinet, newspaper editors, teachers and professors, and judges; clearly they were among "the best and the brightest." In 1969, in their late forties, their average income was $30,000, 95% had been married (though 15% were divorced), most were extremely satisfied with their occupations, but 40% had received psychological counseling at some point in their lives.

Vaillant's (1977) book about the study identifies what he considers four distinct levels of development in an individual's life, and he proposes that there are specific kinds of defense mechanisms, or types of adjustment, typical of each level (see Box 9.5).

Central to the topic of this chapter is Vaillant's procedure in constructing an Adult Adjustment Scale that rated 32 different behaviors with respect to their relative maturity. (This rating scale is reprinted in Box 9.6.) Then, using a separate set of coders, Vaillant classified the types of defense mechanisms used by the men in his subsample. Comparing the 30 "best outcomes" and the 30 "worst outcomes" among these men, based on the ratings they received on the Adult Adjustment Scale, Vaillant found the two groups differed drastically with regard to the types of defense mechanisms they employed. For example, 45% of the "best outcome" men used mature defense mechanisms, whereas less than 20% of the "worst

---

BOX 9.5

Vaillant's Defense Mechanisms

Mature   Immature

   1. suppression   11. acting out
   2. sublimation   12. passive aggression
   3. altruism   13. hypochondriasis
   4. humor   14. fantasy
   5. anticipation   15. projection

Neurotic   Psychotic

   6. displacement   16. denial
   7. intellectualization   17. delusional projection
   8. depression   18. distortion
   9. reaction formation
 10. dissociation

SOURCE: Adapted from Vaillant, 1977.

---

outcome" men did. In contrast, 25% of the "worst outcome" men employed either immature or psychotic defenses, whereas only 5% of the "best outcome" men did. And clearly the use of immature or psychotic defenses was related to future behavioral problems. For example, one third of the men who used the most immature defense mechanisms between the ages of 20 and 45 developed chronic physical illnesses or died during the next decade. Seven of these Vaillant called "perpetual boys." Like earnest Boy Scouts they worked hard at their jobs and required little in the way of counseling for psychological adjustment problems. But they never worked through the Eriksonian life tasks. At middle age, they were still tied to their mothers; only 2 of the 7 ever married. They were downwardly mobile, and had the worst career record in the study.

The Grant study provides strong evidence that adjustment in late adolescence is predictive of "success level" at midlife, even among this highly selected group of subjects. But such a conclusion rests on a subjective foundation, in that Vaillant's (1977) definition of many assessments and terms—such as *successful working, success-*

(Text continued on page 178)

BOX 9.6

Rating Scales Used by Vaillant

ADULT ADJUSTMENT SCALE (a rating from 0 to 32)

Taking the entire twenty-five-year period (from college graduation to 1967) into account, one point was assigned for each of the
following thirty-two items that was true. A score of less than 7 defined
the Best Outcomes; a score of 14 or more defined the Worst Outcomes.

I. Career

    a. Failure to receive steady promotion or increasing responsibil-
       ity, if possible, every five years since graduation.

    b. Not listed in *Who's Who in America* or *American Men of
       Science*.

    c. Earned income is less than $40,000 (unless in teaching, clergy,
       or responsible public service or quasi-charitable work).

    d. Earned income is less than $20,000 (1967 dollars).

    e. Occupation does not clearly surpass father's (income, respon-
       sibility, occupational status).

  *f. Has not actively participated over the years in extracurricular
       public service activities.

    g. However prestigious in the eyes of others, his job either is not
       one that he really wants for himself, or over the years it has
       failed to match his realistic ambitions.

Rater agreement for each item was eighty-five to one hundred
percent, except for items marked with an asterisk, where agreement
was seventy-five to eighty-five percent.

II. Social Health

    a. Failed to achieve ten years or more of marriage (without
       separation) or failed to express overt satisfaction with that
       marriage on two or more occasions after the first year. (Even-
       tual divorce did not affect this item.)

    b. Divorced, separated, or single. (Exclude widowers.)

    c. Never wanted to have or adopt children. (Ignore this item if
       he is single due to external cause—e.g., Catholic clergy.)

BOX 9.6 (Continued)

d. One-third or more of children are markedly underperforming scholastically, delinquent, or getting psychiatric care. [Subsequent data analysis showed that this question would have been useful in 1975, but in 1967, when it was asked, it correlated with nothing.]

e. Maintained no contact with surviving family of origin, except by duty or necessity.

f. Regularly stated that he has less than usual interest in or fewer than average number of close friends. (Subjective evidence.)

*g. Not regularly a member of at least one social club and evidence from less than two occasions that he has more than one close friend. (Objective evidence.)

h. No regular pastime or athletic activity that involves others (family members do not count).

N. B. Items a, b, c, f, g, and h were used to separate the Friendly from the Lonely men.

III. Psychological Health

a. For more than half of years described, did not use full allotted vacation time or spent it at home doing chores or on dutiful visits to relatives.

b. Explicit statement that subject had missed something by being too calm, unruffled, controlled, or unemotional (at two points in time). [Like Item II-d, this item was not significantly correlated with overall adjustment.]

*c. Failure to express satisfaction with job on three or more occasions and once in the past three years.

d. Expressed explicit dissatisfaction with job at three points in time and once in past three years, or had changed occupational field once or job three times since age thirty without evidence of concomitant improvement in personal satisfaction or success.

e. Evidence of detrimental (interferes with health, work, or personal relations at home) use of alcohol, or use of sedative or stimulant drugs weekly for more than three years, or more than six ounces of hard liquor a day for three years, or use of tranquilizers for more than a year.

(Continued)

BOX 9.6 (Continued)

---

   f. Ever hospitalized because of mental breakdown, alcohol misuse, or "physical" illness without evidence of somatic pathology.

   g. Evidence on more than two occasions that he is chronically depressed, dissatisfied with the course of his life, or evidence that he is consistently labeled by himself or others as being emotionally ill.

   h. Has sought psychiatric help for more than ten visits.

IV. Physical Health

   a. One hospitalization or serious accident since college. [Item not significantly correlated with overall adjustment.]

   b. More than two operations and/or serious accidents since college (battle wounds excluded). [Item not significantly correlated with overall adjustment.]

   c. Two hospitalizations since college (excluding those due to surgery, trauma, or physical checkup).

   d. Own estimate of general health since college expressed in less than the most favorable terms on more than one-fourth of occasions.

   e. On the average misses two or more workdays a year due to illness.

   f. On the average misses five or more workdays a year due to illness.

   g. Afflicted with chronic illness (requiring medical care) that significantly limits activity or more than a month of work lost consecutively due to illness.

SOURCE: From *Adaptation to Life* by George E. Vaillant. Copyright © 1977 by George E. Vaillant. By permission of Little, Brown and Company.

---

ful living, or *adaptation*—reflect his own value judgments. He states that adaptation implies success (p. 361) and even acknowledges that healthy success in the study was sometimes confused with materialism (p. 365). He concludes that "a man's capacity to remain happily married over time" (p. 320) is the best indicator of mental health. Even the original selection of subjects has been criticized for being "preselected for their conformity to a perception of the normal and the admirable" (Wolff, 1978, p. 97).

Despite its limitations, the Grant study is so thorough in its processing of information accumulated over a 30-year period that Vaillant's conclusions are worth reporting. He believes that the results provide strong support for Erikson's theory of eight stages of psychosocial development. For example, he notes that a few subjects had very unhappy childhoods; those subjects, failing to have developed a sense of trust in the world about them, were unable to form many friendships in adulthood, nor to develop a playful or humorous attitude toward life. As Dacey (1982) notes in commenting on Vaillant's work, "Although childhood variables had considerably less impact on the later lives of men in the study than psychologists have led us to believe, Vaillant did find a relationship between a seriously unhappy childhood and later difficulties in life" (p. 86).

But Vaillant also proposes the addition of two other stages. He advocates that for men, at least, a new stage that he titled "career consolidation" arises between the stages of intimacy and generativity. In keeping with Gould's and Levinson's observations, he finds that his subjects, between the ages of 25 and 35, were oriented to their careers, worked very hard, and showed unquestioning conformity to work values.

Mentors were usually rejected during this age period. Vaillant (1977, p. 218) reports that many of the men had described mentors at age 19 but had forgotten them by age 47. More of the successful than unsuccessful men had mentors. Thus the Harvard men's reactions give support to Levinson's proposition that there is a period in which "becoming one's own man" is important.

The second additional stage, Vaillant believes, occurs after the generativity crisis, in the late forties and early fifties. Calling this "keeping the meaning versus rigidity," Vaillant argues that those who "keep the meaning" develop an acceptance of the weaknesses of their fellow human beings. These men wish to maintain and protect their culture even while recognizing that it is imperfect. They are more resigned to the inevitability of the future, more contented. In contrast, those who become increasingly rigid also become more and more alienated from their fellow men.

While generating new stages on the basis of his data, Vaillant also fails to find support for some of the central developments in previous theories. For example, little support emerged for the contention of Levinson that fear of one's own death becomes predominant during the generativity stage. Vaillant also saw few examples of *crises;* although change did often occur, mostly it was relatively slow and steady. He notes that for most of the men, fear of the death of their marriage partners was far greater than fear of their own death.

SUMMARY

Early in this century, psychologists assumed that personality traits were consistent over time. Several differing viewpoints in the 1960s agreed in questioning that assumption. These criticisms led personality-trait theorists (a) to seek indicators that there were agreed-on basic units in personality description and (b) to carry out longitudinal studies that might provide empirical evidence for stability in personality over time. One result was the so-called Big Five traits: extroversion, agreeableness, conscientiousness, neuroticism, and openness to experience.

In debating whether personality is consistent over time, one of the problems is the way consistency is operationalized. For the personality trait theorists, who advocate consistency, it is sufficient that each person's score remains in the same *relative* position, compared to others; *absolute* consistency is not required.

Given this definition, the longitudinal studies by Jack Block, by Costa and McCrae, and by others demonstrate impressive levels of trait stability over 20 years or longer. They also present data to challenge the assumption of stage theorists that "midlife crises" frequently occur.

The longitudinal study of Harvard freshmen, coordinated by George Vaillant, provides further support for stability by showing that the quality of defense mechanisms used by these young men when they were 18 or 19 was related to their adjustment to life 30 years later.

10

An Attempt at Integration

*To give ourselves a fair chance to find life-span change, which
is a fairly new undertaking, we need to conceptualize personality as a relatively enduring structure that might under some
circumstances be expected to change.*

Ravenna Helson

A final chapter can sometimes be a futile chapter, if there is nothing
left to be said. This chapter has two major purposes: to search for
any possible ways of integrating the diverse theoretical approaches
described earlier and to examine further the issue of consistency
in personality. A possibility exists for something new to be advanced, although as levels of integration increase, so does the emphasis on speculation rather than demonstrated fact.

An Underlying Factor
in Understanding Development

The issue of stability or change underlies all the previous approaches and each can be placed at a specific place on a stability-

versus-change continuum (Bee, 1992). The psychoanalytic approach reflects early formation and hence inherent stability; stage approaches assume abrupt changes. The dialectical view is extreme; change is frequent and inevitable.

Furthermore, one gets the impression that many theorists and researchers begin their explorations with preconceived biases favoring either consistency or variation. Helson (1992b) reminds us that "personality," as a concept, is usually defined in terms of characteristics that endure over time. Block (1971) is explicit on this point:

> The dominant conceptualizations of the basis and laws of personality development—psychoanalysis, reinforcement theory, and the constitutional-genetic viewpoint—concur in construing later personality as a result primarily of an orderly unfolding of capacities and qualities intrinsic to an individual or laid down earlier . . . [Thus change over time] disappoints the investigator, for he [or she] is prevented from the visible accomplishment of predicting the future. . . . Inconstancy over time is viewed as indicative of poor psychological measurement or as due to an unanalyzable, irreducible, random component in human behavior or as evidence of the unimportance of the variable involved. (p. 11)

Block's position was provided more than 20 years ago, and many—from humanistic psychologists to dialecticians to behaviorists—would challenge his characterization. But as Helson (1992a) notes, the bias against finding change persists. A recent review titled "Personality Continuity and Change Across the Life Course" (Caspi & Bem, 1990) proposes that "a claim of systematic change requires a theory that specifies in what way the observed absence of continuity is systematic" (p. 569).

A goal of this chapter is to examine ways that change can be accommodated within a framework that assumes stability in a broad sense. My bias—to the degree that I can articulate it—is that we should be open to a variety of concepts and approaches, and especially those that take us beyond traditional conceptions. To do so, first we seek to rethink what stability or consistency means.

Rethinking Consistency

If we play by their rules, the consistency theorists can make an impressive claim about the stability of personality throughout adulthood. But their "rules" include their own definitions of consistency, especially the use of correlation coefficients to assess degree of consistency. And even critics acknowledge that certain aspects of personality are relatively stable, including emotional style, introversion/extroversion, anxiety level, and depression. Similarly, interviews with older people directed at identifying their coping styles have noted that these are typically continuations of styles used throughout their adulthood (Reichard, Livson, & Peterson, 1962). But one critic, Orville Brim, is more interested in other aspects of personality, such as people's values, their self-esteem, and their sense of control over their own lives. He concludes that "these are the elements of character that undergo the most important changes over the course of life" (quoted by Z. Rubin, 1981, p. 24). Similarly, Conley (1985) has classified components of personality on the basis of just how stable they are over time. He sees self-esteem and well-being as least stable, with values and personal styles as somewhat changeable, and personality traits as most enduring. A systematic exposition of the levels approach is found in Dan McAdams's ideas in Box 10.1

Daniel Levinson is also critical of stability measures, claiming that these are not what adulthood is really about. The emergence from a midlife crisis, proposes Levinson, leaves one a different person from before.

A different type of reaction to claims of consistency uses a statistical analysis, asking how much consistency is accounted for by a correlation. Assume that over a long interval, say 10 years, there occurs a correlation of, say, .70 between relative positions of individuals on two administrations of the same personality measure. Such a finding is typical of those reviewed earlier in this chapter, and such correlations are usually interpreted as reflecting high degrees of consistency over time. But to determine how much variance is accounted for by a correlation coefficient (i.e., how much of the variation in scores on one measure is determined by variations

(Text continued on page 186)

BOX 10.1

A Levels Analysis in Response
to Issues of Stability and Change

In an invited address to the convention of the American Psychological Association, Dan P. McAdams (1992) poses the question that drives this chapter—"Can personality change?" and he gives the answer I, too, would give—"It depends."

The virtue of his paper is the analysis of personality into three levels, parallel and relatively noninteracting. "As we move from Level 1 to 2 to 3 significant change in personality becomes partially easier to see, even during the adult years, during which time [according to the consistency theorists] personality is no longer supposed to change very much" (McAdams, 1992, p. 1).

Level 1: Level 1 is comprised of traits, the linear, bipolar scales used in the work of the consistency theorists reviewed in Chapter 9. As McAdams notes, for some psychologists, such as Arnold Buss (1989), the trait level is the only one worth considering. McAdams concedes the conclusion of McCrae and Costa (1990) that individual differences in broad personality traits—extroversion, conscientiousness—are remarkably stable over time. But he also observes that the reliance of personality inventories on questions that require only simple and implicitly comparative ratings encourages stability.

Level 2: This middle level of analysis includes plans, goals, striving, tactics—generally what the person is concerned with or "into." McAdams (1992) notes that in recent years, psychologists have become increasingly interested in

> a person's conscious articulations of what he or she is trying to do during a given period of life, what goals and goal-based concerns occupy salient positions in everyday consciousness. Such constructs are explicitly motivational and contextual. They are embedded in and defined by the particularities of the single life. (p. 3)

They cannot be reduced to traits.

Among these "middle-level" units (D. Buss & Cantor, 1989) are "personal strivings" (Emmons, 1986), "life tasks" (Cantor, 1990; Cantor & Kihlstrom, 1987; Cantor, Norem, Niedenthal, Langston, & Brower, 1987), and "personal projects" (Little, 1983; Palys & Little, 1983). But defense mechanisms (Cramer, 1991) and coping styles

---

BOX 10.1 (Continued)

(Lazarus, 1991) are at Level 2, as well as—importantly—developmental-stage-related tasks such as generativity (McAdams & de St. Aubin, 1992).

Here, McAdams (1992) expects personality change; personal strivings and developmentally linked preoccupations "seem to ebb and flow over the life span, in accord with changing situational and developmental demands" (pp. 3-4). McAdams's own work on age differences in generativity, described in Box 4.2 of this book, provides some suggestive evidence for this. (Note, however, that Paul Costa, 1992, as a consistency theorist, concludes that even such Level-2 phenomena as coping mechanisms and defenses stabilize between ages 21 and 30.)

Level 3: Succinctly put, Level 3 refers to making an identity—finding unity and purpose in life—and emphasis is on evolving a narrative quest. For McAdams, these narratives, or stories, are ends in themselves. McAdams writes:

> My research into life stories has identified a number of narrative features, some of which seem relatively stable over time and some of which appear to change markedly. From the most stable to the most changing, these features include (1) a narrative *tone,* ranging from tragic or ironic pessimism to optimistic comedy and romance; (2) distinctive *imagery* containing idiosyncratic and affectively laden meanings; (3) motivational *themes* of agency and communion, power and love; (4) an ideological *setting* or backdrop of relief and value that situates the story in a particular ontological, epistemological, and moral location; (5) key *scenes,* or "nuclear episodes," such as symbolic high points, low points, and turning points in the story; (6) personified main *characters* who represent internalized parts of the self, or what I call "imagoes"; and (7) a generativity *script* that provides a satisfying *ending* to the story by suggesting a way in which the self may generate new beginnings, how the story may give birth to other stories.

Just as the phenomenon at Level 3 is harder to operationalize, so too the data for personality change here are harder to find. But McAdams sees the process at Level 3 not as the emerging stability of traits at Level 1 or the ebb and flow of developmental demands at

(Continued)

BOX 10.1 (Continued)

Level 2, but as a process of "continual fashioning and refashioning narrative in the direction of 'good form' " (1992, p. 5). These would seem to have little to do with generalized personality traits; rather, like George Kelly's personal constructs from Chapter 1, they are unique to the individual and have a self-determined range of applicability.

In summary, "levels" for these may imply too much of a hierarchy.

It may be better to string them out vertically. . . . Think of them as three very different domains, three very different "takes" on personality. They may not have all that much to do with each other. Persons are complex and multiply-arrayed. Everything doesn't need to fit with everything else into a neat, unified personality. (McAdams, 1992, p. 6)

---

on the other measure), we must square the correlation coefficient. The square of .70 is .49; so only about half of the variation is common. Even when a correlation coefficient of .70 has been obtained, a lot of change has occurred. People can change their relative positions on the two measures rather extensively and still contribute to such a "high" correlation.

Similarly, another kind of methodology chosen to study consistency—the retrospective approach—may lead us to see more consistency than was actually there. Most of us want to believe that we are consistent; conversely, unpredictability is not a desirable personal characteristic in our society.

Consistency and Stage Theories

Are there ways of resolving the apparent conflict between consistency and the stage theorists' views of abrupt upheaval and transitions during adulthood? Yes, several perspectives would argue that both can seemingly operate within the same person. Norma Haan, another researcher at the University of California at Berkeley, concludes that well-adjusted individuals do adjust their personalities and values to reflect changes throughout the life cycle. Haan (cited in Casady, 1975) compared the personalities of well-adjusted young and middle-aged adults to those of older persons. She detected that both groups had very similar sets of traits, but they tended to rely on different traits more heavily at specific ages of life. The young and middle-aged adults valued intellectual traits and pursuits, and wanted to see themselves as dependable, productive, likable, and straightforward. The older persons, in their sixties and seventies, emphasized other traits in themselves, such as their capacity for intimacy and close interpersonal relations. They were more protective of others and placed high value on cheerfulness, gregariousness, and a sense of humor. They cared less for manifesting intellectual skills.

Haan (1989) also analyzed the results of the longitudinal studies by the Institute of Human Development at Berkeley (see Chapter 9), covering a variety of responses by the same subjects from ages 6 to 8 to age 55. She concluded that on six personality dimensions, stability was greatest at certain age periods: from early to late childhood, from late childhood to early adolescence, and from early to late adolescence. The transition from late adolescence to early adulthood was the time of least stability. "The two adult intervals from early to middle and middle to late adult years were times of stability for both women and men in the degree of their assertiveness, outgoingness, and dependability" (Haan, 1989, p. 152).

By using a measure of changes, rather than correlation coefficients, Haan (1989) assessed whether the amount of change was superficial or significant. She concluded that midlife was the time when three personality dimensions—assertiveness, extroversion, and cognitive commitment—registered their highest points, followed by drops in late adulthood.

Individual Differences and Metatraits

Another approach proposes that some people are more consistent than others (Borkenau, 1993). The stimulus for this position is an old idea; back in 1937 Allport suggested that a given personality trait will predict behavior better for some people than for others. Bem and Allen, many years later (in 1974), while focusing on behavior, advanced the idea by proposing that people who were consistent in responding to personality inventories may be more consistent in their behavior regardless of the situation.

As Baumeister and Tice (1988; Baumeister, 1991; Tice, 1989) note, these findings have ramifications for the nature of personality. For instance, a dimension of introversion-extroversion "might be a central and consistent aspect of one personality but might be largely irrelevant to understanding someone else" (Baumeister, 1991, p. 633). They came to call these *metatraits;* a metatrait is defined as "the trait of having, versus not having, a given trait—that is, whether the person shows a consistent pattern in behavior on a given dimension" (Baumeister, 1991, p. 633).

Although the major purpose of this line of work is somewhat different from ours, it shows that individual differences in consistency exist. Competing claims of stage theorists that midlife crises occur and consistency theorists' retorts that they do not (see, e.g., Cooper's 1977 study in Chapter 9) may be resolved by expecting that some people do and some do not.

Consistency and the Dialectical Approach

A dialectical approach is also relevant to the dilemma posed here. Consistency versus change can, in and of itself, be viewed as a dialectical issue. Advocates of consistency would describe as a tug a "powerful drive to maintain the sense of one's identity, a sense of one's continuity that allays fear of changing too fast or being changed against one's will by outside forces" (Rubin, 1981, p. 24). But at the same time, most of us feel the pull of a desire to be "a purposeful, striving organism with a desire to be more than [we are] now" (Rubin, 1981, p. 24). An attraction of the dialectical approach is that it provides a formulation by which consistency and change can each be characteristics of the same individuals. It is regrettable that this issue often becomes an ideological debate, because reasonable advocates of each side agree that there exist constraints on their conclusions. Paul Costa has been quoted as saying, "The assertive 19-year-old is the assertive 40-year-old is the assertive 80-year-old unless *something happens to change it*" (Rubin, 1981, p. 26, italics in original). And Orville Brim has stated that people's personalities will keep changing throughout the course of life *unless they get stuck.* Both are essential; a stable personality is necessary to develop a sense of identity, but the potential for growth is the hallmark of humanity.

The Scientific Adequacy of
Methods in Studying Personality Development

Surely the task of accurately portraying personality development in adulthood is among the most challenging that we face. Different explanations abound, which either are in conflict with each other or are so unrelated that they seemingly have nothing in common. They are often advocated by zealots trained in one point of view.

Some observers conclude that preexisting beliefs of theorists preclude a scientific approach. Ann Weick (1989) writes, "Although it is customary for researchers to approach the study of a phenomenon as though it could be addressed solely as a problem of methodology, underlying any investigation is a set of assumptions about the nature of the phenomenon being examined" (p. 235). She concludes that these assumptions reflect such a traditional linear framework that "the formulation of a model of human development is fundamentally a philosophic matter" (p. 235).

Furthermore, we have seen at several places in this book that the methodology offered in support of particular perspectives is problematic; often the research procedures do not satisfy the standards of traditional science. It is rare to see a triangulation of different methods brought to the study of a particular developmental phenomenon. In fact, some of the most fruitful empirical concepts—for example, Levinson's polarities facing a man at midlife—seem to have been generated by the most subjective procedures.

Ironically, the methodology most congenial with scientific tradition—the correlation of two sets of responses by the same sample of people to the same psychometrically validated instrument over a long time interval—gives support to precepts of the approach that receives the most criticism from scientific purists. That is, the indications of stability in responses to personality measures from age 5 to age 55 support the claim of psychoanalysis that personality is formed early in life. Although they are not Freudian in orientation, the pronouncements of consistency theorists give credence to psychoanalytic proposals when they are quoted as saying, for example, that people "grow and change, but they do so on the foundation of enduring dispositions" (Paul Costa, quoted by Adler, 1992, p. 18).

Thus it is necessary, as we saw in Box 10.1, to search for other concepts and methods to give support to concepts from other perspectives. (Box 10.2 provides one recent example.) In regard to methodology, Stewart and Vandewater (1992) make a distinction between "tough" and "tender" methods for studying personality development. "Tough" methods include demographic questions about occupation, marital and parental status, and dates of major events plus the previously referred-to retesting with personality inventories; they state:

> Standardized measures with substantial normative data can provide useful developmental benchmarks for any longitudinal study, particularly if they are repeated over time. The strength of these measures is the way in which they articulate with existing disciplinary knowledge, and help situate the sample in comparison with other samples, and the study within the broader discipline. They also permit tracking of certain lifespan developmental changes over time. (Stewart & Vandewater, 1992, p. 1)

Among what they refer to as "tender" measures are open-ended questions: not objectively scored and less likely to have a past history that provides normative data by which to interpret the responses to them. (Examples: accounts of typical days, descriptions of living situations, high and low points.) But the use of these permits researchers to capitalize on new conceptual frameworks and assess more recent developmental issues, thus remaining "in dialogue with the current discipline" (Stewart & Vandewater, 1992, p. 2) while generating rich data. This is especially important because we are still struggling to understand what the important dimensions of people's lives are, especially people beyond middle age.

One example of tender methods that provide fruitful original knowledge is Helson's (1992b) follow-up study of Mills College graduates in their fifties, in which they were asked what had been the most difficult time in their life. The specific question (Helson, 1992b) asked:

> All of us have times of personal difficulty. Please think of the most unstable, confusing, troubled, or discouraged time of your life since college—the one with the most impact on your values, self-concept, and the way you look at the world. How old are you? About how long did this period last? (p. 336)

BOX 10.2

Linear and Cyclical Ways of Thinking

Hudson (1991) proposes that conventional wisdom, as portrayed by a linear way of thinking, is not sufficient to reflect our changing lives. Instead he advocates a cyclical notion of how life works. The latter is congenial with the spiraling continuities concept offered in this chapter.

Hudson writes:

> *Linear* means "in a straight line," implying that our lives and society are supposed to get better, year by year, generation by generation. According to this point of view, adult lives progress through predictable sequences: learning, loving, working, living, leading, and succeeding. In linear thinking, adult life is viewed as an orderly development following universal principles and rules. Life is lived for future goals and results, and is driven by perfectionism and social constraints. (p. 30)
>
> There are four major characteristics of the linear way of thinking: First, it operates according to a normative and prescriptive picture of how the adult years should happen. It justifies different roles for men and for women, and for adults of different ages. . . . Second, the linear view portrays the adult years as a sequence of events within a social timetable with predictable outcomes. A linear life means a planned linkage of age- and gender-related roles at specific times in the life cycle—marrying, having children, developing careers, and retiring. Third, it assumes a simple equation that if an individual does what he or she is supposed to do to live well, then happiness and success will follow. . . . Fourth, the linear view assumes that control over change is possible. (p. 36)
>
> *Cyclical* implies going in circles, with the repetition of familiar patterns—night and day, the four seasons, birth and death. From this perspective, the purpose of life is to master the repetitive patterns in our ever-changing experience. Cyclical thinking looks for human meaning in the ongoing flow of daily experience, from world news to family events to personal concerns. It assumes that life can make sense in good times and in bad, in growth and decline, in beginnings and

(Continued)

BOX 10.2 (Continued)

---

endings. Cyclical thinking tolerates high levels of ambiguity
and finds pathways for living in dark and unseemly places, if
necessary. (pp. 30-31)

Cyclical concepts are patterns that are repeated but have
different meanings at different times in our lives. (p. 39)

The cyclical picture assumes that life "develops" through
cycles of change and continuity rather than progressive,
straight lines. . . . The cyclical view portrays how the same
basic themes are repeated throughout the adult years—themes
such as love, achievement, and search for meaning. (p. 43)

SOURCE: Hudson (1991). Reprinted with permission from Jossey-Bass, Inc.

Helson acknowledges that such questions are not easy to answer—
they require, for example, some self-discipline and curiosity about
oneself—and some women may pick those times that are relatively
easy to talk about. There may be a recency effect; a study by Reinke,
Ellicott, Harris, and Hancock (1985) finds such. But responses provide opportunities to confirm or disconfirm theories.

For example, Helson sought to determine age of onset of difficult
time; the distribution of ages showed that, of 88 respondents, 17
fell between ages 21 and 20, 14 between ages 27 and 32, 9 between
ages 33 and 39, 34 between ages 40 and 46, and 14 between ages
47 and 53. Thus the thirties were a generally bland period and the
age-40 transition a time of turmoil, reflecting support for part of
Levinson's theory.

At ages 21-26, stories deal primarily with being unhappy, undesired, or helpless. A second type comes from having a bad partner.
In the periods around both age 30 and age 40 the most common
story "concerns a struggle, usually against the husband, in which
the protagonist seeks to affirm herself and her values through graduate training, a career, or sometimes a love affair" (Helson, 1992b,
p. 339).

In the age 36-46 category two themes predominant involved
unpleasant consequences of independence and assertiveness. At

the later ages (47 to 53), themes usually reflected either a destructive relationship or overload.

Is a Higher Level
of Integration Possible?

Chapter 8, dealing with the dialectical approach, noted that change can play a positive role in a cumulative process by which conflicting values force a synthesis in the form of a new level of structural integration. Daniel Levinson capitalized on this idea to propose that men in midlife needed to find creative ways to integrate apparently competing polarities in a new life structure.

A number of different observers, in dealing with such challenges, have proposed a similar resolution: what may be called the phenomenon of spiraling continuities. Styles are established early on, and issues recur, but increased age, experience, and wisdom permit them to be responded to at a higher level each time.

Spotts and Shontz (1985; Shontz, 1986), for example, propose a spiral of individuation in which personal crises cause earlier response patterns to be radically altered or transformed, thus permitting the emergence of new patterns of values, attitudes, and behaviors more appropriate for contemporary circumstances.

In his model of "evolving self," Robert Kegan (1982) uses this symbol of a spiral as he portrays the way people first move beyond certain core issues but then return to them as they develop. Feinstein and Krippner (1988) offer an example:

> If, as a child, you made an uneasy peace with people in authority, you may well find, at different points in your life, that you are challenged by issues related to authority, although perhaps at increasingly subtle and refined levels. Familiar difficulties recur, but at a higher level on the spiral. (p. 201)

Similarly, Frederic M. Hudson's book *The Adult Years: Mastering the Art of Self-Renewal* (1991) proposes that "throughout the life cycle, adults keep rearranging the same basic life issues (such as identity, achievement, intimacy, play and creativity, search for meaning, and contribution) around changing perspectives that our personal development, aging, and social conditions evoke from us" (p. xviii).

UNANSWERED QUESTIONS

An all-encompassing explanation of personality development in adulthood must recognize that change does take place, but still some impressive stability is present. This chapter has sought to provide some theoretical conceptions supportive of this viewpoint. But *why* does personality change? And what generates its stability? These questions propel us into Volume 2, *Adult Personality Development: Applications,* which examines, among other topics, the genetic basis of personality and the nature of career change at midlife.

References

Abrahamsen, D. (1977). *Nixon vs. Nixon: An emotional tragedy*. New York: Farrar, Straus, & Giroux.

Adler, M. J. (1927). *Dialectic*. New York: Harcourt, Brace.

Adler, M. J. (Ed.). (1952). *The great ideas: A syntopicon of great books in the western world*. Chicago: Encyclopedia Britannica.

Adler, T. (1992, October). Personality, like plaster, is pretty stable over time. *APA Monitor*, p. 18.

Adorno, T. W., Frenkel-Brunswik, E., Levinson, D. J., & Sanford, N. (1950). *The authoritarian personality*. New York: Harper & Row.

Aldridge, J. W. (1984, January 8). Part Kafkan, part Puritan. *The New York Times Book Review*, pp. 11-12.

Alexander, I. E. (1982). The Freud-Jung relationship—The other side of Oedipus and countertransference: Some implications for psychoanalytic theory and psychotherapy. *American Psychologist, 37,* 1009-1018.

Allport, G. W. (1937). *Personality: A psychological interpretation*. New York: Holt.

Allport, G. W. (1942). *The use of personal documents in psychological science*. New York: Social Science Research Council.

Allport, G. W. (1961). *Pattern and growth in personality*. New York: Holt.

Allport, G. W. (1965). *Letters from Jenny*. New York: Harcourt Brace.

Allport, G. W. (1967). Autobiography. In E. G. Boring & G. Lindzey (Eds.), *A history of psychology in autobiography* (Vol. 5, pp. 1-26). New York: Appleton-Century-Crofts.

Allport, G. W. (1968). *The person in psychology: Selected essays*. Boston: Beacon Press.

Altman, I., & Christensen, K. (Eds.). (1990). *Environmental and behavior studies: Emergence of intellectual traditions*. New York: Plenum.

Altman, I., Vinsel, A., & Brown, B. B. (1981). Social penetration and privacy regulation. In L. Berkowitz (Ed.), *Advances in experimental social psychology* (Vol. 14, pp. 107-160). San Diego: Academic Press.

Anderson, J. W. (1981). Psychobiographical methodology: The case of William James. In L. Wheeler (Ed.), *Review of personality and social psychology* (Vol. 2, pp. 245-272).

Anderson, P. (1977, March 27). Review of *Nixon vs. Nixon. The New York Times Book Review,* p. 5.

Anonymous. (1946). Letters from Jenny. *Journal of Abnormal and Social Psychology, 41,* 315-350, 449-480.

Apter, T. (1990). *Altered loves: Mothers and daughters during adolescence.* New York: St. Martin's.

Arlow, J., & Brenner, C. (1988). The future of psychoanalysis. *Psychoanalytic Quarterly, 62,* 1-14.

Atwood, G. E., & Tomkins, S. S. (1976). On the subjectivity of personality theory. *Journal of History of the Behavioural Sciences, 12,* 166-177.

Baber, K. M., & Monaghan, P. (1986, August). *Young women's career and parenthood expectations: A new synthesis?* Paper presented at the meetings of the American Psychological Association, Washington, DC.

Bachman, J. G., O'Malley, P. M., & Johnston, L. (1978). *Adolescence to adulthood: Change and stability in the lives of young men.* Ann Arbor, MI: Institute for Social Research.

Bakan, D. (1966). *The duality of human existence: Isolation and communion in western man.* Boston: Beacon.

Bardwick, J. (1980). The seasons of a woman's life. In D. McGuigan (Ed.), *Women's lives: New theory, research and policy* (pp. 35-57). Ann Arbor: University of Michigan Center for Continuing Education of Women.

Barnett, R. C., & Baruch, G. K. (1980). Toward economic independence: Women's involvement in multiple roles. In D. G. McGuigan (Ed.), *Women's lives: New theory, research and policy.* Ann Arbor: University of Michigan Center for Continuing Education of Women.

Bar-Yam Hassan, A. (1989, August). *Stages of interpersonal development in young adulthood.* Paper presented at the meetings of the American Psychological Association, New Orleans.

Baumeister, R. F. (1986). *Identity.* New York: Oxford University Press.

Baumeister, R. F. (1991). On the stability of variability: Retest reliability of metatraits. *Personality and Social Psychology Bulletin, 17,* 633-639.

Baumeister, R. F., & Tice, D. M. (1988). Metatraits. *Journal of Personality, 56,* 571-598.

Bee, H. L. (1992). *The journey of adulthood* (2nd ed.). New York: Macmillan.

Bem, D. J., & Allen, A. (1974). On predicting some of the people some of the time: The search for cross-situational consistencies in behavior. *Psychological Review, 81,* 506-520.

Bergen, C. (1984). *Knock wood.* New York: Simon & Schuster.

Berne, E. (1961). *Transactional analysis in psychotherapy.* New York: Grove.

Berne, E. (1964). *Games people play.* New York: Grove.

Berne, E. (1972). *What do you say after you say hello?* New York: Grove.

Bettelheim, B. (1983). *Freud and man's soul.* New York: Knopf.

Binion, R. (1978). Doing psychohistory. *Journal of Psychohistory, 5,* 313-323.

Block, J. (1971). *Lives through time.* Berkeley, CA: Bancroft.

Bloom, B. (1964). *Stability and change in human characteristics*. New York: John Wiley.

Blumenthal, S. (1991, April 22). Blues for Lee. *New Republic,* pp. 12-13.

Boring, E. G., Langfeld, H. S., Werner, H., & Yerkes, R. M. (Eds.). (1952). *A history of psychology in autobiography* (Vol. 4). Worcester, MA: Clark University Press.

Boring, E. G., & Lindzey, G. (Eds.). (1967). *A history of psychology in autobiography* (Vol. 5). New York: Appleton-Century-Crofts.

Borkenau, P. (1993). To predict some of the people more of the time: Individual traits and the prediction of behavior. In K. H. Craik, R. Hogan, & R. N. Wolfe (Eds.), *Fifty years of personality psychology* (pp. 237-249). New York: Plenum.

Bourne, E. (1978). The state of research on ego identity: A review and appraisal: Part II. *Journal of Youth and Adolescence, 7,* 371-392.

Bowlby, J. (1952). *Maternal care and mental health*. Geneva: World Health Organization.

Brenner, C. (1982). *The mind in conflict*. New York: International Universities Press.

Brim, O. G., Jr. (1977). Theories of the male midlife crisis. In N. K. Schlossberg & A. D. Entine (Eds.), *Counseling adults* (pp. 1-18). Pacific Grove, CA: Brooks/ Cole.

Brim, O. G., & Kagan, J. (Eds.). (1980). *Constancy and change in human development*. Cambridge, MA: Harvard University Press.

Brodie, F. M. (1974). *Thomas Jefferson: An intimate history*. New York: Norton.

Brodie, F. M. (1981). *Richard M. Nixon: The shaping of his character*. New York: Norton.

Brody, E. M. (1990). *Women in the middle: Their parent-care years*. New York: Springer.

Brody, N. (1987). Introduction: Some thoughts on the unconscious. *Personality and Social Psychology Bulletin, 13,* 293-298.

Brown, L. F. (1967, January). Book review of *Thomas Woodrow Wilson*. *Book of the Month Club News,* p. 8.

Brown, L. M., & Gilligan, C. (1992). *Meeting at the crossroads: Women's psychology and girls' development*. Cambridge, MA: Harvard University Press.

Brown, S. A. (1993, March 1). Teen tumult: Why it's harder on girls. *People,* p. 37.

Bush, G., with Gold, V. (1987). *Looking forward*. Garden City, NY: Doubleday.

Bushman, R. L. (1966). On the uses of psychology: Conflict and conciliation in Benjamin Franklin. *History and Theory, 5,* 225-240.

Buss, A. H. (1987). Personality: Primate heritage and human distinctiveness. In J. Aronoff, A. I. Rabin, & R. A. Zucker (Eds.), *The emergence of personality* (pp. 13-48). New York: Springer.

Buss, A. H. (1989). Personality as traits. *American Psychologist, 44,* 1378-1388.

Buss, D. M., & Cantor, N. (1989). Introduction. In D. M. Buss & N. Cantor (Eds.), *Personality psychology: Recent trends and emerging directions* (pp. 1-12). New York: Springer.

Cairns, R. B. (1983). The emergence of developmental psychology. In P. M. Mussen (Ed.), *Handbook of child psychology: Vol. I. History, theory, and methods* (4th ed., pp. 41-101). New York: John Wiley.

Cantor, N. (1990). From thought to behavior: "Having" and "doing" in the study of personality and cognition. *American Psychologist, 45,* 735-750.

Cantor, N., & Kihlstrom, J. F. (1987). *Personality and social intelligence*. Englewood Cliffs, NJ: Prentice Hall.

Cantor, N., Norem, J. K., Niedenthal, P. M., Langston, C. A., & Brower, A. M. (1987). Life tasks, self-concept ideals, and cognitive strategies in a life transition. *Journal of Personality and Social Psychology, 53*, 1178-1191.

Carlson, R. (1981). Studies in script theory: Adult analogs of a childhood nuclear scene. *Journal of Personality and Social Psychology, 40*, 501-510.

Carlson, R. (1988). Exemplary lives: The uses of psychobiography for theory development. In D. P. McAdams & R. L. Ochberg (Eds.), *Psychobiography and life narratives* (pp. 105-138). Durham, NC: Duke University Press.

Casady, M. (1975, November). If you're active and savvy at 30, you'll be warm and witty at 70. *Psychology Today*, p. 138.

Caspi, A., & Bem, D. J. (1990). Personality continuity and change across the life course. In L. A. Pervin (Ed.), *Handbook of personality theory and research* (pp. 549-575). New York: Guilford.

Chesen, E. (1973). *President Nixon's psychiatric profile*. New York: Peter H. Wyden.

Chiriboga, D. A. (1989). Mental health at the midpoint: Crisis, challenge, or relief? In S. Hunter & M. Sundel (Eds.), *Midlife myths* (pp. 116-144). Newbury Park, CA: Sage.

Chodorow, N. (1978). *The reproduction of mothering: Psychoanalysis and the sociology of gender*. Berkeley: University of California Press.

Chodorow, N. J. (1989). *Feminism and psychoanalytic theory*. New Haven, CT: Yale University Press.

Clarke, A. M., & Clarke, A. D. B. (Eds.). (1976). *Early experience: Myth and evidence*. New York: Free Press.

Cocks, G., & Crosby, T. L. (Eds.). (1987). *Psycho/history: Readings in the method of psychology, psychoanalysis, and history*. New Haven, CT: Yale University Press.

Cohen, M. N. (Ed.). (With the assistance of R. L. Green). (1979). *The letters of Lewis Carroll*. New York: Oxford University Press.

Coles, R. (1987). On psychohistory. In G. Cocks & T. L. Crosby (Eds.), *Psycho/history: Readings in the method of psychology, psychoanalysis, and history* (pp. 83-108). New Haven, CT: Yale University Press.

Colson, C. W. (1976). *Born again*. New York: Bantam.

Colson, C. W. (1979). *Life sentence*. Minneapolis: World Wide.

Conley, J. J. (1985). A personality theory of adulthood and aging. In R. Hogan & W. H. Jones (Eds.), *Perspectives in personality* (Vol. I, pp. 81-116). Greenwich, CT: JAI Press.

Cooper, M. W. (1977). *An empirical investigation of the male midlife period: A descriptive cohort analysis*. Unpublished undergraduate honors thesis, University of Massachusetts at Boston.

Costa, P. T., Jr. (1992, August). *Set like plaster?: Evidence for the stability of adult personality*. Paper presented at the meetings of the American Psychological Association, Washington, DC.

Costa, P. T., Jr., & McCrae, R. R. (1976). Age differences in personality structure: A cluster analytic approach. *Journal of Gerontology, 31*, 564-570.

Costa, P. T., Jr., & McCrae, R. R. (1977). Age differences in personality structure revisited: Studies in validity, stability, and change. *Aging and Human Development, 8,* 261-275.

Costa, P. T., Jr., & McCrae, R. R. (1978). Objective personality assessment. In M. Storandt, I. D. Siegler, & M. F. Elias (Eds.), *The clinical psychology of aging* (pp. 119-143). New York: Plenum.

Costa, P. T., Jr., & McCrae, R. R. (1980). Still stable after all these years: Personality as a key to some issues in childhood and old age. In P. B. Baltes & O. G. Brim, Jr. (Eds.), *Life span development and behavior* (Vol. 3, pp. 65-102). San Diego, CA: Academic Press.

Costa, P. T., Jr., & McCrae, R. R. (1985a). Concurrent validation after 20 years: Implications of personality stability for its assessment. In J. N. Butcher & C. D. Spielberger (Eds.), *Advances in personality assessment* (Vol. 4, pp. 31-54). Hillsdale, NJ: Lawrence Erlbaum.

Costa, P. T., Jr., & McCrae, R. R. (1985b). *The NEO Personality Inventory.* Odessa, FL: Psychological Assessment Resources.

Costa, P. T., Jr., & McCrae, R. R. (1989). *NEO PI-R/FFI: Manual supplement for use with NEO Personality Inventory and the NEO Five Factor Inventory.* Odessa, FL: Psychological Assessment Resources.

Costa, P. T., Jr., McCrae, R. R., & Arenberg, D. (1980). Enduring dispositions in adult males. *Journal of Personality and Social Psychology, 38,* 783-800.

Craik, K. H. (1976). The personality research paradigm in environmental psychology. In S. Wapner, S. B. Cohen, & B. Kaplan (Eds.), *Experiencing the environment* (pp. 55-79). New York: Plenum.

Cramer, P. (1991). *The development of defense mechanisms.* New York: Springer.

Crosby, F., & Crosby, T. L. (1981). Psychobiography and psychohistory. In S. L. Long (Ed.), *The handbook of political behavior* (pp. 195-254). New York: Plenum.

Dacey, J. (1982). *Adult development.* Glenview, IL: Scott, Foresman.

Darnton, N. (1990, January 1). She oughta be in pictures. *Newsweek,* pp. 56-57.

de St. Aubin, E., & McAdams, D. P. (1991, August). *Generativity through self-report, behavioral acts, and narrative themes.* Paper presented at the meetings of the American Psychological Association, San Francisco.

Dellas, M., & Jernigan, L. P. (1988). *Relationship of identity statuses to personality characteristics of undergraduates.* Paper presented at the meetings of the American Psychological Association, Atlanta.

Dennis, W. (1968). Creative productivity between the ages of 20 and 80 years. In B. L. Neugarten (Ed.), *Middle age and aging.* Chicago: University of Chicago Press.

Desjardins, C. (1978). *Self perceptions of women across the adult lifespan.* Unpublished doctoral dissertation, Arizona State University.

Deutsch, F. M. (1991). Women's lives: The story not told by theories of development. *Contemporary Psychology, 36,* 237-238.

Digman, J. M. (1988, August). *Classical theories of trait organization and the big five factors of personality.* Paper presented at the meetings of the American Psychological Association, Atlanta.

Digman, J. M. (1990). Personality structure: Emergence of the five-factor model. *Annual Review of Psychology, 41,* 417-440.

Diller, J. V. (1991). *Freud's Jewish identity: A case study in the impact of ethnicity.* Rutherford, NJ: Fairleigh Dickinson University Press/Associated University Presses.

Donovan, J. M. (1975). Identity status and interpersonal style. *Journal of Youth and Adolescence, 4,* 37-55.

Du Bois, W. E. B. (1987). *Writings* (N. Huggins, Ed.). New York: Library of America.

Edelson, M. (1988). *Psychoanalysis: A theory in crisis.* Chicago: University of Chicago Press.

Elkind, D. (1982). Erik Erikson's eight stages of man. In L. R. Allman & D. T. Jaffe (Eds.), *Readings in adult psychology: Contemporary perspectives* (2nd ed., pp. 13-22). New York: Harper & Row.

Ellett, S. O. (1986). *Identity formation and family functioning.* Unpublished doctoral dissertation proposal, University of Kansas.

Ellicott, A. M. (1985). Psychosocial changes as a function of family-cycle phase. *Human Development, 28,* 270-274.

Ellmann, R. (1979, June 17). Fun and games for Alice and others. *The New York Times Book Review,* pp. 3, 29.

Elms, A. C. (1972). Allport, Freud, and the clean little boy. *Psychoanalytic Review, 59,* 627-632.

Elms, A. (1988, August). *The psychologist as biographer.* Paper presented at the meetings of the American Psychological Association, Atlanta.

Elms, A. (1976). *Personality and politics.* San Diego, CA: Harcourt Brace Jovanovich.

Elms, A. C. (1988). Freud as Leonardo: Why the first psychobiography went wrong. In D. P. McAdams & R. L. Ochberg (Eds.), *Psychobiography and life narratives* (pp. 19-40). Durham, NC: Duke University Press.

Elms, A. C. (1993). Allport's *Personality* and Allport's personality. In K. H. Craik, R. Hogan, & R. N. Wolfe (Eds.), *Fifty years of personality psychology* (pp. 39-55). New York: Plenum.

Emmons, R. (1986). Personal strivings: An approach to personality and subjective well-being. *Journal of Personality and Social Psychology, 51,* 1058-1068.

Epstein, C. F. (1970). Encountering the male establishment: Sex-status limits on women's careers in the professions. *American Journal of Sociology, 75,* 965-982.

Erikson, E. H. (1950). *Childhood and society.* New York: Norton.

Erikson, E. H. (1958). *Young man Luther: A study of psychoanalysis and history.* New York: Norton.

Erikson, E. H. (1959). Identity and the life cycle: Selected papers. *Psychological Issues, 1,* 5-165.

Erikson, E. H. (1963). *Childhood and society* (2nd ed.). New York: Norton. (Original work published 1950)

Erikson, E. H. (1968a). *Identity: Youth and crisis.* New York: Norton.

Erikson, E. H. (1968b, Summer). On the nature of psycho-historical evidence: In search of Gandhi. *Daedalus, 97,* Whole No. 3.

Erikson, E. H. (1969). *Gandhi's truth: On the origins of militant nonviolence.* New York: Norton.

Erikson, E. H. (1974). *Dimensions of a new identity.* New York: Norton.

Erikson, E. H. (1975). *Life history and the historical moment.* New York: Norton.

Erikson, E. H. (1980a). *Identity and the life cycle.* New York: Norton.

Erikson, E. H. (1980b). Themes of adulthood in the Freud-Jung correspondence. In N. J. Smelser & E. H. Erikson (Eds.), *Themes of work and love in adulthood* (pp. 43-74). Cambridge, MA: Harvard University Press.

Esterly, G. (1987, June 6). She's the golden girl of romance. *TV Guide,* pp. 19-21.

Evans, R. I. (1967). *Dialogue with Erik Erikson.* New York: Harper.

Evans, R. I. (1970). *Gordon Allport: The man and his ideas.* New York: E. P. Dutton.

Eysenck, H. J., & Wilson, G. D. (Eds.). (1973). *The experimental study of Freudian theories.* London: Methuen.

Farmer, P. (1979). *An exploratory investigation into the nature of the mid-life transition of a group of selected women.* Unpublished doctoral dissertation, Temple University.

Farrell, M. P., & Rosenberg, S. D. (1981). *Men at midlife.* Dover, MA: Auburn House.

Feinstein, D., & Krippner, S. (1988). *Personal mythology: The psychology of your evolving self.* Los Angeles: Jeremy P. Tarcher.

Fine, R. (1973). *The development of Freud's thought.* New York: Jason Aronson.

Fisher, S., & Greenberg, R. P. (1977). *The scientific credibility of Freud's theories and therapy.* New York: Basic Books.

Flavell, J. H. (1991). What young children know about the mind. *Contemporary Psychology, 36,* 741-742.

Foreman, J. (1986, December 16). "Rage" brings wrath from Goetz worshippers. *Kansas City Star,* p. 3C.

Franklin, B. (1961). *The autobiography and other writings.* New York: New American Library.

Franz, C. E., & White, K. M. (1985). Individuation and attachment in personality development: Extending Erikson's theory. *Journal of Personality, 53,* 224-256.

Freud, S. (1933). *New introductory lectures in psychoanalysis* (J. H. Sprott, Trans.). New York: Norton.

Freud, S. (1952). *Collected works* (Vol. 4). London: Hogarth.

Freud, S. (1957). Five lectures on psycho-analysis. In J. Strachey (Ed. and Trans.), *The standard edition of the complete works of Sigmund Freud* (Vol. 7, pp. 125-243). London: Hogarth. (Original work published 1910)

Freud, S. (1963). Introductory lectures on psychoanalysis. In J. Strachey (Ed. and Trans.), *The standard edition of the complete works of Sigmund Freud* (Vols. 15 and 16). London: Hogarth. (Original work published 1917)

Freud, S. (1964). Moses and monotheism. In J. Strachey (Ed. and Trans.), *The standard edition of the complete works of Sigmund Freud* (Vol. 23, pp. 3-137). London: Hogarth. (Original work published 1939)

Freud, S. (1966). *Introductory lectures on psychoanalysis* (J. Strachey, Trans.). New York: Norton. (Original work published 1916)

Freud, S., & Bullitt, W. C. (1967). *Thomas Woodrow Wilson.* Boston: Houghton-Mifflin.

Friedman, W. (1990, July). *Changing theoretical perspectives and the psychobiography of historical figures: The case of Woodrow Wilson.* Paper presented at the meetings of the International Society of Political Psychology, Washington, DC.

Fromm, E. (1941). *Escape from freedom.* New York: Holt.

Fromm, E. (1959). *Sigmund Freud's mission.* New York: Harper & Row.

Frosh, S. (1987). *The politics of psychoanalysis: An introduction to Freudian and post-Freudian theory*. New Haven, CT: Yale University Press.

Gardner, M. (Ed.). (1960). *The annotated Alice*. New York: Clarkson Potter.

Garrow, D. J. (1986). *Bearing the cross: Martin Luther King, Jr., and the Southern Christian Leadership Conference*. New York: William Morrow.

Gay, P. (1988). *Freud: A life for our time*. New York: Norton.

Gelman, D. (1991, November 25). Revival sessions. *Newsweek*, pp. 60-61.

George, A. L., & George, J. L. (1956). *Woodrow Wilson and Colonel House*. New York: John Day.

Gilligan, C. (1980). Woman's place in man's life cycle. *Harvard Educational Review, 49*, 431-446.

Gilligan, C. (1982). *In a different voice: Psychological theory and women's development*. Cambridge, MA: Harvard University Press.

Gilot, F., & Lake, C. (1964). *Life with Picasso*. New York: McGraw-Hill.

Goldberg, L. R. (1993). The structure of phenotypic personality traits. *American Psychologist, 48*, 26-34.

Goldman-Eisler, F. (1951). The problem of "orality" and of its origin in early childhood. *Journal of Mental Science, 97*, 765-782.

Goleman, D. (1987a, February 10). Lost paper shows Freud's effort to link analysis and evolution. *The New York Times*, pp. 19, 22.

Goleman, D. (1987b, November 29). Taking sides, then and now. *The New York Times Book Review*, p. 11.

Goodman, E. (1990, December 18). "Home Alone" quiets modern fears. *Lawrence Journal-World*, p. 5A.

Goodman, S. F. (1980). *Women in their later years: A study of the psychosocial development of women between 45-60*. Unpublished doctoral dissertation, School of Education, Boston University.

Gould, R. L. (1972). The phases of adult life: A study in developmental psychology. *American Journal of Psychiatry, 29*, 521-531.

Gould, R. (1975, January). Adult life stages: Growth toward self-tolerance. *Psychology Today*, pp. 74-78.

Gould, R. (1978). *Transformations: Growth and change in adult life*. New York: Simon & Schuster.

Greenacre, P. (1955). *Swift and Carroll: A psychoanalytic study of two lives*. New York: International Universities Press.

Gutmann, D. (1964). An exploration of ego configurations in middle and later life. In B. Neugarten (Ed.), *Personality in middle and later life* (pp. 114-148). New York: Atherton.

Gutmann, D. (1977). The cross-cultural perspective: Notes towards a comparative psychology of aging. In J. E. Birren & K. W. Schaie (Eds.), *Handbook of the psychology of aging* (pp. 302-326). New York: Van Nostrand Reinhold.

Haan, N. (1989). Personality at midlife. In S. Hunter & M. Sundel (Eds.), *Midlife myths* (pp. 145-156). Newbury Park, CA: Sage.

Haan, N., Millsap, R., & Hartka, E. (1986). As time goes by: Change and stability in personality over fifty years. *Psychology and Aging, 1*, 220-232.

Hall, C. S., & Lindzey, G. (1970). *Theories of personality* (2nd ed.). New York: John Wiley.

Hall, C. S., & Lindzey, G. (1978). *Theories of personality* (3rd ed.). New York: John Wiley.

Hargrove, E. C. (1966). *Presidential leadership: Personality and political style.* New York: Macmillan.

Harris, R. L., Ellicott, A. M., & Holmes, D. S. (1986). The timing of psychosocial transitions and changes in women's lives: An examination of women aged 45 to 60. *Journal of Personality and Social Psychology, 51,* 409-416.

Hartshorne, H., & May, M. A. (1928). *Studies in the nature of character: Vol. I. Studies in deceit.* New York: Macmillan.

Havighurst, R. J. (1972). *Developmental tasks and education* (3rd ed.). New York: David McKay.

Hawley, G. A. (1986). *Construction and validation of an Eriksonian measure of psychosocial development.* Unpublished doctoral dissertation, University of North Carolina at Chapel Hill.

Hazan, C., & Shaver, P. R. (1987). Romantic love conceptualized as an attachment process. *Journal of Personality and Social Psychology, 52,* 511-524.

Helson, R. (1992a, August). *Contexts of personality change.* Paper presented at the meetings of the American Psychological Association, Washington, DC.

Helson, R. (1992b). Women's difficult times and the rewriting of the life story. *Psychology of Women Quarterly, 16,* 331-347.

Helson, R., & Mitchell, V. (1978). Personality. *Annual Review of Psychology, 29,* 555-585.

Helson, R., Mitchell, V., & Moane, G. (1984). Personality and patterns of adherence and non-adherence to the social clock. *Journal of Personality and Social Psychology, 46,* 1079-1096.

Helson, R., & Moane, G. (1987). Personality change in women from college to midlife. *Journal of Personality and Social Psychology, 53,* 176-186.

Henry, W. A., III. (1986, December 15). Reliving a poignant past. *Time,* pp. 72-78.

Herbert, W. (1987, January). A national morality play. *Psychology Today,* p. 80.

Hogan, R. (1986). *Hogan Personality Inventory.* Minneapolis, MN: National Computer Systems.

Holmes, D. S. (1972). Repression and interference: A further investigation. *Journal of Personality and Social Psychology, 22,* 163-170.

Holmes, D. S. (1974). Investigations of repression: Differential recall of material experimentally or naturally associated with ego threat. *Psychological Bulletin, 81,* 632-653.

Holt, R. R. (1985). The current status of psychoanalytic theory. *Psychoanalytic Psychology, 2,* 289-315.

Holzman, P. (1985). Psychoanalysis: Is the therapy destroying the science? *Journal of the American Psychoanalytic Association, 33,* 725-770.

Horney, K. (1937). *The neurotic personality of our time.* New York: Norton.

Horney, K. (1950). *Neurosis and human growth.* New York: Norton.

Hudson, D. (1954). *Lewis Carroll.* London: Constable.

Hudson, F. M. (1991). *The adult years: Mastering the art of self-renewal.* San Francisco: Jossey-Bass.

Huffington, A. S. (1988). *Picasso: Creator and destroyer.* New York: Simon & Schuster.

Hunter, S., & Sundel, M. (Eds.). (1989). *Midlife myths: Issues, findings, and practice implications*. Newbury Park, CA: Sage.

Huyck, M. H., & Hoyer, W. J. (1982). *Adult development and aging*. Belmont, CA: Wadsworth.

Jackson, P. F. (1975). Disruption and change in mid-life: An exploratory study of women in their fifth decade. *Dissertation Abstracts, 35*(12-B), 6074. (University Microfilms No. 75-13, 194)

Jahoda, M. (1977). *Freud and the dilemmas of psychology*. London: Hogarth Press.

Jankowicz, A. D. (1987). Whatever became of George Kelly? Applications and implications. *American Psychologist, 42,* 481-487.

John, O. P. (1990). The big five factor taxonomy: Dimensions of personality in the natural language. In L. Pervin (Ed.), *Handbook of personality theory and research* (pp. 66-100). New York: Guilford.

Johnson, K. (1986, October 19). Review of *Quiet Rage*. *The New York Times Book Review,* p. 31.

Josselson, R. (1987). *Finding herself: Pathways to identity development in women*. San Francisco: Jossey-Bass.

Jung, C. G. (1961). *Memories, dreams, recollections*. New York: Vintage.

Kandel, D. B., & Lesser, G. S. (1972). *Youth in two worlds*. San Francisco: Jossey-Bass.

Karl, F. R. (1984). *American fictions 1940/1980*. New York: Harper & Row.

Kaye, E. (1991, March). Nureyev: Dancing in his own shadow. *Esquire,* pp. 122-128, 154-158.

Keaton, B. (with C. Samuels). (1960). *My wonderful world of slapstick*. Garden City, NY: Doubleday.

Kegan, R. (1982). *The evolving self: Problem and process in human development*. Cambridge, MA: Harvard University Press.

Keil, F. C. (1989). *Concepts, kinds, and cognitive development*. Cambridge: MIT Press.

Kelly, E. L. (1955). Consistency of adult personality. *American Psychologist, 10,* 659-681.

Kelly, G. A. (1955). *The psychology of personal constructs*. New York: Norton.

Kelly, G. A. (1963). *A theory of personality*. New York: Norton.

Kernberg, O. (1976). *Object relations theory and clinical psychoanalysis*. New York: Jason Aronson.

Kihlstrom, J. F. (1990). The psychological unconscious. In L. A. Pervin (Ed.), *Handbook of personality theory and research* (pp. 445-464). New York: Guilford.

Kimmel, D. C. (1980). *Adulthood and aging: An interdisciplinary developmental view* (2nd ed.). New York: John Wiley.

Kimmel, D. C. (1990). *Adulthood and aging: An interdisciplinary, developmental view* (3rd ed.). New York: John Wiley.

Koenig, J. (1991, June 30). Favored by suicides. *The New York Times Book Review,* p. 34.

Kolakowski, L. (1991, May 6). The man who made modernity. *New Republic,* pp. 40-41.

Kroszarski, R. (1976). *Hollywood directors 1914-1940*. New York: Oxford University Press.

Kutner, L. (1990, July 19). Parent and child. *The New York Times,* p. B7.

Lasswell, H. D. (1930). *Psychopathology and politics*. Chicago: University of Chicago Press.

Lazarus, R. S. (1991). *Emotion and adaptation*. New York: Oxford University Press.

Lehman, H. C. (1953). *Age and achievement*. Princeton, NJ: Princeton University Press.

Lehman, H. C. (1962). The creative production rates of present versus past generations of scientists. *Journal of Gerontology, 17,* 409-417.

Leichtman, M. (1987, December). *Developmental psychology and psychoanalysis: Vol. 1. The context for a contemporary revolution in psychoanalysis.* Paper presented at the meetings of the American Psychoanalytic Association, New York.

Leon, G. R., Gillum, B., Gillum, R., & Gouze, M. (1979). Personality stability and change over a 30-year period—middle age to old age. *Journal of Counseling and Clinical Psychology, 47,* 517-524.

Levinson, D. J. (1978). *The seasons of a man's life*. New York: Knopf.

Levinson, D. J. (1979). Adult development—or what? *Contemporary Psychology, 24,* 727.

Levinson, D. J. (1980). Toward a conception of the adult life course. In N. J. Smelser & E. H. Erikson (Eds.), *Themes of work and love in adulthood* (pp. 265-290). Cambridge, MA: Harvard University Press.

Levinson, D. J. (1985, July 8). Personal communication.

Levinson, D. J. (1986). A conception of adult development. *American Psychologist, 41,* 3-13.

Levinson, D. J. (1990, August). *The seasons of a woman's life: Implications for women and men.* Paper presented at the meetings of the American Psychological Association, Boston.

Levinson, D. J., Darrow, C. N., Klein, E. B., Levinson, M. H., & McKee, B. (1977). Periods in the adult development of men: Ages 18 to 45. In N. K. Schlossberg & A. D. Entine (Eds.), *Counseling adults* (pp. 47-59). Pacific Grove, CA: Brooks/ Cole.

Levinson, D. J., in collaboration with Darrow, C. N., Klein, E. B., Levinson, M. H, & McKee, B. (1978). *The seasons of a man's life*. New York: Knopf.

Lindzey, G. (Ed.). (1974). *A history of psychology in autobiography* (Vol. 6). Englewood Cliffs, NJ: Prentice Hall.

Little, B. (1983). Personal projects: A rationale and methods for investigation. *Environment and Behavior, 15,* 273-309.

Loevinger, J. (1976). *Ego development: Conceptions and theories*. San Francisco: Jossey-Bass.

Lorr, M. (1986). *Interpersonal Style Inventory: Manual*. Los Angeles: Western Psychological Services.

Lowenthal, M. F., Thurnher, M., Chiriboga, D., & Associates (1975). *Four stages of life: A comparative study of women and men facing transitions*. San Francisco: Jossey-Bass.

Maas, H. S. (1979). Book review of *The seasons of a man's life*. *Psychiatry, 42,* 188-191.

MacKinnon, D. W., & Dukes, W. F. (1963). Repression. In L. Postman (Ed.), *Psychology in the making* (pp. 662-744). New York: Knopf.

Marcia, J. E. (1966). Development and validation of ego-identity status. *Journal of Personality and Social Psychology, 3,* 551-558.

Marcia, J. E. (1967). Ego-identity status: Relationship to change in self-esteem, "general maladjustment," and authoritarianism. *Journal of Personality, 35,* 118-133.

Marcia, J. E. (1980). Identity in adolescence. In J. Abelson (Ed.), *Handbook of adolescent psychology.* New York: John Wiley.

Marcia, J. E. (1992, August). *Ego psychoanalytic perspectives on identity.* Paper presented at the meetings of the American Psychological Association, Washington, DC.

Marcia, J. E., & Friedman, M. L. (1970). Ego identity status in college women. *Journal of Personality, 38,* 249-263.

Markman, E. M. (1989). *Categorization and naming in children: Problems of induction.* Cambridge: MIT Press.

Masson, J. M. (1984). *The assault on truth: Freud's suppression of the seduction theory.* New York: Farrar, Straus, & Giroux.

Masson, J. M. (Ed. and Trans.). (1985). *The complete letters of Sigmund Freud to Wilhelm Fliess 1887-1904.* Cambridge, MA: Harvard University Press.

Mazlish, B. (1973). *In search of Nixon.* Baltimore, MD: Penguin.

McAdams, D. P. (1985). *Power, intimacy, and the life story: Personological inquiries into identity.* Homewood, IL: Dow Jones-Irwin.

McAdams, D. P. (1987). A life-story model of identity. In R. Hogan & W. H. Jones (Eds.), *Perspectives on personality* (Vol. 2, pp. 15-50). Greenwich, CT: JAI Press.

McAdams, D. P. (1988). Biography, narrative, and lives: An introduction. In D. P. McAdams & R. L. Ochberg (Eds.), *Psychobiography and life narratives* (pp. 1-18). Durham, NC: Duke University Press.

McAdams, D. P. (1992, August). *Can personality change? Levels of stability and growth in personality across the lifespan.* Invited address presented at the meetings of the American Psychological Association, Washington, DC.

McAdams, D. P., & de St. Aubin, E. (1992). A theory of generativity and its assessment through self-report, behavioral acts, and narrative themes in autobiography. *Journal of Personality and Social Psychology, 62,* 1003-1015.

McAdams, D. P., Ruetzel, K., & Foley, J. M. (1986). Complexity and generativity at mid-life: Relations among social motives, ego development, and adults' plans for the future. *Journal of Personality and Social Psychology, 50,* 800-807.

McClelland, D. C. (1981). Is personality consistent? In A. I. Rabin, J. Aronoff, A. M. Barclay, & R. A. Zucker (Eds.), *Further explorations in personality* (pp. 87-113). New York: John Wiley.

McCrae, R. R. (1989, Fall). The big five. *Dialogue,* p. 9.

McCrae, R. R., & Costa, P. T., Jr. (1985). Updating Norman's "adequate taxonomy": Intelligence and personality dimensions in natural language and in questionnaires. *Journal of Personality and Social Psychology, 49,* 710-721.

McCrae, R. R., & Costa, P. T., Jr. (1990). *Personality in adulthood.* New York: Guilford.

McGuire, W. (Ed.). (1974). *The Freud/Jung letters.* Princeton, NJ: Princeton University Press.

Mercer, R. T., Nichols, E. G., & Doyle, G. C. (1989). *Transitions in a woman's life: Major life events in developmental context.* New York: Springer.

Meyerhoff, H. (1987). On psychoanalysis as history. In G. Cocks & T. L. Crosby (Eds.), *Psycho/history: Readings in the method of psychology, psychoanalysis, and history* (pp. 17-29). New Haven, CT: Yale University Press.

Miller, A. (1990). *The untouched key: Tracing childhood trauma in creativity and destructiveness*. Garden City, NY: Anchor Books.

Miller, J. (1984, February 6). An attack on Father Freud. *Time,* pp. 86-87.

Mischel, W. (1968). *Personality and assessment*. New York: John Wiley.

Montemayor, R. (1983). Parents and adolescents in conflict: All families some of the time and some families most of the time. *Journal of Early Adolescence, 3,* 83-103.

Movers & Shakers. (1987, January/February). *Washington Journalism Review,* pp. 6-8.

Murchison, C. (Ed.). (1930). *A history of psychology in autobiography* (Vol. 1). Worcester, MA: Clark University Press. (Vol. 2, 1932; Vol. 3, 1936)

Neuber, K. A., & Genthner, R. W. (1977). The relationship between ego identity, personal responsibility, and facilitative communication. *Journal of Psychology, 95,* 45-49.

Neugarten, B. L. (1968). The awareness of middle age. In B. L. Neugarten (Ed.), *Middle age and aging* (pp. 93-98). Chicago: University of Chicago Press.

Neugarten, B. L. (1976). Adaptation and the life cycle. *Counseling Psychologist, 6,* 16-20.

Neugarten, B. L. (1979). Time, age, and the life cycle. *American Journal of Psychiatry, 136,* 887-894.

Neugarten, B. L., & Neugarten, D. A. (1987, May). The changing meanings of age. *Psychology Today,* pp. 29-33.

Newman, C. (1991, June). The wonderland of Lewis Carroll. *National Geographic,* pp. 100-129.

Oates, J. C. (1988, August 28). Adventures in abandonment. *The New York Times Book Review,* pp. 3, 33.

Ochse, R., & Plug, C. (1986). Cross-cultural investigation of the validity of Erikson's theory of personality development. *Journal of Personality and Social Psychology, 50,* 1240-1252.

Ogilvie, D. M. (1984). Personality and paradox: Gordon Allport's final contribution. *Personality Forum, 2,* 12-14.

Orlansky, H. (1949). Infant care and personality. *Psychological Bulletin, 40,* 1-48.

Orlofsky, J. L., Marcia, J. E., & Lesser, I. M. (1973). Ego identity status and the intimacy versus isolation crisis of young adulthood. *Journal of Personality and Social Psychology, 27,* 211-219.

Page, M. (1983). Introduction: Personality—Current theory and research. In M. Page (Ed.), *Nebraska Symposium on Motivation, 1982* (pp. 1-2). Lincoln: University of Nebraska Press.

Palys, T. S., & Little, B. R. (1983). Perceived life satisfaction and the organization of personal project systems. *Journal of Personality and Social Psychology, 44,* 1221-1230.

Paris, B. J. (1989). The importance of Karen Horney. *Contemporary Psychology, 34,* 568-569.

Parkes, C. M. (1971). Psycho-social transitions: A field for study. In C. M. Parkes (Ed.), *Social science and medicine* (Vol. 5). London: Pergamon.

Paul, E. L. (1989, August). *Individual differences in young adult intimacy development.* Paper presented at the meetings of the American Psychological Association, New Orleans.

Peck, R. (1968). Psychological developments in the second half of life. In B. L. Neugarten (Ed.), *Middle age and aging* (pp. 88-92). Chicago: University of Chicago Press.

Petersen, A. C. (1988). Adolescent development. *Annual Review of Psychology, 39,* 583-608.

Phelps, E., Savola, K. L., & Young, C. H. (1991). *Inventory of longitudinal studies in social sciences.* Newbury Park, CA: Sage.

Poitier, S. (1980). *This life.* New York: Knopf.

Popper, K. (1957). *The poverty of historicism.* London: Routledge & Kegan Paul.

Popper, K. R. (1963). *Conjectures and refutations.* London: Routledge & Kegan Paul.

Pritchett, V. S. (1980, March 3). Lewis Carroll. *New Yorker,* pp. 123-128.

Pudney, J. (1976). *Lewis Carroll and his world.* New York: Scribner.

Quinn, S. (1987). *A mind of her own: The life of Karen Horney.* New York: Summit Books.

Raines, H. (1986, November 30). Driven to martyrdom. *The New York Times Book Review,* pp. 1, 33-34.

Raskin, P. M. (1984). Procedures in research on identity status: Some notes on method. *Psychological Reports, 54,* 719-730.

Reichard, S., Livson, F., & Peterson, P. G. (1962). *Aging and personality.* New York: John Wiley.

Reinke, B. J. (1982). *Psychosocial change among women from early adulthood to middle age as a function of chronological age and family cycle phase.* Unpublished doctoral dissertation, University of Kansas.

Reinke, B. J. (1985). Psychosocial changes as a function of chronological age. *Human Development, 28,* 266-269.

Reinke, B. J., Ellicott, A. M., Harris, R. L., & Hancock, E. (1985). Timing of psychosocial changes in women's lives. *Human Development, 28,* 259-280.

Reinke, B. J., Holmes, D. S., & Harris, R. L. (1985). The timing of psychosocial changes in women's lives: The years 25 to 45. *Journal of Personality and Social Psychology, 48,* 1353-1364.

Reynolds, B. (1991, April 5). Ex-pit bull Atwater an unlikely prophet. *USA Today,* p. 13A.

Rice, E. (1991). *Freud and Moses: The long journey home.* New York: SUNY Press.

Riegel, K. F. (1976). The dialectics of human development. *American Psychologist, 31,* 689-700.

Roazen, P. (1976). *Erik H. Erikson: The power and limits of a vision.* New York: Free Press.

Robert, M. (1976). *From Oedipus to Moses: Freud's Jewish identity* (R. Manheim, Trans.). Garden City, NY: Anchor Books.

Roberts, P., & Newton, P. M. (1987). Levinsonian studies of women's adult development. *Psychology and Aging, 2,* 154-163.

Robinson, F. G. (1992). *Love's story told: A life of Henry A. Murray.* Cambridge, MA: Harvard University Press.

Rogers, C. R. (1967). Autobiography. In E. G. Boring & G. Lindzey (Eds.), *A history of psychology in autobiography* (Vol. 5, pp. 343-384). New York: Appleton-Century-Crofts.

Rosenfeld, A., & Stark, E. (1987, May). The prime of our lives. *Psychology Today,* pp. 62-72.

Rubin, L. B. (1979). *Women of a certain age: The midlife search for self.* New York: Harper & Row.

Rubin, L. B. (1986). *Quiet rage: Bernie Goetz in a time of madness.* New York: Farrar, Straus, & Giroux.

Rubin, Z. (1981, May). Does personality really change after 20? *Psychology Today, 15,* 18-27.

Runyan, W. McK. (1982). *Life histories and psychobiography: Explorations in theory and method.* New York: Oxford University Press.

Runyan, W. McK. (1988). Alternatives to psychoanalytic psychobiography. In W. McK. Runyan (Ed.), *Psychology and historical interpretation* (pp. 219-244). New York: Oxford University Press.

Rutter, M. (1979). Maternal deprivation, 1972-1978: New findings, new concepts, new approaches. *Child Development, 50,* 282-305.

Rybczynski, W. (1991). *Waiting for the weekend.* New York: Viking.

Ryff, C. D., & Heincke, S. G. (1983). Subjective organization of personality in adulthood and aging. *Journal of Personality and Social Psychology, 44,* 807-816.

Ryff, C. D., & Migdal, S. (1984). Intimacy and generativity: Self-perceived transitions. *Signs: Journal of Women in Culture and Society, 9,* 470-481.

St. Clair, M. (1986). *Object relations and self psychology: An introduction.* Pacific Grove, CA: Brooks/Cole.

Sanford, N. (1980). *Learning after college.* Orinda, CA: Montaigne.

Sayers, J. (1991). *Mothers of psychoanalysis: Helene Deutsch, Karen Horney, Anna Freud, Melanie Klein.* New York: Norton.

Schaeffer, D. L. (Ed.). (1971). *Sex differences in personality: Readings.* Pacific Grove, CA: Brooks/Cole.

Schlein, S. (Ed.). (1987). *A way of looking at things: Selected papers of E. H. Erikson from 1930 to 1980.* New York: Norton.

Schultz, D. (1990). *Intimate friends, dangerous rivals.* Los Angeles: Jeremy B. Tarcher.

Schultz, D. (1992). *Theories of personality* (4th ed.). Pacific Grove, CA: Brooks/Cole.

Sears, R. R. (1943). *Survey of objective studies of psychoanalytic concepts.* New York: Social Science Research Council.

Sears, R. R. (1979a, June). Mark Twain's separation anxiety. *Psychology Today,* pp. 100-104.

Sears, R. R. (1979b). Mid-life development. *Contemporary Psychology, 24,* 97-98.

Segal, J. (1992). Ego, superego, and yid: Analyzing the Jew in Freud. *Contemporary Psychology, 37,* 886.

Sheehy, G. (1976). *Passages: Predictable crises of adult life.* New York: E. P. Dutton.

Shogan, R. (1991, March 30). Ex-GOP chief Atwater dies. *Kansas City Star,* pp. A-1, A-9.

Shontz, F. C. (1986). Who are the drug users? *Drugs and Society, 1,* 51-74.

Simmel, G. (1950). *The sociology of Georg Simmel* (K. H. Wolff, Trans.). New York: Free Press.

Smelser, N. J. (1980). Issues in the study of work and love in adulthood. In N. J. Smelser & E. H. Erikson (Eds.), *Themes of work and love in adulthood* (pp. 1-26). Cambridge, MA: Harvard University Press.

Smith, M. B. (1977). A dialectical social psychology? Comments on a symposium. *Personality and Social Psychology Bulletin, 3,* 719-724.

Smith, M. B. (1993). Allport and Murray on Allport's *Personality:* A confrontation in 1946-1947. In K. H. Craik, R. Hogan, & R. N. Wolfe (Eds.), *Fifty years of personality psychology* (pp. 57-65). New York: Plenum.

Snyder, C. R., & Fromkin, H. L. (1980). *Uniqueness: The human pursuit of difference.* New York: Plenum.

Spitz, L. W. (1973). Psychohistory and history: The case of *Young man Luther. Soundings, 56*(2), 181-209.

Spotts, J. V., & Shontz, F. C. (1985). A new perspective on intervention in heavy, chronic drug use. *International Journal of the Addictions, 20,* 1545-1565.

Stannard, D. E. (1980). *Shrinking history: On Freud and the failure of psychohistory.* New York: Oxford University Press.

Staude, J. R. (1981). *The adult development of C. G. Jung.* London: Routledge & Kegan Paul.

Steiner, C. M. (1974). *Scripts people live: Transactional analysis of life scripts.* New York: Grove.

Stern, D. (1985). *The interpersonal world of the infant.* New York: Basic Books.

Stern, D. N. (1990). *Diary of a baby: What your child sees, feels and experiences.* New York: Basic Books.

Stewart, A. J., Franz, C., & Layton, L. (1988). The changing self: Using personal documents to study lives. In D. P. McAdams & R. L. Ochberg (Eds.), *Psychobiography and life narratives* (pp. 41-74). Durham, NC: Duke University Press.

Stewart, A. J., & Vandewater, E. A. (1992, August). *Combining tough and tender methods to study women's lives.* Paper presented at the meetings of the American Psychological Association, Washington, DC.

Stewart, W. A. (1977). *A psychosocial study of early adult life structures in women.* Unpublished doctoral dissertation, Columbia University.

Stolorow, R. D., & Atwood, G. E. (1979). *Faces in a cloud: Subjectivity in personality theory.* New York: Jason Aronson.

Strouse, J. (1974). *Women and analysis: Dialogues on psychoanalytic views of femininity.* New York: Dell.

Strozier, C. B. (1976). Disciplined subjectivity and the psychohistorian: A critical look at the work of Erik H. Erikson. *Psychohistory Review, 53,* 28-31.

Swogger, G. (1989, April 18). *Carl Sandburg and American optimism.* Unpublished paper presented at the meetings of the Mid-America Psychosocial Study Group, Topeka, KS.

Tamir, L. M. (1980). Men at middle age. In D. G. McGuigan (Ed.), *Women's lives: New theory, research, and policy.* Ann Arbor: University of Michigan Center for Continuing Education of Women.

Tamir, L. M. (1989). Modern myths about men at midlife: An assessment. In S. Hunter & M. Sundel (Eds.), *Midlife myths: Issues, findings, and practice implications* (pp. 157-179). Newbury Park, CA: Sage.

Tavris, C. (1990, July 1). Mothers are a girl's best friend. *The New York Times Book Review,* p. 9.

Thurnher, M. (1983). Turning points and developmental change: Subjective and "objective" assessments. *American Journal of Orthopsychiatry, 53,* 52-60.

Tice, D. M. (1989). Metatraits: Interitem variance as personality assessment. In D. Buss & N. Cantor (Eds.), *Personality psychology: Recent trends and emerging directions* (pp. 194-200). New York: Springer.

Tomkins, S. S. (1979). Script theory: Differential magnification of affects. In H. E. Howe, Jr., & R. A. Dienstbier (Eds.), *Nebraska Symposium on Motivation, 1978* (Vol. 26, pp. 201-236). Lincoln: University of Nebraska Press.

Tomkins, S. S. (1987). Script theory. In J. Aronoff, A. I. Rabin, & R. A. Zucker (Eds.), *The emergence of personality* (pp. 147-216). New York: Springer.

T R B. (1985, October 14). Dohrn again. *New Republic,* pp. 4, 41.

Troll, L. E. (1982). *Continuations: Adult development and aging.* Pacific Grove, CA: Brooks/Cole.

Tucker, R. (1977, June). The Georges' Wilson re-examined: An essay on psychobiography. *American Political Science Review,* No. 2.

Usdansky, M. L. (1993, February 12). Young adults return to nest. *USA Today,* p. 2A.

Vaillant, G. E. (1977). *Adaptation to life.* Boston: Little, Brown.

Vaillant, G. E., & Milofsky, E. (1980). The natural history of male psychological health: IX. Empirical evidence for Erikson's model of the life cycle. *American Journal of Psychiatry, 137,* 1348-1359.

Vobejda, B. (1991, September 23-29). Declarations of independence. *The Washington Post National Weekly Edition,* p. 9.

Wachtel, P. (1977). Interaction cycles, unconscious processes, and the person-situation issue. In D. Magnusson & N. Endler (Eds.), *Personality at the crossroads* (pp. 317-331). Hillsdale, NJ: Lawrence Erlbaum.

Waite, R. G. L. (1977). *The psychopathic god: Adolf Hitler.* New York: Basic Books.

Walker, C. (1974, June 2). The cycle of life. *Parade,* p. 20.

Waterman, C. K., & Waterman, A. S. (1974). Ego identity status and decision styles. *Journal of Youth and Adolescence, 3,* 1-6.

Weick, A. (1989). Patterns of change and processes of power in adulthood. In S. Hunter & M. Sundel (Eds.), *Midlife myths: Issues, findings, and practice implications* (pp. 235-252). Newbury Park, CA: Sage.

Weinberg, S. (1992). *Telling the untold story: How investigative reporters are changing the craft of biography.* Columbia: University of Missouri Press.

Wellman, H. M. (1990). *The child's theory of the mind.* Cambridge: MIT Press.

Westen, D. (1990). Psychoanalytic approaches to personality. In L. A. Pervin (Ed.), *Handbook of personality theory and research* (pp. 21-65). New York: Guilford.

Whitbourne, S. K. (1991). Of clocks and looking glasses: A social interactionist perspective on adult development and aging. *Contemporary Psychology, 36,* 885-886.

Whitbourne, S. K., & Weinstock, C. S. (1979). *Adult development: The differentiation of experience.* New York: Holt, Rinehart & Winston.

Wicker, T. (1991). *One of us: Richard Nixon and the American dream.* New York: Random House.

Winter, D. G. (1993). Gordon Allport and "Letters from Jenny." In K. H. Craik, R. Hogan, & R. N. Wolfe (Eds), *Fifty years of personality psychology* (pp. 147-163). New York: Plenum.

Wolff, G. (1978, January 9). Vaillant effort falls short. *New Times,* pp. 96-97.

Woodward, C. V. (1987, March 16). The black and the red. *New Republic,* pp. 32-36.

Wright, J. E., Jr. (1982). *Erikson: Identity and religion.* New York: Seabury Press.

Yerushalmi, Y. H. (1991). *Freud's Moses: Judaism terminable and interminable.* New Haven, CT: Yale University Press.

Young-Bruehl, E. (1988). *Anna Freud: A biography.* New York: Summit Books.

Zuckerman, M. (1986, August). *What lies beyond E and N?* Paper presented at the meetings of the American Psychological Association, Washington, DC.

Author Index

Subject Index

About the Author

Lawrence S. Wrightsman (Ph.D., University of Minnesota, 1959) is Professor of Psychology at the University of Kansas, Lawrence, and a former department chair there. He is an author or editor of 18 books, including *Social Psychology in the Nineties* (6th edition, authored with Kay Deaux and Francis C. Dane). He has taught a course on personality in adulthood for more than 10 years and has participated in several workshops on the topic. He is a former President of the Society for the Psychological Study of Social Issues and of the Society of Personality and Social Psychology.